MW00610880

# SUPER SLICK

## Life and Death in a
## Huey Helicopter in Vietnam

STORY BY TOM FEIGEL
WRITTEN BY LARRY WEILL

# STACKPOLE
# BOOKS

*Essex, Connecticut*
*Blue Ridge Summit, Pennsylvania*

# STACKPOLE BOOKS

An imprint of Globe Pequot, the trade division of
The Rowman & Littlefield Publishing Group, Inc.
4501 Forbes Boulevard, Suite 200,
Lanham, Maryland 20706
www.rowman.com

Distributed by NATIONAL BOOK NETWORK

British Library Cataloguing in Publication Information Available

**Library of Congress Cataloging-in-Publication Data**

Names: Feigel, Tom, author. | Weill, Larry, author.
Title: Super Slick : life and death in a Huey helicopter in Vietnam / Tom
  Feigel, Larry Weill.
Other titles: Life and death in a Huey helicopter in Vietnam
Description: Essex, Connecticut: Stackpole Books, 2024.
Identifiers: LCCN 2023049470 (print) | LCCN 2023049471 (ebook) | ISBN
  9780811775663 (cloth) | ISBN 9780811772969 (ebook)
Subjects: LCSH: United States. Army. Assault Helicopter Company,
  336th—Biography. | Vietnam War, 1961-1975—Aerial operations, American.
  | UH-1 (Helicopter) | Flight crews—United State—Biography. | Vietnam
  War, 1961-1975—Personal narratives, American.
Classification: LCC DS558.8.F454 2024  (print) | LCC DS558.8 (ebook) |
  DDC 959.704/1092 [B]—dc23/eng/20240129
LC record available at https://lccn.loc.gov/2023049470
LC ebook record available at https://lccn.loc.gov/2023049471

♾️™ The paper used in this publication meets the minimum requirements of
American National Standard for Information Sciences—Permanence of Paper
for Printed Library Materials, ANSI/NISO Z39.48-1992.

*This book is dedicated to the memory of the crew of Lucky Strike,*
*whose lives were sacrificed in unselfish service to their country.*
*Your memory lives on in the hearts of your shipmates.*
*We will always miss you, and we will always remember.*

# CONTENTS

# ACKNOWLEDGMENTS

This book has been a collaborative effort that has called upon the efforts and resources of a great many people. The events recorded in this volume transpired over fifty years ago. The collective memory of our entire crew has been put to the test to recall everything as factually as possible. Each member of that group, including our pilot, Randy Olson, and our door gunners, Robert Sandwith and Tom Wilkes, have contributed their time and patience throughout endless telephone calls and emails to fill in the blanks of these episodes. Their practical expertise in various aspects of helicopter flight and weapons engagement were also critical to the technical merit of many of the chapters.

Our Platoon Leader, John Leandro, was instrumental in detailing several stories of combat flight and inspirational leadership during his time with our platoon. His assistance in recalling and corroborating these incidents was invaluable to the accuracy of this book.

Dana Brown, who served with our crew after Randy Olson completed his tour, was also a major contributor to several chapters in this book. His recollections of events, including not only the mission-related details but the human emotions of those involved, have made this a much more engaging and entertaining volume.

Numerous other individuals who provided their own personal accountings of their interactions with our crew have vastly enhanced this story. SEAL Team 1 member Ray Smith, who detailed his perilous rescue from a near fatal AK-47 wounding, and Sady Caicedo, the sole survivor of a Huey helicopter crash in hostile territory, have provided massive infusions of personal drama to the battle scenes.

A number of organizations and officials have also provided indispensable assistance in the care and upkeep of our helicopter, call sign Super

Slick (Warrior 21). Jeff Greene, manager of the Marion County Vietnam Veterans Memorial, worked with us to coordinate our visits and activities around the site of our beloved ship.

John Moon, along with other officials of Bombardier Inc., welcomed us into their Bridgeport, WV, facilities as part of their outstanding work and support in voluntarily maintaining and preserving Super Slick at the memorial site.

We gratefully thank John Brennan, author of numerous reference books on helicopter nose art, for reaching out to us and making us aware that our helicopter was stateside and housed at the Marion County Vietnam Veterans Memorial in Fairmont, WV.

We are most grateful to my cousin, Donald Feigel, and his wife Karen for donating their time, resources, and expertise to produce the documentary *Fate's Call*. Their many contributions in driving this production have raised awareness of the memorial and our ship's story among thousands of viewers and veterans' organizations.

Many thanks are extended to Bruno Petrauskas of Rochester, NY, for donating his professional proofreading and editing skills. He continues to teach writing and composition to our US Armed Forces at bases and installations across the country.

We also extend our gratitude to the entire towns of Fairmont and Grafton, WV, for adopting us and inviting us to join in their Memorial Day parade and ceremonies. Just as our ship, Super Slick, has become a part of their community, so have we as individuals and families. We gratefully acknowledge your warmth and hospitality in making us feel as honored citizens of your towns.

Finally, we'd like to thank those unknown individuals who were responsible for bringing our ship, Super Slick, back to the United States so it could eventually be placed in its current spot of honor at the Marion County Vietnam Veterans Memorial. That ship was responsible for each member of our crew making it home to our beloved country and families. Thank you for returning the favor.

# FOREWORD

Vietnam. A country that will be forever linked to a catastrophic era in the history of our nation. A place where over fifty-eight thousand American service members lost their lives fighting for a cause that very few could define.

Americans remember this war and those times for a variety of reasons. Even for those who served in-country within what was then South Vietnam, the experience differed based upon a plethora of factors, including location, timing, and just plain luck. For a country so small that it exceeds the area of only nine US states, Vietnam has left an indelible mark on the men who served inside its borders.

My own time in Vietnam had its share of highs and lows, as it did for every one of the 2.2 million service members who landed there. My time spent aloft as Crew Chief of my UH-1 (Huey) helicopter, Super Slick, was exciting, distressing, insightful, exhilarating, terrifying, and just about any other adjective that can be linked to the adrenaline-junkie syndrome we all experienced above the tree lines, fields, and rice paddies of Vietnam. We were fighting an enemy we seldom saw while witnessing the loss of our many crewmates with whom we flew side by side on a daily basis. And every day we wondered, Who would be next? Maybe it would be me.

Throughout my two-year enlistment, especially the twelve months I spent flying combat missions in Vietnam, the common issue of fate hung over everything. It was all prevailing and seemed to determine the day-to-day question of my existence. Would I live to see another day? Would my crewmates survive? Would any of the bullets that seemed to emboss the outer hull of our ship on a daily basis find their intended mark and end my life? Or worse yet, would they hit a critical component of the rotor head or fuel line that would send us spiraling out of control into the ground below, killing us all?

So many times over the years since returning from Vietnam, I've found myself pondering that factor.

Fate.

The *Merriam-Webster.com* dictionary defines fate as "the will or principle or determining cause by which things in general are believed to come to be as they are or events to happen as they do." I've thought a lot about that definition and how it applies to me, both today and as a soldier in 1969–1970. Was fate the overriding factor that decided what happened to me on a daily basis? Was fate to blame for whether I lived or died, regardless of my own actions? I doubt it, but looking back, many of my decisions seemed to lead me down the right path, even when I didn't realize the consequences of my actions. Fate.

How much of what happened to bring me home alive was directly linked to that one factor? I think about it a lot as I consider my string of good luck, day after day and week after week, considering all the elements that brought me home alive.

My mother, Betty, made me promise in advance to keep my head down and "never volunteer for anything." I heeded her attention for a matter of weeks before veering off from her request and asking for the Crew Chief position. It was a combat mission, but I accepted it anyway. Had I remained onboard the air ship Lucky Strike for another two weeks, I would have never been here to write this book. Six of my best friends and crewmates perished in the fiery crash, while my life was spared. Fate.

The fact that I was assigned to the US Army instead of the Marines Corps position in the thick of the fighting and killing. It could have easily been me. Fate.

The very fact that I had been assigned to aviation, where I could hide out in our very own safe hangar, isolated from much of the fighting that enveloped our infantry troops on a daily basis. They fought and died while I worked on helos inside a corrugated metal building on a protected base. Fate.

The day that Lucky Strike was shot down, my pilot, Mr. Olson, was supposed to be copiloting that ship. But instead he was asked (against his wishes) to ride in a Jeep leading a supply convoy. He completed that mission, "bringing home the bacon," while fuming that someone else got to take his place that night. No one survived the crash of Lucky Strike; all six men onboard perished. Fate.

My day-one assignment, made by a nameless, faceless clerk whom I would never see again and that sent me south toward the Mekong Delta instead of northwest into the deadly Central Highlands. Those mountains and high plateaus seemed to be the origin of many of the body bags seen on the nightly news across our country. But our area was much quieter by comparison. And so I got to live. Fate.

The fact that I didn't participate in the defoliation missions, one which so many fellow crew members decided to accept. The mission, which utilized the now infamous Agent Orange, turned out to be one of our deadliest endeavors in Vietnam. At the time little was known about the defoliant or its toxic ingredient, dioxin. Yet its presence can serve as a catalyst for an entire lineup of health problems, including cancer, diabetes, liver problems, birth defects, and more. The numbers of soldiers who spent time deployed in that country and have since passed away due to cancer and other side effects of the chemical is horrifying. It has even been linked to birth defects in offspring up to twenty years after the initial exposure. But for some reason, I declined and was never involved in the use of Agent Orange. Fate.

Even the fact that I had been assigned as Crew Chief to one of the best, most experienced Huey crews in southern Vietnam seemed to be pure, dumb luck. We had Randy Olson, pilot, and Rob Sandwith and Tom Wilkes, door gunners, and anyone else who flew with us, especially when entering zones that were "hot" and full of Vietcong fighters. Mr. Olson possessed an innate sixth sense that told him when we were safe versus when we had to "get the hell out of there." These were men who were the very best at what they did, and they knew how to survive when facing adversity.

Fate.

I am convinced that a small number of the people we lost in Vietnam were lost to fate, just as it was the cause for my own survival. In a land where there were so many hostile fighters and so many deadly projectiles aimed at us as the enemy, a certain percentage of our platoon and company were not coming home. That part was simply the application of logical statistics. Some bullets were going to find their targets.

Yet it never happened to me. True, I had been hit by an AK-47 round on at least one occasion—thus my Purple Heart, which still sits on a table inside my house as a reminder of my close call. But even more scary were the bullet holes that appeared in our ship's skin, uncomfortably close to the position of my head just a few feet away. What would have happened if the high-powered shell had struck a metal frame member and diverted downward by six inches? What would have happened had I repositioned to take a better gun position? I shudder to think about those possibilities.

So many of these chance incidences were linked to that one factor: fate. And while I didn't recognize it at the time (or perhaps just didn't have the time to consider it), I do today. The fact that I am alive today and living a good life instead of being just another name on The Wall is proof that fate exists.

What follows is the story of my life, as well as the lives of my fellow crew members, who shared with me my time, life, and tribulations in that embattled hellhole called Vietnam. God bless them all, the living and the deceased, for helping us to assist fate and get us home alive.

# I

## THE EARLY YEARS

# 1

# BEGINNINGS

The story of my life in a US Army air crew was never part of my family DNA. I was born in a regular working-class, middle-income family in upstate New York. The town of Webster, NY, is located about fifteen miles east of Rochester and is situated on the shoreline of Lake Ontario. At the time of my birth in 1950, the population of the town was only about 7,100, but that was soon to grow dramatically as major corporations and businesses moved into the area. One of these corporations, Xerox, would later become my employer for most of my adult years.

Life was good for our family and neighbors in the quiet little community. My father, Joseph, and my mother, Elizabeth, or "Betty," provided a secure home for us in our little town, and we grew up as respectful children with a love of our family and country. I attended R. L. Thomas High School, later to become known as Webster Thomas High School, along with my sister Kathy. Throughout high school, I was an average student with grades that could have earned me admission into most of the local colleges, if I had selected to go that route. Life was very busy with all the extracurricular activities, sports, and friends that compete with the classroom for the overwhelming majority of teenage boys' attention.

Another major interest of mine throughout high school was working on cars, a hobby that started early in my youth when I drove my first go-cart. I loved every aspect of it and became fairly well versed in its mechanics from the time I was knee-high to a grasshopper. With that background, I had no problem at all passing my driver's test when I attained the legal age. It was a piece of cake since I'd already been driving for seven to eight years.

I had a large group of friends who were similarly engaged in the hobby of automotive work. There were at least eight or ten of us "gearheads" who enjoyed nothing more than immersing ourselves in tearing apart cars and engines, then rebuilding them into even hotter machines. This became a passion that consumed much of my extracurricular time. We would gather in one or another of our garages and help each other out, especially when performing major jobs like pulling an engine or transmission. Before long, there were friendly competitions between us to see who could have the highest-performance car.

One advantage I had was that I was employed at a local commercial gas station that had two attached bays for automobile repairs. I worked in that garage a few days a week, performing routine maintenance and assisting on some of the repairs that came into the garage. Later on, when I needed a place to work on my own car, the owners granted me permission to use their facility after hours, which was handy because it was difficult to find hydraulic lifts that enabled you to work beneath the car. Sometimes I ended up staying there the entire night. As a teenager, time had little meaning, and I was truly working in my preferred environment.

I remember several of my favorite cars, including a 1957 Chevy that we used for cruising in our off time. I also had a Volkswagen "Bug" with a Chevy engine up front. I bought it partially finished from another local car enthusiast and continued working on it until the time I left for Vietnam. It would be my final automotive project in that era of my life, and my father continued to labor on it after I was deployed. I was always grateful for the days and weeks that I spent beneath the hoods of various cars. The knowledge I'd gained from that pursuit would later come in handy as I trained for my pending job as a helicopter Crew Chief.

I was fairly well disciplined from an early age, although I also had a bit of a rebellious streak ingrained in my personality. My father taught me discipline and respect, and I took my lead from his example. I was also well trained in athletics, as I wrestled for my school and competed at the high school varsity level. Wrestling is one of those competitive endeavors that is little understood by most sports enthusiasts, yet it requires more training and dedication than most team sports. It taught me to work hard, train hard, and pay attention to details. All of these things would become valuable attributes in the years to come.

My father introduced me to aviation and flying at an early age and encouraged me to follow him in this lifelong pursuit. Growing up on a farm in Penfield, NY, he'd developed an everlasting love of flying that would remain his primary passion for the rest of his life. He started flying while still in his teens, and he became the youngest commercial pilot in Rochester by 1934.

Even before Japan bombed Pearl Harbor, which marked our official entry into World War II, my father was involved in training military pilots. As a civilian, he taught US Navy pilots in Norfolk, Virginia, which he followed by instructing British aviation students as part of the Lend–Lease deal with Great Britain. (Prior to the declaration of war in 1941, the United States functioned only in a support role for England and its allies.)

Once the US formally joined the war following Pearl Harbor, the US Navy wanted him to become a Naval officer on active duty. Before that could happen, in 1941, he was sworn into the Royal Air Force and become an RAF officer. He spent the entirety of World War II training new RAF pilots, many of whom fought in the Battle of Britain. They arrived by boat from England and immediately commenced basic aviation training using PT-17s (a basic trainer aircraft). Upon graduation from their primary basic training, they moved up to advanced training, where they used AT-6 trainers, which had a bit more power and maneuverability. It made no difference what aircraft they used; my father was an expert pilot and instructor in them all.

Throughout those years, my father was actually an employee of Embry-Riddle College, which is located in Daytona Beach, Florida. Embry-Riddle is an aviation and aerospace college that focuses entirely on aviation science. It was funded almost entirely by the US State Department, which arranged compensation for "employees" like my father, who were involved in the early war efforts.

My father remained in Clewiston, Florida (about eighty miles northwest of Fort Lauderdale), in his capacity as an RAF officer for the rest of the war. He also married my mother, Elizabeth (Betty), while stationed there. He did not leave the Clewiston base until the end of the war, in 1945.

Long after the end of World War II, my father got me involved in flying lessons in our part of New York State. I was only twelve or thirteen years old when I took my first lesson, but I quickly became hooked. He owned a seaplane, which he operated off of Irondequoit Bay, located along the western boundary of our home town. I did my first "solo" at age sixteen, flying an Aeronca Champ from the Williamson/Sodus Airport. It was a comparatively minor facility with small aircraft and a single runway, but for me, it was everything I ever dreamed of. I was hooked. The single-engine, high-wing aircraft took me into the blue skies over our town and gave me a birds-eye view that I would never forget. It was easy to see how my father had become so transfixed on a life based on aviation.

Even as I continued to train toward getting my pilot's license, my father pursued his love of flying. He went on to serve as a commercial airline pilot, flight instructor, and a Federal Aviation Administration (FAA) flight examiner, becoming one of the region's most noted authorities on aircraft and aviation.

By my senior year in high school, more and more thoughts about life after graduation occupied my mind. What would follow receiving my diploma that summer of 1968? Would I apply for a job while still in school? Would I remain in the area? Would I look at the possibility of going on to college?

College was something that I'd discussed with my family—briefly. My father had tried to convince me to attend Embry-Riddle College in Daytona Beach to continue my interest in aviation. I did give it some serious consideration—but not for long. It seemed like a good idea for some time down the road, but as I already mentioned, I had a bit of a rebellious nature, and I was itching to get out into the real world and do something. (I would later return to school, when my employer and the military would pay for my college degrees.)

While all these events transpired in my life, another major news story was developing in the country: the Vietnam War. It was always there, in the background, looming as a slow and ominous ticking that could be heard above all else. The war was in full swing by 1968, and the bloody news could be heard every night on our black-and-white television sets. It was forced into the living rooms of every American household, with the horrible stories and body counts appearing for all to see. There was no way to escape it. The Selective Service draft had started in 1964 and was continuing to snag young men ages eighteen through twenty-six, who were required to register. I was well aware of the chances of being called. Of the eligible 27 million men who fell into that age group, some 2.2 million had already been tagged for military duty. A great many of those would be deployed to South Vietnam. I worried that my turn was rapidly approaching.

While I worried about the prospects of being drafted, my entire being was tugged in a totally different direction: Whitney, or "Whit" for short. She was the early love of my life, and I could think of nothing but being together constantly and sharing our lives forever. Whit and I had only started dating in our senior year, but it was a flame that exploded like a spark in a gasoline can.

Whit was also a senior at R. L. Thomas High School, and we were introduced by a friend of hers named Anne. That was in February 1968, and it didn't take long for us to go out on our first date. She was a petite girl with beautiful blonde hair. I was instantly attracted to her, and we seemed to form an almost-immediate connection between us. It wasn't long before we were an inseparable couple, doing everything together.

The bond between us grew through the spring and into the summer, when we spent the time out cruising in my 1957 Chevy. We hung out with our group of friends and became regulars at the local drive-in. It really didn't matter what the movie was or whether we'd seen it before or not. In fact, our group of friends spent so many nights together at the outdoor movie venue that we adopted our own area of the parking lot. No one else parked there because our cars had staked our claim in the parking lot. It was reserved territory.

We also spent a lot of time hanging out in the local parks, where once again, we usually had a good-sized group. We often brought some cold beer along for the ride, and times were good. You couldn't get away with that in today's world, but no one bothered us, and we usually kept it pretty restrained, not causing trouble for anyone else.

As that final summer progressed, Whit and I continued to get closer and closer. We spent a lot of time with each other's families, including over the holidays. My mother and father really loved Whit, and I got along great with her parents as well. Sometime in that period, we discussed getting married, and Whit suggested that I ask her father's permission for her hand. I was very nervous about that, but her father was fine with the idea. He only wanted to know one thing: did I love her? Once I professed to him that I did, it was all smiles and hugs.

By the end of the summer of 1968, Whit and I were engaged and were planning on tying the knot sometime over the next few years. It was a fairly common thing to do back then; teenage sweethearts graduating from high school often pledged themselves to one another in the hopes of finding a lifetime of wedded bliss. We had talks of a house, children, and all the other trappings of married life in our little hometown. But these were unsettled times in a world filled with uncertainty.

With the exception of the possibility of being drafted, life charged right ahead at a fast and furious pace. Even before graduation, I'd applied for a job at Xerox, which had major facilities on the Webster Campus of our town. Xerox, which got its humble beginnings under the name of Haloid, achieved its first commercial success with the introduction of the 914 Xerox copier in 1959. It was a product that literally launched a new era in American business, and the effects were immediate. Major tracts of land that been open fields were transformed overnight into a huge industrial megacomplex, and almost anyone looking for work was hired instantly.

Not knowing what was in store for my future, I filed my application for employment with Xerox over Easter in 1968. I was amazed at the speed of the hiring process. The person doing the hiring asked me if I could start the following day! He was astounded when I informed him that I was still in high school. Hearing that, he backed off and asked if I would come back following graduation, which is what I did. I, an ambitious eighteen-year-old kid with a ton of energy, started working there in July 1968.

In the late 1960s, Xerox was a booming business that was hungry for people to assemble machines, which they could not keep in stock. As fast as copiers were built, they were sold, and the company couldn't seem to hire enough people to meet their manufacturing needs. I was put to work in a cavernous assembly building, piecing together Xerox copy machines along with an army of other assemblers. It was good work that paid a generous hourly wage, and I enjoyed earning a weekly paycheck instead of spending my time in a classroom.

And still, the clock ticked.

It was somewhere around my eighteenth birthday when I had to satisfy the requirement to notify our town clerk of my status for the Selective Service. That time arrived late in the spring of 1968. It was something that all of us had to do around the time of our eighteenth birthday, and now it was my turn. All my friends were doing the same thing as their birthdays rolled by. It was part of life at the time. Tick, tick, tick . . .

As we moved ahead into the fall of 1968, all my schoolmates who were not bound for college began contemplating their next course of action. For most, that meant deciding whether to enlist or wait until they were drafted. There were advantages and disadvantages to both. If you enlisted, you could make your own choice as to which branch of the service you would report, including, Army, Navy, and the others. However, enlisting also meant a thirty-six-month commitment. If you were willing to wait until you were drafted, the commitment was only twenty-four months, but you had no say over your assignment, which most likely would be infantry in the Army or the Marine Corps. It all depended on the risks you were willing to accept.

It was around that time (the fall of 1968), that I received my draft-card status. It read "1A" in big, bold characters. That pretty much said it all: no deferments, no exceptions. If called, I would be there on the first bus out of town.

My "greetings" (induction) letter from the Selective Service arrived in February 1969, as I had a 1A draft status. We always called it the "Greetings" letter because that is how it always started out. Even before opening it, I knew what was inside. It arrived by regular mail in the standard Selective Service envelope and was printed on their standard stationery. It confirmed that I was to report to the induction center in Buffalo, NY. Attending college could have deferred my date for reporting until after graduation. But college was not in my plans. So there were no surprises; I had been expecting this for at least three months.

The following weeks and months literally flew by in an eye-blurring burst, and my departure date arrived before I felt ready. I knew that I'd be in transit for a few days, passing through a gathering point in downtown Rochester, then on to the induction center in Buffalo, where we'd all get sworn in. Immediately following our induction into the Army, it would be a quick flight to my basic training site at Fort Dix, New Jersey. Things were happening so fast, it hardly felt I had time to breathe. But that was just a precursor of things to come.

My final recollection of departing was saying my goodbyes on the steps of my house. My mother was there, as were Kath and Whit. Everyone was crying and reaching for one last hug. We then said our forced goodbye, and my father and I climbed into our car for the trip downtown.

It was a difficult ride, and I didn't know when I would return to see my family and fiancée again. The only certainty was uncertainty, and I only hoped that I was up to the task.

# 2

# BOOT CAMP

The first leg of my transformation from civilian to US Army soldier started in downtown Rochester. It was just my father and me in the car, and the ride was both awkward and silent. Normally, we had so much to say to one another, so much to discuss. But this ride was different. Few words were said as we headed west along Route 104 toward the city of Rochester. I know my father would have liked to talk this one last time, but there was very little to say. It was as though a noxious pregnant pause had filled the car and lingered throughout the full thirty-minute ride.

We soon headed over the Irondequoit Bay Bridge, still in relative silence. The bridge was only two years old at the time, and as we passed over the expanse of steel and pavement, I looked at the ground in the rear-view mirror and wondered when I would return.

Our destination was a building that the Selective Service used as an initial gathering spot for newbies who were just starting their first steps into military service. It was an old brick building that had previously served as Rochester City Hall. I only remember the dark bricks on the outside edifice of the fortress-like building. It looked old and tired. The building is still there today, even older and more tired than before.

Outside the building a group of local war protestors gathered to express their sentiments about the war—and possibly even about us.

"You don't have to go," they screamed at the top of their voices, over and over again.

"Come with us to Canada," others shouted. They created quite a commotion, yelling and hollering at the tops of their lungs. We walked right past them and into the building. I know I never gave them a second thought, and I doubt that any of the others did either. It was just part of the scene in our country at the time.

Our stop was primarily to gather together everyone from the Rochester area for the ride down the thruway to Buffalo. We did little or nothing in the way of administrative processing. We were just herded together in a room to wait for everyone to arrive.

Looking around the room at all the other arrivals, I was able to find one familiar face. His name was Pat, and he was a fellow student at R. L. Thomas High School. He wasn't in my normal circle of close friends in Webster, but it was nice to have a familiar face in the crowd. I did recognize a few other folks as they entered the room and checked in, but no one I knew by name. Webster was a small, close-knit town; we didn't get out and about often to socialize with students from neighboring townships.

We spoke casually as more recruits arrived, the place filling until we numbered about forty. About that time, we were herded once again onto a bus. (The word "herded" is used a lot here. It just fits.) They must have carefully planned the size of our entourage, because we filled the bus to capacity just about perfectly. The whole process had taken just a little over an hour.

Pat and I sat together on the bus heading to Buffalo. It was a different kind of experience—not because I was chatting with someone who wasn't a close friend as much as from the uncertainty of the voyage. I remember the two of us laughing as we verbalized our thoughts, the common mental bond screaming, "What the hell are we doing here?" Neither of us could provide a logical answer. And at this point, there was nothing we could do about it, so we were just along for the ride.

The day had started quite early in Rochester. We'd left the building in Rochester for the bus ride to Buffalo by about 8:00 a.m., so we arrived shortly after 9:00 a.m. I already knew it would be a very long day, but I didn't realize just how long it would be extended. And extended. At different times of the day, I would be transported by car, bus (twice), and by plane. Of the seemingly indefinite legs of the trip, we were still on leg number three—a very long day.

The building in Buffalo was more of an induction center, where we would be initially processed, sworn in, and dip our toes into the waters of the military pool for the first time. The structure itself looked more like an office building than anything connected with the military. It was about five or six floors in height, concrete, and commercial in appearance. It was located downtown, right on Main Street, although I doubt I could point it out today.

All forty of us were herded once again into a large holding room on the second floor of the building, where we ran into another similar-sized group. Whereas our entire block of men was from the Rochester area, the other assemblage was from Buffalo. I imagine that there were similar groupings of men being pushed together in countless other induction centers across the country, just like ours. Well over two million men served in Vietnam, so there must have been a great many forty-man clusters on any day of the week. We were not unique.

Contrary to our first stop in Rochester, this function seemed to last forever. We were there most of the day, filling out paperwork and forms that hit us in a never-ending stream. It went on for hours and hours, with little time to rest in between. I continued to talk with Pat, mainly because I knew no one else. "At least there are two of us," I thought to myself. It made it a bit easier to have some companionship.

The day continued in unbroken monotony until sometime around 3:00 p.m., when a spit-shined Marine Corps Sergeant marched into the room. I still remember him to this day. He was an African American wearing the most perfect Marine Corps uniform I had ever seen. His shoes were polished until they had a mirror-like finish from the toes to the heels. His uniform was perfectly starched and pressed. The crease in his pant leg could have sliced a loaf of rye bread in half without leaving any crumbs. He was a Marine Corps Sergeant, and he fit the description to a T.

The Sergeant strode purposefully to the front of the room, where he did a crisp facing move to address the entire assembled crowd. In perfectly timed cadence, his voice boomed over our heads and drowned out all other sounds.

"I'm looking for five volunteers. I want a show of hands; who wants to be a Marine?"

The silence following his request was absolute. You could have heard a mosquito sneeze from across the room as we all looked at one another, no one daring to make a move or a sound. Evidently, everyone else had heard the same stories about the rugged combat faced by the Marines in the jungles of Vietnam: the fierce firefights and the ever-escalating body counts. The Sergeant would have no volunteers on this day.

After surveying our silent and motionless group for ten or fifteen seconds, the Marine concluded that he'd have to resort to plan B.

"OK then, we'll do it my way," he intoned. Then he left the room in the same, stiffly choreographed march. He was 100 percent Marine Corps to the core, and there wasn't a single soul among us who would have willingly taken him on. In fact, there was only one thing wrong with this man: We knew he'd be coming back.

It didn't take long. About fifteen or twenty minutes later, he repeated his earlier entrance and steps to the front of the room but, this time, accompanied by a small packet of papers. They were orders that instantly identified those individuals who would become members of the United States Marine Corps. In a toneless bark, he read the five names aloud. Thankfully, neither Pat nor I were on the list. I remember breathing a sigh of relief and hoping that no one could see my heart beating through the front of my shirt. Of all the bullets I would see over the next two years, I felt like I had just dodged my very first.

A short while later, we were gathered together and sent down the hall to a smaller room that was dressed out in American flags and other decorations from the various services. We quickly established that this would be the swearing-in room, if such a thing existed. We stood in straight lines and rows and were asked to raise our right hands. At that point, a noncommissioned officer in the front of our formation led us through the formal oath, using the "repeat after me" format.

We had almost made it through the entire swearing-in ceremony when a commotion arose on the other side of the room. There were other voices accompanied by some scuffling, and the "non-com" performing the ceremony went silent. Evidently, of the five men selected to go into the Marines, three of them objected and said they were not going to be sworn into any branch other than the Army. After some verbal badgering by the soldiers in charge, one of the three consented, leaving only two detractors. A Sergeant then prepared to take the two out of the room.

At this point, one of the recruits asked, "Where are we going?"

"We're taking you to jail," replied the Sergeant.

At this point, one of the two dissenters gave up and went through with the swearing-in process. The other did not. He was quickly and unceremoniously taken away. We never saw him again.

I remember thinking to myself that this was heavy stuff. A lot of these kids had probably never been away from home before. Now here they were, facing these big life-and-death decisions away from their parents, their families, their friends, and with no legal counsel whatsoever. I remember thinking that everything else in my life up to this point had been a cakewalk.

After the swearing-in ceremony, we were shepherded back into the bigger room, where we sat for a while without doing much of anything. It was obvious that they were preparing our bus transportation to the Buffalo Airport, where we would be flown out to our next point of accession. It was already getting dark out by the time we left the building: step four in the very long day.

Our bus dropped us off at the Buffalo Airport terminal, where we were led to a rather isolated part of the terminal. Our gate area seemed to be reserved for just us, and we waited quietly for a couple of hours before we were asked to board our plane. Throughout this waiting period, Pat and I remained together, and we found ourselves getting to know each other much better than we had through all those years of high school.

I don't know whether Pat had ever flown before, but I had logged a great many hours in the air. However, I still found this aircraft to be amazing. All my hours had been spent in single-engine prop planes, but this was a 727. I had never flown in a jet before, much less something this large. It was obviously a chartered aircraft, as only military personnel were onboard.

I remember taking off in the plane and being astounded at how rapidly it climbed into the nighttime sky. Had it been a prop plane attempting this rate of ascent, it most definitely would have stalled out and crashed into the city not far from the airport. But this powerful, multiengine jet soared rapidly into the clouds at a rate I could barely fathom. It was yet another new experience—and step five of the very long day.

Our plane touched down at Newark Airport in New Jersey sometime around 10:00 p.m. From there we boarded buses that took us to Fort Dix, which was some distance away. It may have been after midnight by the time we arrived and pulled through the gates. It made little difference, as by this time, time itself had little meaning.

Our bus pulled up to a reception center, where an Army Sergeant got on and gave us "greetings." (The term "greetings" seldom has a good connotation in the military.) He marshalled us off the bus and ordered us to form up in two lines.

"We're going to march you down to the warehouse," he shouted. "There, you will pick up your bedding. After that, you will carry your bedding back to your barracks and take your bunk. Now let's go, double time!"

At the warehouse, we each picked up our sheets, pillows, and blankets in rapid order before exiting for the barracks buildings, which, thankfully, were not far away. It must have been after 1:00 a.m. by the time we arrived at our barracks, and I was amazed that I was still able to stand. Once inside, we each grabbed the first available bunk, made our beds, and collapsed for a few hours' sleep.

Literally.

The Sergeant's voice seemed to explode inside our craniums within an hour of our falling asleep. It would be an early morning, the first of many, as we strained to pull our unrefreshed bodies from our bunks.

After a quick breakfast, our first stop of the day was back at the reception center, where the first order of business was haircuts. I found it hard to believe that a number of the recruits arrived with long hair—I mean, very long hair. I knew that this would not bode well in forming a good impression with my Drill Sergeant, so I'd had my head fairly well buzzed before I ever left home. As such, my appearance really didn't change much after my obligatory haircut. But the transformation of some of the fellows with long hair was almost comical. To see the expressions on some of them as they were seated in the barbers' chairs was priceless. I've seen worse on the faces of individuals facing root canal surgery.

One other thing I thought unusual was that the barbers were civilians rather than military. What that meant to us was that we had the regretful responsibility of paying for our own haircuts. I found this to be a bit ironic, as none of us wanted the standard buzz cut that was provided, but we had no choice. I still wonder what would have happened if one of our fellow recruits had arrived with no cash. I doubt they would have escaped the chair.

A lot more happened on day two, much of which took place in the reception center. For one thing, Pat and I (who had stayed together since our first stop in Rochester) got separated. He went one way, and I went another. I never saw him again.

In the reception center, there were a lot of people, perhaps one hundred recruits in a big room. As we were sitting there, a Lieutenant stood up in the front of the room and called out just two names. One of them was mine. I tensed up as I rose and approached the officer, not knowing what kind of trouble I had caused to be singled out like this.

The Lieutenant didn't immediately say anything but asked the two of us to accompany him to a desk at the back of the auditorium. He was a young-looking fellow who looked to be only a year or two older than myself. He also appeared to be very friendly and open, which I appreciated. I also noted that, while being very clean-cut, he didn't seem like a career officer. I couldn't put my finger on it, but that was just the impression I got.

Once he had me aside, he asked me about the tests I'd taken a few months earlier, during my discussions with the recruiters in Rochester. I had inquired about going into a warrant officer program for aviation, as I wanted to fly. The Lieutenant had access to the recruiter's notes as well as my test results. My tests had scored high enough to permit me admission to the program. He wanted to know why I hadn't accepted the offer.

I quickly explained that the recruiter told me I'd have to satisfy a seventy-two-month (six-year) enlistment period in order to go through the aviation warrant officer program. That explanation drew an incredulous look from the Lieutenant.

"That is simply not true," he said as he gazed at me with a level stare. "Your commitment would be only forty-eight months, no more."

To this day, I still don't know whether the recruiter had intentionally lied to me to gain enlistment points, or perhaps he was just ignorant of the basic requirements. But either way, I been given bad information that had led me to my current placement.

"You know, I could still get you into that pilot program," he added. "It isn't too late if you still want to fly."

I considered it briefly but then compared the commitment periods; it was still four years of piloting versus two years in my current route. The two-year enlistment won out. But the officer wasn't finished, and he made one more generous offer.

"I'll tell you what," he said. "In my opinion, you've been wronged. So if you'd like, I'll put you into an enlisted program that will still involve aviation but in a support role. Instead of infantry, you'll have a different MOS [military occupation specialty] that will have you working with aircraft in one capacity or another."

I readily agreed to that offer, as I would prefer almost any form of aviation over infantry. I didn't know where that would take me, but I figured I had enough time to figure it all out before I left my eight weeks of basic training.

Our first several days in the reception center were interesting because there were all kinds of recruits going through the same process, just at different points of the process. Behind us there were numerous day-one folks who still had their long hair and civilian clothes, just as we'd had when we arrived. The day-two recruits had their haircuts but were still in civilian clothes, having not yet received uniforms and combat boots, and so forth. The day-three people had uniforms and were much closer to commencing the actual training that toughened us up for future combat.

Following all the in-processing, we were next sent to the basic training area and the training center. There would be four platoons, which formed a single company. Of those, I was assigned to the 4th Platoon, which contained only about six members on the first day. We would have to wait for the rest of the forty men to arrive, but in the meantime, we had a barracks all to ourselves.

During one of the first days in the barracks, our Drill Sergeant came inside to address us. He looked at me and asked, "What's your name?" When I replied that it was Feigel (which is pronounced "Fie-gel," he responded by telling me that I was to become the Platoon Leader and that I should go to pick up an arm band to pin on that had three stripes on it. For the life of me, I didn't have a clue what a Platoon Leader's duties entailed; I only knew that I was it.

Another interesting bit was that the Sergeant never quite got the hang of pronouncing my last name. Throughout the entirety of basic training, my name was "Fuh-gelly" or various combinations and permutations of that pronunciation. But I answered to almost anything, so it made very little difference.

One other issue I quickly recognized was that the Platoon Leader had many places to go, including the company orderly room to pick up orders every day, as well as to other administrative locations. I was the only one who was required to visit all these daily offices, and we were *always* required to run between stops. That was a problem. Although in pretty good condition, I was not a runner, and the constant surging over countless locations quickly took a toll on my legs, ankles, and feet. I was always naturally flat-footed, which added to the anguish I experienced from the very first day. The stiff, heavy combat boots certainly didn't help either, instead adding to the constant agony.

The only benefit I gained from my leadership position was that I was never scheduled for details. If we were assigned the task of scrubbing the floors, polishing the brass, or loading/unloading trucks, I was exempt from that duty. But there was many a time when I would have gladly traded places and performed the details in exchange for the endless miles of running between buildings.

The running persisted whenever our platoon had to move between any two locations. Every movement was done as a run; we *never* walked anyplace. Ever. Platoons were required to run as double columns, and I (as Platoon Leader) had to run alongside the columns calling out a cadence to keep us all together in stride. It was very difficult for me, and it became worse by the week as my feet and ankles systemically fell apart. Our Drill Sergeant noticed that my problems were worsening, and he sympathized with my handicapped gait. But still, I persisted and kept up the pace as best I could.

The barracks in which we lived were comfortable, but they were genuine relics of World War II. They were two-storied wooden structures that were very run-down but simultaneously spit shined to extremes. Sometimes I wondered if the second-story floors had been polished so many times that the floor would give way. Every day they were cleaned, then waxed, then cleaned again. It would have been safe to eat chow off any tile on the floor.

The barracks were also old enough that they were heated with coal furnaces, which were located in the cellars of the buildings. In colder times a recruit trainee would be in the cellar, shoveling coal into the furnace to heat the buildings through the cool nights. However, thankfully, the weather in New Jersey was warm enough in April and May that it was unnecessary.

Sometime during the first few weeks, we received our M14 rifles, though without any ammunition. These would become ours to "love, honor, and cherish" for the rest of basic training. The M14 had been the standard combat rifle in Vietnam up until about 1965, when they were officially replaced by the M16. By 1970, most of the rifles in use by Americans in Vietnam were the M16s. However, we still used the M14 throughout basic training prior to deploying.

Through constant drilling, we became extremely familiar with each part of those rifles and took classes instructing us on how to take them apart, field clean them, and then reassemble them in rapid time. The Sergeant was constantly inspecting these pieces to ensure that we were keeping them perfectly clean. We also completed training on all the commands, including "Present arms," "Order arms," and "Right shoulder arms." It became second nature; we could do it in our sleep.

As we moved through week six of the eight weeks, my feet and ankles continued to deteriorate. My ankles got so bad that I had to swab them with alcohol on a daily basis, then wrap them with heavy ace bandages. This helped somewhat, but it made my feet and ankles almost impossible to squeeze into my combat boots. It made my ankles feel as though they were breaking every time I had to run, which was several times each day. I really needed to go to the hospital, but my pride and my daily commitments restrained me from taking this course of action.

I finally arrived at a point during week six when I knew I could not go on in my current condition. My Drill Sergeant knew it as well. He arranged a swap of duties; I traded places with a Squad Leader. A Squad Leader was below a Platoon Leader (there were four squad leaders who reported to each Platoon Leader), so I was actually requesting a demotion in position and responsibility. But the Squad Leaders did *much* less running and still were exempt from working details, so I gladly accepted the new job.

Sometime near the end of week six, we had to go out to the rifle range to qualify with our M14s. We were given three rounds for our magazines, which we used on targets that were placed roughly twenty-five yards away. The range instructors observed us and helped us to correct for sighting errors. As our training progressed, we moved up to combat scenarios where we had to run forward, then drop and provide cover fire for the next man moving forward. It included pop-up targets that provided for even more realistic training.

During the final rifle qualification firing, I surprised myself by achieving the expert level, which was not easy to attain. In fact, it was so difficult to achieve that the Army rewarded that performance with a two-day pass. This was very rare, and I gladly took advantage of the opportunity. I flew from Newark back to Rochester and spent the forty-eight hours with Whit and my family. I still had to wear my uniform and the buzz-cut hairstyle, but I was home again for those two days.

It seemed like it was taking forever, but we were rapidly approaching week eight, when we would graduate and move on—that is, *if* we passed our final qualifications, which would be difficult. I remember two of the hardest parts of the final testing were the run and the man-carry. The run was a couple of miles long, timed, around an oval track, and in all our gear. It was very close, but I made it across the finish line with seconds to spare.

The second part of the testing was much harder. The man-carry involved picking up another recruit and physically carrying him one hundred yards across another finish line. By this point, running one hundred yards *without* carrying anything seemed hard enough. But performing this task with a man on my back, on ankles that were completely shot, and in a timed run over a stone track? That seemed impossible. But one thing the Army had taught me by that point was that you had to push yourself. You had to push yourself to the very end of your limitations, and then go beyond.

As I started down the track, the finish line seemed to be at least a mile away rather than one hundred yards. But I knew that if I didn't make it in time, I would fail and be forced to start basic training all over again from the day-one start. I was not willing to do that.

Push, push. Put one foot in front of the other. Keep going. Keep moving. Never stop. Never give up.

The stop watch was within a couple seconds of hitting the end when I fell across the finish line—and I did literally fall across the finish line. The fellow on my back came tumbling over the top of me, and I did a face-plant into the gravel. I'm sure my "rider" didn't appreciate it, nor did I. But I had made it. I had passed. The Drill Sergeant just looked at me, shaking his head, concealing a smile as he walked away.

Once we'd all completed our qualifications, the only thing remaining in front of us was graduation itself. It was to be conducted on a big lot, somewhat similar to the scene in the iconic movie *Stripes*. There was a large gathering of all the other companies, stands for the three hundred to four hundred spectators in attendance, a band, a pass-in-review stand with the high-ranking officials, and more. As we marched out to our positions, my eyes scanned the bleacher seating as I looked for my family. My father had told me that he was going to fly his plane down to Newark with a friend of his, and he was going to bring Whit along as a second passenger. I had looked forward to seeing them in the stands, and I spent most of the ceremony in a failed attempt to pick them out of the crowd.

Following the ceremony and still unable to locate my family, I called home to inquire about their absence. My father told me that the weather in Rochester was abysmal, preventing them from getting airborne. It was disappointing, but I certainly wouldn't have wanted them to risk their safety by flying under those conditions.

Finally, basic training was over. Done. In the rear-view mirror. We didn't have much to do over the following days as we prepared to move on to our next course of training. For almost all the men in our platoon, that meant advanced infantry training, which was also held at Fort Dix. In other words, the vast majority of our men would be staying in place for the next few months.

The very next day, our platoon was sitting outside in a grassy area, taking apart our rifles and cleaning them. As we worked, our 4th Platoon Sergeant came outside with a stack of papers and a staff clerk.

"I have orders for the 4th Platoon," he announced. He then proceeded to read off all the orders and MOS (job descriptions) for all forty men in our unit. Of those, thirty-eight were assigned to attend advanced infantry training at Fort Dix. Only one other soldier and I received orders to another training school in another location. I learned that I would be driven to Fort Eustis, located in Virginia, to attend some other school. I was also told that my MOS would be 67N20. I had no idea just what that meant. I only knew that it was *not* infantry.

I did make one casual attempt to find out the meaning of 67N20. Before departing, I asked a Sergeant if he could translate the letters and numbers into something resembling a job description. He glanced at a sheet of paper and was able to come up with the word "transportation."

"I don't know," he mumbled. "Maybe you're going to drive a truck."

And so I prepared for the drive the following day that would take me all the way down to the middle of Virginia. I didn't know what to expect in this next step of my military journey other than that I should prepare for another very long day.

# 3

# AVIATION SCHOOL

It's very seldom that I go somewhere without having any idea why it is that I am going. But the morning I departed Fort Dix fits that description. I knew that I now possessed a 67N20 MOS, but I didn't know what that meant. I only knew that it was different from all my classmates from basic, who were going into the infantry. I also knew that because of the mysterious number, I had to climb on a big old bus with about forty other men for the long ride south.

The trip was about 340 miles, but it felt much longer. We boarded the bus in the early morning and were on the road until late afternoon. We did make several stops to permit our men to use the bathroom facilities along the way, but that was about it. We ate our "box lunches" that had been packed for us back at Fort Dix. The obligatory ham sandwich and apple were enough to keep us going, but they did not measure up to the food we'd enjoyed back on base.

One saving grace about the extended duration of the bus trip was that I had the chance to cement in place a new friendship. Toward the end of basic training, I had met another soldier by the name of John Foley, who was from Danbury, Connecticut. He was a nice fellow, very levelheaded, who seemed to share a lot of the same interests as me. I spotted him waiting for the same bus on the morning of the trip to Fort Eustis, and we began to talk. We boarded the bus together and ended up sitting next to each another for the duration of the trip. It was nice to have friends during our initial training classes, as it gave me someone to hang with rather than doing everything by myself. John quickly became a good friend.

We finally pulled through the gates of Fort Eustis (or, as we called it, Fort Useless) around 4:00 p.m. We were hot, tired, and in need of stretching our legs. It felt good just to walk off the bus and look around the place.

One thing I noticed immediately was the climate. It was June, and the air was both hot and *extremely* humid. I found this to be surprising because we weren't all that far south of Fort Dix. But the difference was very noticeable, and I was glad that all the hard running of basic was now just a bad memory.

The base itself was significantly smaller than Fort Dix and also not as well-known. When you consider the area surrounding Norfolk and Virginia Beach, most visitors think of the many Naval installations (bases and air centers) without realizing that it is also home to the facilities of other branches of our armed forces. The land along the James River that was once known as Mulberry Island, now part of Newport News, was acquired by the US Army in 1918 and used to establish Camp Eustis in 1923.

Our arrival process was so much different than our first hour at Fort Dix had been. We had graduated from basic training and were now real US Army soldiers, so the pressure was off. There were no Drill Sergeants screaming in our faces or roughly demanding that we line up in regimented formations. Instead there was a clerk with perhaps a corporal directing us from the reception center to our barracks. It was much more relaxed, as we were now students instead of recruit newbies.

We all noticed there were a lot of interesting things to see around the base entrance, one of which appeared to be a transportation museum. There were train cars and vehicles, boats and aircraft, all arranged for viewing both indoors and out. As a matter of fact, transportation seemed to be the main theme that tied almost everything together on this base.

I stopped the clerk who was assisting the men coming off our bus and asked him about my MOS. Just what was a 67N20?

"Helicopters," he replied matter-of-factly. "You're going to take a helicopter repair course that is going to teach you everything you'll ever want to know about repairing and maintaining Army helicopters."

It all made sense now.

The clerk escorted us down to the platoon barracks, which looked exactly like the buildings we'd occupied at Fort Dix. They must have all been built around the same time, as their size, shape, and proportions were identical. There were four of these barracks built together in our platoon area, which were accompanied by a mess hall and an orderly room. The orderly room housed the Platoon Captain's offices, which also served as the work spaces for various clerks and administrative assistants.

This area would be home to the sixty-one students in our class, so there were a lot of people moving around at any given time. As we entered the building, John and I noticed there were already a lot of our classmates who had picked out bunks on the first floor, so he and I skipped up to the second floor to pick out our quarters. We found a lot of empty space up there, so we quickly claimed a bunk and some lockers. John took the top bunk while I dropped my gear on the bottom. It was a comfortable arrangement—old, but comfortable.

I also found it interesting how little locker space I needed. We had sent almost all of our civilian clothes home since the start of basic training, so there was very little left. We had extra uniforms, our toiletries, notebooks, and, of course, our orders and other paperwork, but that was about it. Life as a transient soldier doesn't permit you to acquire a large volume of personal effects.

Another thing that I instantly enjoyed was the lack of running. At Fort Dix, we ran *everywhere*. It was required of all recruits, and it just became part of life. Once we arrived at Fort Eustis, we didn't run anyplace. We did have to march in rows and formations, but no more running. Slowly but surely, my feet began to recover until I was fully functional again.

Our classes didn't begin for a week or two, so we had some time to tour the base and relax a bit. We visited the museum and the post exchange (PX), as well as the base bowling alley, which was quite close by. It gave us a chance to unwind, which we hadn't been able to do since starting basic training a few months earlier. The bowling alley served beer, which we were all able to enjoy since the legal drinking age in that day was still eighteen. On some nights, a good percentage of our class could be found in the bowling alley.

It turned out that our helicopter repairman course of sixty-one students would include about twenty Army Reservists from Texas. One of those individuals was already a "Spec 4," or Specialist 4. This was equivalent to a corporal, which was the fourth pay level up the enlisted ranks. It was a relatively low rank but still the highest in our platoon, so he was designated our Platoon Leader. This meant that he not only had to do the reporting on our platoon, but he also had to march alongside our double column of men, calling out the cadence as we marched between classes. He was a pretty decent sort of fellow, short and slender, with a very serious demeanor. I quickly got the impression that he was grooming himself for a career in the Army.

A week or two later, we started our classes in the Helicopter Repairman Course, and I realized right from the start that I loved it. The instruction was a combination of mechanics and aviation, which had been two of my favorite pursuits since I was quite young. The training followed a curriculum that mixed about 70 percent classroom learning with 30 percent hands-on work. A lot of the hands-on sessions were held in work spaces inside large hangars, but we often operated in smaller buildings that were designated for other uses. Either way, it was all good as we studied about everything needed to maintain a Bell UH-1 helicopter, from power plant to hydraulics to electrical and maintenance. Every day was a different topic, although some of the more involved subjects, such as power plants and hydraulics, remained on our agenda for three or four days. Everything was covered in excruciating detail, and our instructors were really top-notch.

As a group, almost all of us were quick learners because the majority of students in our platoon had the same "gearhead" background. We had all tinkered with our own cars in high school, and a number of my classmates brought their own cars to the Newport News base. I noticed that a number of those cars had been fixed up with some pretty impressive improvements, and most of them could really move. Gearheads.

Our progress through the eight-week course was carefully monitored, and we received a form of report card every week. It was an old-fashioned, IBM-style card that gave us a weekly score, which was presumably tallied up for a final grade. I noticed that for many weeks, I had the highest or second-highest score of all sixty-one members of our platoon, which felt fantastic. After all, attending high school and learning my math and science and reading had been one thing. I paid attention as best I could, sometimes getting better results than others. But this was different. Every procedure, every technique, and every turn of the wrench could easily determine whether our air crew survived or perished. Our instructors were good, but we were forced into being quick learners.

The majority of our instructors had all been through at least one tour in Vietnam, so they were intimately familiar with our ships and the problems they faced on their daily missions. They also knew that we needed more good people to repair and maintain those craft in order to support all the combat missions. Because of that, they were very supportive and encouraging of students to pursue the job of Crew Chief.

"Our Hueys are dropping like flies over there, men, so we need all the good people we can get." Eight weeks didn't seem like a long time to gain all that knowledge, so we worked as hard as we could every day.

In a way, the eight-week duration of the course afforded us a reprieve. Eight weeks was a long time, but it meant that much longer to stay in our own territory, shielded from the dangers of war and combat. Those two months seemed like such a long period of time—at least at first. Being away from home like this, with other troops my age and with all the freedoms we enjoyed, was a new experience. We had been extremely regulated through boot camp, with no time to enjoy ourselves with our comrades. Here in Newport News, we were permitted time to travel off base once the classroom hours ended. The insouciances of our risk-free environment enabled our carefree attitudes as we enjoyed the pleasures of the town while intentionally deferring our thoughts on what would come after graduation.

Our schedules were a bit irregular, as our platoon followed a second-shift workday. There were so many student soldiers on the base taking the same courses that they had to conduct two completely separate class sessions. While many attended classes during the day, our platoon attended theirs later in the day, from 4:00 p.m. until 11:00 p.m. Every day, we'd get up by 8:00 a.m. and take care of our other needs on base. Sometimes that might mean taking clothes in for cleaning or visiting the PX to pick up supplies. A lot of us studied during the day as well since we had a lot of material to learn.

On other days, we would gather in an open area for physical training, which usually meant performing an hour of calisthenics. It was nothing compared to the rigors of basic training, and it never included running. My feet and ankles had healed by then, but I still wanted to avoid running if at all possible.

Around 4:00 p.m., we would fall out for muster in the parade area, where we would line up in formation and march to our class, wherever it was on that given day. Sometimes that march would be a distance of almost a mile. On most days, we each carried a stack of notebooks and tech manuals, sometimes piled eight- or nine-inches thick. It was pretty intense. It is amazing just how many tech manuals are required to maintain a single aircraft, and we used them all. (I had heard it said that the number of manuals printed to maintain a B-52 bomber would completely fill a B-52. After going through Helo Repairman School, I believed it.)

Even before starting classes at Fort Eustis, I had heard of another student from a neighboring town back in upstate New York. His name was Juddy, and he had grown up in Irondequoit, which was located on the other side of the bay bordering my town. We never attended the same school, but he was a fellow gearhead, and most of us were friends with the car enthusiasts in neighboring communities. It was a bit of a brotherhood, and we all felt fairly connected.

A few weeks into our course, John and I traveled down to the other end of the base to search for Juddy. I can't remember whether he knew I was there at the time, but I figured he couldn't be too difficult to find. Juddy was working his way through the course for the CH-47, which was a much larger ship than our Bell UH-1. Because of the difference in size and complexity, his course was ten weeks in duration, two weeks longer than mine.

Without knowing where to find Juddy, we ended up walking through their mess hall, as that was where the most people were congregated. It was lunch hour, and the place was very crowded. It didn't take long before I spotted him sitting at a table with a group of other students. I approached him quietly from behind but then accidently bumped into the back of his chair. He was in the middle of transporting a piece of chocolate cake from his plate to his mouth. The cake fell off his fork and splashed into a glass of milk. Juddy, not knowing who had committed that foul, spun around, ready for action. The expression on his face when he saw me was priceless.

"What the hell are YOU doing here?" he cried out.

Juddy's surprise was extreme, and we all had a good laugh about our fortunes (or misfortunes?) that had brought us together so far from home. We spent quite a while talking and just catching up, which was good to do with someone from so close to home. We also made tentative arrangements to get together over the weekend. Not only was it nice to have another friend on base, but Juddy had a car, which made it even better.

As I got to become even better friends with Juddy, we decided to make a few weekend excursions back to Rochester using his car. We were granted two-day weekend passes every week, which we always used to get away somewhere off base. Most of the time John came with us, and we headed out to Virginia Beach, which was a great place for single guys in the military. We didn't have to report in until our platoon formation on Monday afternoon, so we had the time to ourselves to do whatever we desired.

The weekend excursions to Rochester were a lot more ambitious, not to mention against the regulations. Our two passes had a stipulation that required us to remain within one hundred miles of the base. Any fool with a map and pair of dividers could quickly determine that one hundred miles would take you about as far as Fredericksburg, which was still in Virginia. Rochester was a whopping 550 miles from Newport News, which required a solid twelve hours of driving. To make matters worse, I never got out of class and back to my barracks before 11:00 p.m., which meant that we'd have to drive through the entire night to arrive in Rochester by 11:00 a.m. the following morning. We'd get to spend the entire day on Saturday at home, then have to leave sometime around 10:00 a.m. on Sunday to make it back at a decent hour. Naturally, we shared the driving time, which was the only way we could stay awake and safely cover that kind of distance. It was just nice to be able to see my family and Whit, if even for part of a day.

Back on the base, week followed week all too quickly as we counted down toward our departure for parts unknown. The heat and humidity was brutal at times, but we learned to put up with it. Many of the classrooms were air conditioned, as was the bowling alley. It would have been nice if our barracks shared the same luxury, as we were there during the hottest months of the year, but unfortunately, they did not. This might have made it difficult to sleep at night had we not been so tired by the late hour of our return each day. We were usually pretty exhausted, and almost nothing would have kept us awake.

Only once during my course was I able to obtain a pass that was longer than twenty-four hours, but it was provided to me under fraudulent circumstances. I remember being in my barracks one afternoon early in July. One of the platoon clerks approached me and said that our Platoon Commander wanted to see me. This was highly unusual; under normal circumstances, we had no reason to interact with officers unless there had been trouble. It was seldom a good thing to be called on the carpet.

As I followed the clerk across the common area and into the orderly building, my level of angst rose accordingly as I wondered what I had done wrong. After all, I was one of the best students in my class, and I had never been put on report for anything. So what was all this about?

The clerk led me into the orderly building and into the Captain's office, where I snapped to my best at-attention pose and snapped off a crisp salute, all while stating my name and unit in a clipped military voice.

The Captain looked at me for a moment before speaking. "Where do you come from, Private?" he asked.

"Webster, New York, Sir!" I responded. I still wasn't sure where this was going.

"What happens in Webster, New York, over the Fourth of July?" he continued.

Huh? OK, now I was completely baffled. "We have parades and fireworks, Sir," I answered.

"Exactly!" shouted the Captain. I'm sure the officer saw the look of bewilderment in my eyes and decided to put me out of my misery.

"Private Feigel, I received a letter from Mayor Chris Pantis of Webster this morning. He said it was urgent that you return to Webster in time to lead the military members of the armed forces in your town's Fourth of July parade."

"Yes, Sir, I would be happy to do that," I replied. However, inside, I was in hysterics, and the laughter almost burst through my façade to give it away. If only the Captain knew that Chris was not the mayor of Webster.

In fact, he was not an official of the town in any capacity. Instead he owned a popular restaurant in the middle of Webster and was well-known for being a bit of a prankster—but in a good way.

The conversation and official request from the "mayor" resulted in a four-day pass back to Rochester. But the most humorous part of the entire thing was that I never even marched in the parade. I should have felt guilty, but I didn't.

As we moved into the final couple weeks of our Helicopter Repairman Course, things began to change a little. We all knew that we would soon be deploying mostly overseas, and the destination was never really in doubt for most of us. Our moods turned a bit more serious, more somber, as we contemplated the journey ahead.

Sometime near our final week of training, they gave us a Vietnam Orientation Course, where they taught us about the Vietnamese culture, lifestyle, and even a few basic words in their native language. It was interesting, but I didn't think it would be of much use.

Next, the instructors led us down a trail that took us into the woods, presumably to show us some booby traps and how they were activated. Once again, as an aviation troop, I really couldn't see the purpose of this training, unless perhaps we were shot down in enemy territory. I guess it was possible.

We continued along the trail until we came to an entirely authentic Vietnamese village, built right there in the middle of the Fort Eustis woods. It was amazing; not one of us knew it was there. We strolled through the village, passing a fire in the middle of the clearing that was probably used for cooking. But none of us paid it much attention.

We continued for about fifty more feet before a series of loud, staccato sounds cracked behind us. "Pop! Pop-pop-pop-pop!" We all whirled around and stared at the Vietcong imitator who was standing next to the fire. A trap door had been raised, exposing a small underground compartment in which he had been concealed. Not one of us had seen him until the shooting was done.

"Congratulations, you are all dead!" said our instructor. "Nice job."

The bullets were all blanks, of course, but it taught us some valuable lessons. Know your enemy, always keep your eyes and ears open, and never assume you are safe. You are always surrounded by threats and should always expect the unexpected. Always.

Back on the base, we wrapped up our classes and took our final exams, most of which were written. To the best of my knowledge, we all passed, as everyone was processed in similar fashion. I was very pleased to learn that I had finished with a class rank of two out of sixty-one students. I also learned that my high class rank meant that I got a promotion up to Spec 4, which was an E-4 in Army terms. This was great. I had been in the Army for only four months and had already been promoted from E-1 to E-4. I must admit, I was quite proud of my progression.

Funny as it seemed, I spent much of my final few days at Fort Eustis just trying to avoid running into the Sergeant. He was always trying to track down members of our platoon to work on one detail or another. It was always some lame duty that we did not feel up to working, so we all became well versed in his search patterns. I wouldn't call it hiding as much as "intentional avoidance." But whatever, it worked.

We had a number of administrative tasks to complete before leaving the base, including picking up our orders, returning library materials, and more. But there was one more group-session schedule, and it drove home the seriousness of our duty in dramatic fashion. It was our last day in the classroom, and the Sergeant stood before the group and asked the front third of the room to rise. We all stood up, looking at one another and not knowing the point of the exercise. Then the Sergeant spoke again.

"If this platoon of sixty men were Crew Chiefs and door gunners actually stationed in Vietnam, those of you standing would not be returning home." That was one-third: twenty out of sixty. Those were our odds operating as flight crew members over enemy territory. Of every three men, one would not be coming home.

It was a very somber statement, much like the simulated sniper in the woods: one in three. We have no idea whether those statistics were real or just meant to scare us. Either way, it got the point across. It was better to know the odds before we left.

Our final acts of departure were simple. There were no graduation ceremonies, no marching bands, and no crowds of spectators watching from the stands. It was just us, picking up our papers and taking care of last-minute details.

One of the last things we did before leaving Fort Eustis was to receive our orders. Lists were read out loud, and we learned that all but two of our entire platoon were heading to Vietnam. That was anything but a surprise. We all knew where we were going. If nothing else, the lists perhaps took away the suspense and simply confirmed our fates. We were heading to Vietnam and the middle of the action.

# 4

# LEAVE—LAST DAYS OF FREEDOM

Considering how long we'd spent at Fort Eustis and the intensity of the training, we certainly departed with very little in the way of fanfare. Not much was said. We just left.

I remember stuffing all my clothing and belongings into my duffel bag, with the exception of my "civvies" (civilian clothes) that I'd wear and the large brown envelope containing my orders that I'd carry all the way to Vietnam. The only emotional part I'd experience would be saying goodbye to Juddy, as his helicopter course would continue for at least two more weeks.

John and I ended up sharing a taxi cab ride with a couple of other members of our platoon in route to the airport. Since John was flying directly home to Connecticut and I was heading north to Rochester, we knew we'd be splitting up at the Newport News airport. But we had become very close friends during our eight weeks of school, and we knew we wanted to spend some time together before heading overseas. To facilitate this, we coordinated our travel plans following our leave period so that they would align for much of our trip. We were both scheduled to fly from Chicago to our final stopover point at Fort Lewis, in the state of Washington, so we decided in advance to meet up in Chicago and travel together from there.

It was sometime around 6:00 p.m. when my plane touched down in Rochester, NY. It was a fairly small airport back then, and security was not yet much of an issue. My father and Whit were at the gate, waiting for me, and we had a quiet little celebration marking my arrival.

Twenty-five days of leave. Twenty-five! Everyone I knew had gotten the same amount, and it seemed like such a lot of time. And yet, we all knew what awaited us at the end of those few weeks, and it attenuated the joy and anticipation of my time at home. I would have to make the best of every moment and enjoy it to the fullest.

Unlike in my basic training days, we were not required to wear uniforms when off on our own time. I was glad to be able to wear civilian clothes, as I would be wearing uniforms continuously once I headed off to my final station.

My days and weeks of leave were wonderful, with only the background ticking of time interrupting my peaceful bliss with visions of the hazardous upcoming duty. It was now early September. Even in upstate New York, the leaves had yet to begin turning color, though the air was beginning to show signs of the change in season.

I spent all my time with my family, relatives, and, of course, Whit. My family was really good about this, surrounding me with love and support, and all the while attempting to divert my thoughts away from the trip to Vietnam. This was almost impossible to do, as the daily news was always loaded with the terrible storylines, the lists of names, all while playing Taps in the background. We all tried living in denial, focusing instead on the present day and looking forward to my safe return.

My mother was wonderful throughout this entire interval and arranged a continuous stream of dinners, picnics, and other functions that seemed to follow on a daily basis. Family, aunts, uncles, cousins—everyone was invited, and everyone came. I think I must have regained any weight I'd lost through all the running and calisthenics of the past four months. In the back of my mind, I wondered whether all my uniforms would still fit.

At one of these family gatherings, my Aunt Mary pulled me aside and hugged me, then gave me a small card with a printed verse called "Prayer to St. Joseph." It read as follows:

> This prayer was found in the fiftieth year of our Lord and Savior Jesus Christ. In 1505 it was sent from the Pope to Emperor Charles when he was going into battle. Whoever shall read this prayer or hear it, or keep it about themselves, shall never die a sudden death or be drowned, nor shall poison take effect on them; neither shall they fall into the hands of the enemy, or shall be burned in any fire or shall be overpowered in any battle.

I took this card and placed it in my wallet, where it remained through my entire tour of duty in Vietnam and beyond. I still carry it with me today, some forty years later, although it is now laminated to hold together the now-frayed remainder of the treasured original piece.

I was happy to be able to spend some quality time with my dad as well. We spent a lot of time just talking, filling the hours with discussions about aviation and who was doing what amongst our group of mutual acquaintances. But sometimes our conversation also stalled, as we felt awkward about discussing the really heavy topics about my upcoming year in Vietnam. It seemed as though neither of us knew quite what to say. Yet I somehow think we could read each other's minds and thoughts, even if we couldn't voice them to one another.

We also went flying together a couple times, once again taking the Aeronca Champ out of the Williamson/Sodus Airport. I still hadn't fully qualified for my pilot's license (I wouldn't achieve that until after returning from the war), but we had fun flying together over the local towns and shoreline of Lake Ontario to the north. Being up in the aircraft, soaring beneath the clouds, always provided a temporary relief that soothed my soul like nothing else.

I also spent as much time as possible with Whit, and we shared just about everything throughout my leave. Every moment we could be together, we were. She attended most of our family picnics and gatherings, becoming almost a real member of our family. In essence, she was just that, as she was living in our house by that time. She was working in downtown Rochester in the same building as my mother, so they shared a ride every day. To save time, she moved into a room in our house, so she was always around.

Whit and I passed our time over those weeks by reliving many of the same activities we'd enjoyed in high school. We'd ride over to Webster Park and leave our car where our high school group had once parked, then stroll over to the picnic tables and talk for hours. There were memories there—the friends, the cars, the beers—and we took comfort with being alone with each other and the memories.

In comparison to those earlier times, it was a quiet time, as almost all our high school friends had left the area. Those who enlisted or were drafted had already deployed. Meanwhile, those classmates who received college deferments from the Selective Service had departed for college, leaving almost no one but Whit and me. And even that was just temporary.

Much of what we did together over those few weeks in September was a replay of our senior year. We frequented the drive-ins, the parks, and everywhere else we could think of. One day we drove down to Letchworth Park, located about forty miles south of Rochester, to take in the beautiful forests, cliffs, and waterfalls. We spent the day enjoying each other as much as the scenery.

While touring around the area, we made use of my mother's car, as I had sold my 1957 Chevy when I went off to basic training. My mom had a white 1968 Barracuda, which they had purchased new and was a beautiful car. She let me use it whenever she didn't need it for work or other required transport.

I also ran into Chris, the owner of the Candy Kitchen restaurant, who had used duplicitous means to get me the four-day pass over the Fourth of July. Chris had served on PT boats during World War II, which was combat duty in that war. Chris was one of the only people with whom I could discuss actual combat, as my father had spent all his time training pilots in Florida. Chris was a real character, but he had been through hell in the Pacific and lived to talk about it. I respected him and enjoyed our conversations.

Another acquaintance who helped put things in perspective was George Fischer, a good friend of my father's. George's only child was a son, George Jr., who had gone off to Vietnam about two years earlier as part of the infantry. He had stepped on a land mine and perished during his first year of duty (in 1967), which traumatized the family beyond words. I met George at a family function once, but he was too distraught to address the subject.

George was also an auto mechanic, and he happened to own a garage in the area. He and his son had worked on cars together, and his son was an avid racer, having won numerous stock car races on the local tracks. That summer George Sr. asked if he could take home my Volkswagen on which I had worked to tinker with it in his own garage. He later ended up racing himself for a few years, although he never experienced the same levels of success as his son. He held on to the VW until I returned home from Vietnam.

One thing I was glad to see was that there was no resentment for those classmates who chose to attend college over the military. It was easy to understand how some people would have felt angered over this choice or held the sentiment that only the wealthy members of the high school class could have afforded college and, thus, avoided Vietnam. But there was none of that. It was just accepted that some men wanted to attend college to pursue a degree, while others did not, and we let it go at that.

I was also grateful to our little community for always providing continuous support to all our men in uniform. We were seeing nightly scenes on the television about war protests and backlash against soldiers but never in Webster or our neighboring towns. We were a working-class town that always displayed a dose of heavy patriotism. Many of the fathers had served in World War II, while the mothers had performed their share of support roles stateside. No one thought of running off to Canada to escape the draft. Service was considered honorable, and our community supported us 100 percent.

As the days of my twenty-five-day leave wound down to the final week, the feeling of dread grew exponentially. Every day became more precious than the day before. Whit and I attempted to fill every day, every hour, and every moment with meaningful activity. Although she tried to maintain a brave exterior, sometimes I would catch her crying, unable to hold back her tears. At those times, I would take her in my arms and hold her passionately, telling her that it was only for one year. One year. Twelve months. It seemed like an eternity to both of us. Little did she know that I was living through my own sleepless nights, my own tears, my own vision of surviving for an entire year without having each other to hold. It led to even more tears and more sleepless nights.

I had flashbacks to the final session with my Sergeant at Fort Eustis, when he asked one-third of our class to stand up and then told us, "You will not be coming home." Would I become one of that one-third? Would I ever return home? Would I ever see Whit and my family again? I couldn't say which one of those horrors scared me the most.

The final morning in Webster, when I was to catch my flight across the country, I awoke early and pulled out my khaki uniform, which I had not worn in almost a month. At least it still fit. As I got dressed, I repeated to myself, over and over again, "I have to be strong today. I have to be strong today."

I had already decided that I did *not* want my family to accompany me to the airport. The scene would have been too emotional to handle—not just for them but for me as well. I would have my friend Jerry drive me, and we'd bring along Whit for support.

Jerry had been a friend of mine through high school. His father had passed away, leaving him as the only male in the family. The Selective Service assigned a special deferment for males in that situation, with the thought being that they were crucial to support the family in the absence of the father. Thus, Jerry was still at home.

As Whit and I left the house, my mother, father, and Kath were standing on the steps on the side of the house. My mother kept repeating her instructions: "Don't volunteer for anything." We exchanged hugs and a lot of tears before getting into Jerry's GTO. As we pulled out of the driveway, I remember looking back at the house, my parents and sister still rooted in place, still crying. I also remember wondering whether I would ever see any of them again.

Jerry kept us company into the airport, shook my hand, then hugged me. "Remember to keep your head down," he said in a wavering voice. Then he backed off so Whit and I could say our final goodbyes.

Whit's eyes were filled with tears as we tried to exchange goodbyes. We held each other for what seemed like hours before the very last "Last call for boarding." Then, we had that final kiss before I turned and walked to the gate door. I turned back one last time to wave, then passed through the door.

At that moment, I didn't need Vietnam to experience life and death. I felt like part of me had already died.

Yearbook photograph of Tom Feigel taken in Webster, NY, in 1968. (Photographer unknown.)

Spec 4 Tom Feigel, 1969, Profado Studios, East Rochester, NY.

*Photograph of Tom's father, Joseph Feigel, in his RAF uniform in Clewiston, FL, 1942. (RAF official photo.)*

*Tom's father (Joseph) in RAF uniform with three unidentified RAF cadets in 1942. (Official RAF photograph.)*

*Tom Feigel with Cessna sea plane on Irondequoit Bay, 1962. (Photo taken by father Joseph Feigel.)*

*Tom with Aeronica Champ aircraft taken at Williamson Airport in 1965. (Photograph taken by father, Joseph Feigel, following flight lesson.)*

*Tom (center) with mother (Betty) and father (Joseph) in front of home in Webster, NY. (Photo taken in 1969 by sister Kathlene.)*

*Photograph of Tom (center) with sister (Elizabeth) and John Foley (left), taken in Chicago Airport in 1969. (Taken by sister Kathlene.)*

# 5

# JOURNEY TO THE UNKNOWN

The first leg of my marathon two-day journey took me through Chicago, which is where John and I had planned to rendezvous for the rest of our trip. It was also home to my sister Betty Jo and her husband Tom, so they came to the airport to say both hello and goodbye. Airport security really didn't exist in those days, so they were able to come right to the gate to give their farewells.

There wasn't a lot to say to my sister and brother-in-law, and we didn't have much time between flights anyway, so our conversation was very short. No one seemed to know exactly what to say, just like back at home. It was an awkward mixture of sadness, anxiety, concern, and dismay that led to a stilted conversation. My sister put on a brave face but, at a later time, confessed that she had been in tears the entire drive home. She had experienced a premonition that I would not be coming home and was hiding the fact that internally, she was a nervous wreck.

Before my departing, my sister took a final photo of me and John, both still hanging onto our large brown envelopes as we were heading toward the boarding door of the plane. We both looked back and waved, and her photo caught us in an iconic pose as we prepared to walk through that final door. It was a scene that was being recreated at hundreds of airports across the country every day. I still have that photograph today, and I still recall the emotions I experienced as we crossed that threshold.

I was glad to have another person in uniform sitting next to me on the long flight across the country. There were no protestors at the airports in either Rochester or Chicago, but there were definitely strong antiwar sentiments across the country, and accidental encounters sometimes led to touchy situations. It felt better to be with another serviceman as we made the transit to Washington.

We arrived in the Seattle airport, which was the closest major airfield near Tacoma, home of Fort Lewis. It was late in the day, so the traffic was light for our nine-mile taxi ride to the base. The time made little difference anyway, as John and I were arriving a full day later than ordered. That was not an accident; we had arranged that. We had agreed on a "self-approved extension" of our twenty-five-day leave period, and we met in Chicago one day later than ordered. After all, we figured, what the heck could they do to punish us? Make us Army soldiers and send us to Vietnam? Would they do anything at all to reprimand us for our tardiness? Would anyone even care?

No one cared. As a matter of fact, no one said a thing about it. They were mostly civilian clerks who were processing us, and I'm sure they didn't care either. We had probably missed our intended flight, but there were multiple flights going across every day, so that made little difference either.

Fort Lewis is a massive installation that covers over eighty-seven thousand acres of Washington prairie land. Named after Meriwether Lewis of the Lewis and Clark Expedition, it is a very modern base that is the most requested duty station in the US Army. However, as we arrived at 11:00 p.m. following a lengthy cross-country flight, none of that mattered to us. We just wanted to find an empty bunk and collapse for the night.

Following our first night at Fort Lewis, we ran into a number of our classmates from the Helicopter Repairman Course at Fort Eustis. Unlike us, they had arrived on time and were just hanging out, waiting for our flight across the Pacific. We'd all be traveling on the same flight, as we were all going to the same place: Vietnam.

We stayed at Fort Lewis for two days and two nights before flying out. Most of that time seemed to be spent completing paperwork, and I remember filling out and signing so many forms that I developed cramps in my finger. At one point, I was sitting next to another fellow whose only brother was already stationed in Vietnam. A civilian clerk, noticing that fact, informed him of his choice.

"You know, you don't have to go over there," she said in a kindly voice. "If your brother is already serving in Vietnam, you can decline the deployment and stay in the States."

"Thanks anyway, but I'll go," he replied.

I remember looking at him through the corner of my eye, shocked at his answer. I don't know what I would have said given the same circumstances. Perhaps he would have felt ashamed if he had remained home, safe from the war and the killing. I also wonder what his mother would have said had she been able to hear his response.

I remember very little else about Fort Lewis other than the paperwork and the constant flurry of motion. Throngs of people were headed in every direction, and I was soon to join them. Those of my classmates who were still there were spread out over multiple barracks, so we were no longer a single, cohesive group.

Part of my checkoout process included passing through another supply warehouse, where I would receive five pairs of jungle fatigues and another pair of sturdy combat boots. This took quite a bit of time, as the uniforms had no names or rank insignias attached. We had to pass through a slow-moving line and provide all the required information to customize the uniform shirts for ourselves, which also included the sewing and embroidering.

After picking up all the new fatigues and boots, which we stuffed into our duffel bags along with everything else, we then trudged through even more stops inside the supply depot, receiving additional items that we pushed inside our already-bulging sacks. I remember thinking to myself that I'd be hard-pressed to carry this thing for even the shortest of marches. And I learned later that we weren't even done with it yet. There would be more to pack later on.

The evening before the third morning, I was told that I'd be flying out. John was ordered onto the same flight, so we would continue on for at least one more stop together. Our flight was to take off extremely early, hours before dawn. There would be 225 of us flying together, so the buses had to make many stops to pick us all up.

Predawn we were bused to an airstrip and loaded onto a Flying Tiger Stretch 8. These aircraft had been around for many years and had a reputation for being able to fly over great distances. (A specially modified Flying Tiger had once flown around the world, a flight spanning over sixty-two hours, carrying extra fuel tanks.) John and I were the first two passengers to board the plane, and I remember being in shock as I looked back along the cavernous interior. It was enormous. We sat in rows of six along the entire length of the cabin, with three seats on each side of the central aisle.

Another very noticeable item as we prepared for take off was the almost cathedral-like silence inside the aircraft. No one was talking. The mood was very quiet, very somber. It seemed as though words would have been superfluous. We all knew where we were going, and we probably shared the same thoughts.

Because the aircraft was so heavily burdened with men, equipment, and fuel, it seemed to take forever to leave the ground. We accelerated and accelerated and accelerated, experiencing bumps and jolts as we sped along the extended-length runway. I remember thinking back on our local airport in Williamson, NY, and that we not only would have gone beyond the end of the runway but probably through much of the town as well.

After what seemed like hours, we finally lifted off into the air and gained altitude. Even the start of the flight seemed long: We were airborne for a couple hours before the sun came up astern of our plane. We flew on and on, following the great-circle route westward until the sun set again behind us.

We made a refueling stop in Japan, which was twenty-two hours later. Out the windows we could make out the vast bulk of Mount Fuji, its conical summit injecting itself into the lightening skies. This would only be a refueling stop, perhaps an hour or two. But we were still permitted the luxury of deplaning, which we all accepted to stretch our legs and move around the small area inside the terminal. Even in that short-duration stop-over, we realized just how much the world differed from the United States, where everything was so new and modernized. Looking back toward the runway, we spied a small army of sweepers who were walking down the asphalt with brooms, clearing away any debris to prevent foreign object damage (FOD) to the plane. I remember thinking to myself, "We're not in Kansas anymore, Toto."

Inside the terminal, I could read the look in the eyes of my fellow servicemen. Many probably had never been out of their own state, much less flown halfway around the world. For me, it was a definite case of culture shock: the different people; the foreign languages; the different appearances, sights, sounds, and smells. It was very, very different, and we had yet to reach our remote destination.

Within two hour, we reboarded the same aircraft and took off for our next stop, which would be Cam Ranh Bay, Vietnam. Even though we knew this was just another stop, the entire mood changed once again. What had been somber was now abysmal. No one spoke, no one made a sound. We all shared thoughts of what we'd seen on the television for years. In addition to the gloom, there was the additional fear of the unknown.

The flight was much shorter than the trip across the Pacific, about three hours in a southerly direction. Then we felt the plane throttling back, the craft losing altitude as the wing flaps came down. Many were craning their necks to get a view of the shoreline outside the front windows.

At one point, the pilot came on the cabin loudspeaker with an announcement that sounded halfway between a greeting and a prayer. I still remember both his tone of voice and his words:

"Guys, I want to wish you all good luck, and I hope you'll be making the trip home again sometime real soon. So take care, and God bless."

It was both calming and disquieting at the same time. When his voice went silent, I glanced at John, and he returned my eye contact in a silent exchange. We never spoke a word, but our eyes alone spoke volumes.

Thump!

Our plane touched down on the tarmac. Welcome to Vietnam—the place that had been part of an American nightmare for so long, dominating the thoughts of Americans young and old. The war that had torn our country apart at its very soul and claimed our president (Lyndon Johnson) as one of its victims. Never in my wildest dreams did I imagine being a part of this. My heartbeat quickened as the plane slowed. I looked out the window and gained my first view of this godforsaken place.

Cam Ranh Bay is a major port that is located on the South China Sea, about halfway down the coast of South Vietnam. It is one of the United State's largest bases and also a gateway for military personnel in transit to and from the United States. We knew there would be further connection flights for us before arriving at our final destinations, but we were now "in-country."

As soon as the door opened, an Air Force noncommissioned officer stepped onboard and addressed us in a throaty yell. Our aircraft was very long, and his voice had to project through to the very back row.

"Listen up, men, and pay attention to everything I'm telling you. I need you to get off this plane as quickly as you possibly can, then get into the buses next to the runway. Quickly, now go, go, go, go!"

We didn't know why the speed was required, but we moved as fast as we could hustle down the aisle of the plane, then the steps leading to the row of buses. I noticed with some degree of concern that the buses were covered with steel mesh, including the spaces over the windows. We inquired about this once inside the transport vehicles and were told that the mesh had been placed there to stop hand grenades from being tossed through the windows. Nope, this was definitely not like Rochester. Even our worst city neighborhoods were totally void of grenades.

The buses filled, then gradually pulled off the airstrip. I found myself thinking, "Where am I going to end up, and what will I be doing when I get there?" I know a lot of the other men were thinking similar thoughts, especially the Marines and the Infantry.

I was also acutely aware of the intense heat and humidity that hung in the air, forming a suffocating blanket that was chokingly intense. And there was something else: The air had a pungent and *really bad* aroma that seemed to attack your nose and taste buds at the same time. I didn't know what it was, as I had never smelled anything like it before. I was hoping it was only temporary, perhaps something rotting on the ground or burning in the woods. But I soon realized that it hung in the air everywhere in our surroundings, unidentified but gag-inducing. I wasn't sure if I could ever get used to it.

Our bus pulled out onto a dirt road (there were a lot of dirt roads in Vietnam) and started the ride to the reception center. As we headed down the unimproved route, I noticed two *mamasans* walking along the side of the road. Officially, a *mamasan* is defined as a female in a position of authority—that is, a manager or supervisor of an establishment. However, for most of my fellow servicemen, it became a common name for any Vietnamese woman, so I assigned the same meaning to the term.

The two women were strolling along through the dusty dirt, seemingly not noticing the extremely high temperature and humidity. I suppose if you were born and raised there, you'd become totally immune to the extreme conditions. They both had on the stereotypical black pajama-style-baggy pants and white top, accompanied by the cone-shaped woven hat. This is exactly how I expected people to look, although I wasn't sure they would actually look that way.

The terminus of our bus ride was the base reception center, which was much less attractive and modernized than the one at Fort Eustis. We didn't have a lot to do there other than check in and take care of a few more administrative items, one of which was to surrender all our American greenback money and exchange it for the US military payment certificate (MPC) currency, or what we affectionately referred to as "Monopoly money." We were required to clear our wallets of all coinage and currency because of the black market value of American money. We exchanged it all for military bills that went as high as twenty dollars and as low as five- or ten-cent coins. Everything was paper, right down to the small stuff. It was just part of life over there. The Monopoly money didn't come close to looking authentic, but everyone accepted it as the real deal, so it worked the same for all practical purposes.

At Cam Ranh, we received even more supplies to take with us to our final station. This allotment came in the form of a large waterproof bag that contained even more gear. As I recall, it included a helmet, a poncho, and other items to protect us from the enemy and the elements. It turned into even more hours of tedious boredom as we moved along at a snail's pace. Meanwhile, we continued to drag around our oversized duffel bags along with our newly issued waterproof bags. It became an expression we all heard every day; we did the "duffel bag drag and the waterproof bag" everywhere we went. I couldn't wait to ditch them in a locker somewhere. As least it gave me *some* reason to look forward to arriving.

We didn't stick around the base at Cam Ranh for too many days, just a few. We found that the barracks were really, really terrible. The heat and humidity still hung in the air, and the smell somehow got even worse. Many urban regions of Vietnam have long suffered from air pollution, but this was nothing of an industrial odor. It smelled like a rotting combination of organic materials and mold in the humid environment, which was amplified by the dampness of the monsoon season. I never really got used to it, and just when I thought I was becoming acclimated, a new scent would join the pungent mix, containing rotting fish heads and other spoiled foodstuffs.

The food at the Cam Ranh base was also terrible. No matter what it was, it all had a deplorable taste that I just could not ingest. It was American food, just inedible. I had never before consumed powdered milk and could not get it down with my food. My very first time in the mess hall, I found myself wondering, "How am I going eat enough to keep myself alive?" After a few weeks, we all found a way to close our nose and eyes and swallow the stuff, although I cannot remember how we managed it.

There wasn't much to do at Cam Ranh. It was mostly a way station that was used to hold troops until they were shipped out in one direction or another. We weren't allowed to go into town here, so we slogged around the base to one administrative office or another. While parked there, we were called to two formations every day, one in the morning and the other in the afternoon. Sometimes the Sergeant would read out some names, and those individuals were shipped out to head to their final duty stations.

John and I somehow managed to stay together for those days while we were waiting for our next set of travel instructions. During those days, we noticed that the Sergeant had a daily routine. At the formations he would climb onto the stage at the front of the assemblage and pick out "volunteers" for the daily details. Sometimes it was kitchen police (KP) duty, which involved peeling mountains of potatoes or other food prep tasks. Sometimes it might have been cleaning the dining room or other tedious work. Regardless of the assignment, neither John nor I wanted any part of it.

To avoid these details, we discovered a little trick. The Sergeant always made his selections from the front of the group, which was fairly large. So we made sure that we always arrived later than most of the crowd and stood in the very back. I doubt the Sergeant could even see us from his position up front. But one day, they tripped us up by reversing their strategies. From the front of the group, we heard the Sergeant say, "OK, we need four people for KP detail this afternoon. We'll take the following people." Then, in a different voice, we heard, "You, you, you, and you." The voice was from a different Sergeant, who was standing in back of us. He tapped each of us on the shoulder as he singled us out for the manual-labor duty. Sometimes it was impossible to win, and you couldn't fool the Sergeants all the time. We peeled potatoes for the next three hours.

At least the soldiers were not asked to do dishwashing duty. That task fell on the kitchen workers, who were almost all civilians. Civilians also did most of the cooking. These people were mostly Vietnamese, with a few military folks thrown in as well. The workers from the town were paid in Vietnamese currency, the dong. We were all asked to help contribute to their paychecks, which was collected by Disbursement Officers at our own payday lines. We would receive our own pay and then have to dish some out to pay for the work of the mamasans who served us. Sometimes they also did chores like our laundry and more of the same, and they were compensated accordingly.

There was one volunteer task that we wanted to avoid at all cost. That would be shit-burning detail. At both Cam Ranh Bay and, later, at Long Bin, we used elevated latrines that were primitive at best, employing fifty-five-gallon drums that were cut off twelve inches from the bottom, leaving only a short rim wall around at the base of the drum. These large tubs were then pushed beneath the latrine seats to catch all the feces that fell through the latrine seats. If you happened to be one of the lucky individuals selected for the duty, you had to pull the tub out from the latrine structure, pour in several gallons of kerosene, and burn it. You also had to use a stick to keep stirring the potent mixture throughout the combustion cycle to ensure that the feces and the kerosene remained in ignitable proportions, adding more kerosene if needed.

To this day I'm glad that I was never assigned to the shit-burning detail. When I arrived at my final duty station farther south, I was pleased to learn that they had regular outhouses distributed around the base. These often became overfilled to the point where they were unusable. When this happened, the men complained and complained, often without any action being taken. If the situation was ignored for too long, someone would set the outhouse on fire, and they have to set up a new one. I never saw one actually on fire, but I knew it happened on a fairly regular basis.

Inside our barracks, the conditions were equally as poor. Many of the bunks had no mattresses, so we slept on the bunk springs. We had to use our duffels as pillows, which was a bit rough, as they were stiff, lumpy, and rough in texture. The only saving grace was that you were so tired by the end of most days that you simply didn't notice the discomfort. You just passed out along with everyone else.

Every morning, the Sergeant read more names at our muster, and those men gathered their duffels and other belongings and prepared to be shipped out. It seemed like about thirty names each day were read out loud for movement, although John and I somehow avoided this process for a few days. Once their names were read, they disappeared onto a bus that would take them to a plane flying to parts unknown, and we never saw them again.

Each day, after not hearing our names called, we'd head back to our barracks and prepare to spend another day at our "lovely" base. All the while, new men kept arriving, so it was a continuous process of people passing through our barracks and our lives. I spoke to several of them but never really got to know anyone new.

Finally, on the third morning, the clerk at formation read both John's name and my own. We still didn't know our direction, whether it would be to the north, Central Highlands, or south. We were then informed that we were assigned to the 1st Aviation Brigade and would be heading somewhere to the south. This was all decided by fate; it was in the hands of some clerk whom we'd never met and would never see again.

There was a lot of murmuring among the men about which direction was considered more dangerous. Was it the North or South? From those with prior experience in-country, we heard that the territory in the North was considered more dangerous. This was where many of the Marines and some of the Army Infantry units were wrapped up in heavy fighting, and the Marines were taking losses. This northern territory was our US I Corps. It was located along the northern border of South Vietnam, near the demilitarized zone (DMZ) between North and South Vietnam. The entire central part of the country, known as the Central Highlands, was where our II and III Corps were engaged in battle. This mountainous territory was where both Marines and Army Infantry found themselves pitted against the North Vietnamese, and the fighting was also very heavy.

As for me and my 1st Aviation Brigade, we learned that we would be operating from inside the IV Corps, which was south of Saigon and the Mekong Delta. By comparison, this region was safer than those to the north, but it was not without its dangers. Both the Army and Navy were operating out of this territory, with numerous units from the Brown-Water Navy, which performed a lot of the riverine patrol work. We worked a lot with the men on the patrol boats as well as the US Navy SEALs. The SEALs also ran a special platoon of Huey gunships, so we saw them quite often. We also operated with a lot of the South Vietnamese Army in the IV Corps, as they did a lot of the ground fighting in that area. Our 1st Aviation Brigade became quite familiar with these soldiers, as we often flew them into combat.

Regardless of which direction we were heading, I can honestly say I was overjoyed at the thought of leaving Cam Ranh. I truly hated the place, with its putrid smells and bare-spring bunks and shit-burning details. I'd been ready to leave within five minutes of our arrival and shed no tears as I packed up my possessions.

After gathering our gear, we were herded back onto the mesh-covered bus and driven to the airport. There we were loaded onto a C130 transport for the flight to Long Bin, which was farther down the coast. The flight on the C130 bore no resemblance at all to that on a passenger aircraft. There was no air conditioning and no comfortable seating. John and I still found a way to sit next to each other, although there were nu-

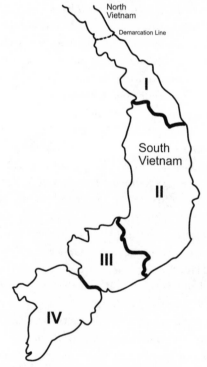

*The four operational regions of South Vietnam.*
*(Photo credit: Archie Woodworth)*

merous crates and pieces of equipment surrounding us, thus limiting our mobility. It was roughly configured to carry some troops in addition to the spare parts, crates, and other supplies that filled the rest of the fuselage. The only saving grace was that it wasn't a particularly lengthy flight, perhaps an hour at most, and we soon detected the now-familiar sounds of the engines throttling back as we started our descent.

Bump.

The sound of our wheels hitting the ground signaled our arrival at Long Bin, located near Saigon. By now, there were very few surprises in store for us upon arrival. We were once again herded onto buses and transported to a reception center. But the further into our trip we progressed, the more dilapidated the facilities appeared.

The barracks at Long Bin were worse than at our previous stop. I scanned the bunks and noticed that less than half had mattresses, while none (again) had pillows. We suffered through two more nights at our new home, Long Bin, enduring all the same torments as in our previous base at Cam Ranh. The scary part was that I think we were all getting used to it.

I can't remember much about Long Bin other than hanging around even more and going to countless formations, where we did very little of importance. It was all just part of a blur by now, one day following another. On our third morning at Long Bin, we were all taken out to a large field that must have been half the size of a football field. The field was entirely dirt and studded with a series of telephone poles arranged in rows. Each pole held a placard sign with the name of a town or city, which presumably represented the location of a duty station.

We understood that the phone poles with their destination signs would serve as gathering points for those men selected to deploy to each city. Until now, John and I had always been assigned to the same destinations. Whenever my name was read, John's name quickly followed. We had become used to traveling together and hanging out at the same base, regardless of how short the stay was. However, this is where it all ended. Our coincidental partnership would go no further.

I listened attentively as my name was read off a list, followed by a number of others—but not John's. Instead he was included in another grouping and marched off in a different direction. My pole was identified by the town name Can Tho, while John's assignment was to Vinh Long. Each pole was surrounded by about twenty men, none looking all too happy. None of us knew what the signs meant or anything about the towns they represented. I looked across the span of empty field to where John was mustered. It was roughly thirty yards from my own phone pole, but that distance might as well have been one thousand miles. I knew I wouldn't see him again as long as we remained in Vietnam.

Silently, across the empty distance, I mouthed, "Good luck," and waved goodbye. He replied with a similar gesture. They were herded in a different direction, and then he was gone.

Following our short game of "musical phone poles," we headed back to the airport and boarded yet another aircraft, also a C130. Everyone who had accompanied me to the Can Tho telephone pole joined me onboard.

At Can Tho, the pattern repeated itself once again. Deboard the plane and climb aboard a bus that took us to yet another reception center. And again, this reception center was worse than any of the others we had seen.

The barracks at Can Tho were similarly broken and disheveled, and less than 20 percent of the bunks had mattresses. (We had long since stopped looking for them.) I still remember one bunk in particular that was not only missing its mattress but also the springs that held the base of the supporting mesh to the frame. If the person occupying that bunk had shifted positions during the night, they probably would have been dumped unceremoniously to the floor below. I chose to avoid that bunk in favor of another in a lesser state of disrepair.

As we were getting moved into our bunks, a Sergeant came inside and started giving us a warning. In his best Sergeant's voice, he barked out:

"Now if mortars start falling inside the compound, just run outside and jump into the ditch you saw out there. It's the safest place to hide, but remember to wear your helmet and keep your head down."

I remember seeing the Sergeant trying to conceal a smile as he was providing the instructions. None of us really believed him. And anyway, the ditch had water in it.

We were only in Can Tho for two days before shipping out for the final time—one last flight, one last C123, one last takeoff and landing. Our destination on this leg would be Soc Trang, the farthest US Army base on Vietnam's Mekong Delta. It was November of 1969, and this would be my home for the next year.

I was rather surprised at my touchdown in Soc Trang, as it didn't resemble the other airstrips I'd seen in my last couple stops. This one actually had a hard-surface runway, which had been built by the Japanese during World War II. It was the only hard surface runway on the Mekong Delta south of Saigon, which contributed to its noteworthiness.

After landing at the airport in Soc Trang, I was met by a clerk in a Jeep who drove me to the 13th Combat Aviation Battalion Headquarters. There I was assigned to the 336th Assault Helicopter Company, which served as home of the Warriors and Thunderbirds.

The Jeep dropped me off about two hundred yards from the 336th Headquarters building, leaving me to conduct one more performance of the "duffel bag drag and the waterproof bag." Once inside, I was greeted by the administrative cadre of assistants and asked to complete yet another packet of forms. I can only imagine how many forests of hardwood trees I killed to produce the mountains of paperwork I signed during my tour. It must have been impressive.

Next, one of the other clerks escorted me to my barracks, which was a welcome stop. For the first time since leaving the United States, I would be staking my claim (a bunk) that would actually be *mine* for the next year. As we entered the barracks building, I was even more pleased to see that all the bunks had real mattresses—and pillows! Luxury of all luxuries! I could get used to this.

I spent the next fifteen minutes unpacking my duffel and getting my gear stashed away into a locker. As I was unbuttoning my fatigues shirt to pull on a fresher set, I realized something rather disquieting. I stunk. We had been on the move for the past two weeks, living out of a duffel bag, and almost everything contained therein had been worn for several days without washing. By that point, I really couldn't remember how long it had been since I had showered. The combination of those factors resulted in a rather foul-smelling scent that had me heading to the showers as quickly as possible.

While I was still arranging my belongings, a mamasan entered my room and attempted to speak to me in broken English.

"You want wash?" she asked, pointing at my clothes.

Apparently, she was the mamasan for the inhabitants of half the barracks, and in addition to the general sweeping and cleaning, she was also responsible for all our wash. I nodded my head to her to signal that I did indeed want all my clothes laundered.

As I was attempting to communicate with this native employee, a Sergeant entered the room and addressed me in an impatient tone.

"You Feigel?" he demanded.

"Yes, Sergeant," I replied quickly.

"Let's go," he ordered, and without waiting for any further response, he turned on his heel and marched out of the room.

I hadn't had the chance to fully unpack or even change my shirt. Instead I rebuttoned the top of my fatigues and trotted after the Sergeant, who bore a striking resemblance to Barney Fife. As I chased him down from behind, I remember thinking to myself, "I'll be here for a whole year. Couldn't he have waited an hour or two before dragging me off like this?"

Without further conversation, the Sergeant led me directly up to the hangar to introduce me to the hangar maintenance crew. As I entered the large building, I could feel the attentive stares of everyone watching me. All eyes were directed at me, the newbie. There was no hiding it, especially since I was wearing the newest, brightest set of green fatigues in the entire compound. That was one good way of determining who had been in-country the longest. Those with the most extended tenure had the most faded fatigues, while the more recent arrivals appeared in varying shades of darker green. It ran the full spectrum, from light to dark, but I was by far the most colorful.

My first introduction was to Ron Knight, who was in charge of our hangar helicopter repair team. There were four teams operating from our hangar, and each team had five members. These men worked together as cohesive units. Everyone was well trained and well versed in their responsibilities. One of these duties was taking the ships through their one hundred-hour maintenance inspection. It was detailed work, and Ron was the one responsible for overseeing all our work and making sure that our individual tasks came together in the finished package.

Ron was tall and thin with a head full of thick dark hair, and he spoke with a thick New England accent. He was a Spec 5, which was only one pay grade above me. Yet he was incredibly well respected for his knowledge and experience, as well as his ability to get things done. A native of Boston, he was close to completing his second tour in Vietnam. He knew everyone, and everyone knew him.

I spent a short while being led around the hangar and introduced to all the guys on the various teams. After that, I was put to work assisting Ron in some rather mundane tasks, which I think were assigned to see whether I had picked up the basic concepts back in Helo Repairman School. Regardless, I appreciated getting the chance to work side by side with Ron. Not only could he instruct me in the basics of their team processes, but he could observe my own strengths and weaknesses and make recommendations on improving my skills.

Ron had learned a lot from his two tours in Vietnam. He had been a Huey Crew Chief for most of his time, spending the majority of his days flying combat missions with the rest of his platoon. But now, entering his last two months of service in-country, Ron had made the decision to go from the Huey to the hangar. He had tempted fate long enough and now had decided to stay just slightly further out of harm's way.

My respect for Ron was soon enhanced tenfold by an incident that happened shortly after we met. It started while we were having supper together in the mess hall. Suddenly, a pair of piercing *boom* sounds split the air. I had no idea what those sounds meant, but Ron catapulted up from the table as if shot from a cannon. In the same motion, he sprinted for the door, headed for the runway. The rest of us followed as quickly as we could—but not as fast as Ron. He was already gone by the time we cleared the door.

We pursued Ron in the direction of the runway, dread filling our guts as we approached the tarmac area. As the runway came into view, we saw the source of the booms, and it tied my insides into a constricted knot. One of our Hueys was laying on its side in the middle of the runway, its blades twisted in grotesque shapes against the hard surface below. (The blades hitting the tarmac had been the source of the explosive sounds we'd heard from the mess hall.) Then, as we approached the wrecked craft, another horrifying spectacle appeared before our eyes.

Fire!

It started out small, the bright orange flames originating from inside the fuselage and licking the exterior walls of the airframe. The crew was frantically trying to escape the approaching holocaust as the intensity of the fire grew. One crew member stood in the doorway, screaming for help as his arms pinwheeled furiously to attract attention.

None of us immediately understood the source of the crew member's consternation, but Ron didn't wait around to find out. As the fire continued to grow in intensity, he sprinted to the open doorway of the ship, climbed up, and then dove in. It turned out that the Crew Chief's legs had become pinned between the base of the aircraft and the runway. Ron shimmied his way through the burning helicopter toward the crew chief while the rest of the crew focused their adrenaline on the Herculean task of lifting the ship from the tail boom. As they accomplished this, Ron pulled the Crew Chief's legs free and then dragged him out of the burning Huey.

Thinking back on the events of the day, I realize that absolutely anything could have happened to Ron as he performed heroically to save the Crew Chief. The flames could have easily reached a ruptured fuel line, or fuel could have spilled from a tank or line onto the tarmac and come into contact with the fire. Ron never would have known a thing. He might have briefly heard the explosion as the entire aircraft exploded in a single fireball, snuffing out the lives of everyone brave enough to be within twenty feet of the burning craft. But thankfully, that never transpired that memorable day, and everyone involved lived to "fly another day."

Ron's unselfish and heroic actions that day, performed without regard for his own personal safety, earned him the Soldier's Medal. This is the highest award that can be given to an Army soldier for an act of bravery in a noncombat situation. Its precedence (importance) is *above* the Bronze Star, and it is one of the Army's less-awarded medals.

As it turned out, this was one of Ron's last acts while still serving on our base. A few days later, he received his detaching orders and was headed back home. And as uniquely incredible as his bravery appeared to me that day, it was just a taste of things that followed. We were at war, and I was to witness many other such acts in the weeks and months to come.

Welcome to Vietnam.

Over the next few months, I fell into the standard routine that featured extended days from 7:00 a.m. through 6:00 p.m. in the evening (0700–1800 for those used to a twenty-four-hour clock). Those of us who spent our entire days in the hangar were known as hangar rats, although the term was not used in a derogatory way. Some days were packed with excitement as a ship arrived back from a mission peppered with bullet holes that we had to fix. On other days (or nights), we experienced enemy mortar attacks, which had us running for our bunkers. For the most part, though, our lives as hangar rats were dull—but safe when compared to those who were airborne.

It didn't take long before I came to know all the men in our company; the pilots, Crew Chiefs, and door gunners. We were all different ranks and had very different responsibilities. We had about thirty helicopters to maintain in our company, all of them variants of the UH-1. This craft, which was first released as the HU-1 (thus the nickname "Huey"), has been in the US inventory since 1959. In 1962, the official designation was changed to UH-1. About seven thousand of these Hueys eventually found their way over to Vietnam, where they became one of the main workhorses of the Army's forces. Half of them never came back to the States. They were also used by the Air Force and Navy, not to mention at least a dozen other countries.

Our company operated two flight platoons of ten aircrafts called "slicks" (used to carry troops).[1] There was also a gunship platoon comprised of five to six UH-1C Hueys outfitted with rocket pods and miniguns. There was also one Command and Control (C&C) ship, one Maintenance Huey, and one "Night Hawk/Firefly," which was used for conducting night patrols. It was a lot to repair and maintain, but we managed to keep our entire fleet of ships in the air most of the time.

The gunships were incredibly impressive between their loadouts of rocket pods and the miniguns. Each rocket pod held 2.75 rocket launchers, while the "miniguns" were basically 6-barelled Gatling guns that fired four thousand to six thousand 7.62 mm caliber rounds per minute. The rocket pods usually came in pairs, one on either side of the Huey, and launched simultaneously (left and right) in order to maintain the weight stability of the ship.

Over those first several months, I worked extremely hard to gain proficiency in all aspects of aviation maintenance. I had learned a lot in my school back at Fort Eustis and had finished second in my class. But this was different. This was real life, where the rubber met the road. I felt like I had to prove myself every day, and I wanted to have a reputation that showed I could be counted on to do anything and get it done right. I think I accomplished that goal rather quickly.

By January 1970, I found that I was spending a majority of my time with the Crew Chiefs. I had been out on a few tests flights, mostly circling the airfield, but I really had not left the base in over two months. Then one day, I was approached while working in the hangar and asked if I'd like to fly on a maintenance operation that would take us to a remote location some distance from our own base. The mission would be to replace a tail rotor on a downed gunship.

This would be way out of my wheelhouse, as I had never done anything like this before. I felt my pulse surging as I considered the request. I also remembered the promise I'd made to my mother to not volunteer for anything. "Keep your head down and don't volunteer" was the mantra that ran through my mind over and over again. But in the back of my mind, I knew that I wanted to at least try it: flying. In Vietnam. Just to see what it was all about. And so I raised my hand.

"I'll do it."

Even before the words left my mouth, I found myself questioning my own decision. I had heard all the stories, and I had been to the memorial

---

1. Slicks received their nickname due to an absence of weapons pods. Gunships had their own informal nomenclature: They were called "frogs" or "hogs" if they were outfitted with rockets or "guns" or "cobras" if they carried guns.

services. I had also worked on numerous aircraft that returned to our air-field shot full of bullet holes. So I knew the risks, and I knew that statistics don't lie. Flying meant taking risks, and you seldom got a second chance.

During that first flight, I spent most of my time looking down at the flooded rice paddies below and listening to the radio chatter of the pilots talking to one another. We landed in a field to perform our mission and then got the hell out of there. It didn't take long, but I became instantly hooked. I knew that's what I wanted to do: I wanted to fly, to look down at the land and water as it flashed beneath our ship. I decided right there that this was what I wanted, and I never second-guessed myself.

My new title was Crew Chief Warrior 28, 2nd Flight Platoon. It was a huge step. Warrior 28 was the oldest ship in the fleet, but I didn't care in the least. It was mine, and I was going to make it shine. I started on it right away, cleaning it up and pulling some needed maintenance.

Crew Chiefs were a rare breed in Vietnam; they were very well re-spected and heavily laden with a lot of responsibility. There was no formal school for this job. It was pretty much on-the-job training, passed down from generation to generation of Crew Chiefs; the old ones schooled the new. You had to learn quickly, or the consequences were harsh and im-mediate. I would need to up my game.

I quickly realized that the ship was the shared responsibility of the pilot and the Crew Chief. The crew normally consisted of four members: the pilot (or AC, which meant Aircraft Commander), the Crew Chief, the door gunner, and the copilot. The copilot was often called the Peter pilot, and he was not actually a permanent member of the Huey's crew. Instead he rotated from one ship to the next, gaining experience from the extra air time. In other words, he was a pilot "under instruction" until he was designated an Aircraft Commander in his own right and assigned a ship of his own.

My AC on Warrior 28 was Warrant Officer Randy Olson. He was a great pilot who was highly experienced with a great number of hours be-hind the controls. I learned later just how skilled he was and how fortunate I was to have him as my AC and, later, as a friend.

I had the additional good fortune of having Rob Sandwith assigned to my ship as the door gunner. He was a top-notch soldier and one of the best door gunners in the company. He was tough, reliable, and always all business. He made sure the guns always fired. (The operation of the M60s and the M16s was the door gunner's responsibility.)

It was with this good fortune that I took over as Crew Chief of War-rior 28. I felt as though I had the best crew I could possibly hope for as we got ready for my first combat mission. I only hoped that my crew had as much confidence in me as I did in them.

# 6

# FIRST COMBAT MISSION

It was sometime in January 1970, and there I was, on the brink of starting combat mission number one. I had requested it, I had prepared for it, and now I was about to embark on it. I hoped I had done the right thing. Please forgive me, Mother.

It was to be an early start that morning, liftoff by 0700, so I was up a couple hours earlier to take care of my personal matters and run through some preflight checkouts. Somehow I managed to eat my breakfast, though it didn't go down as easily as usual due to the butterflies dancing around in my stomach. I chalked this up to it being my first time in a combat role, then did my best to ignore it.

As I walked from the mess hall to the 2nd Flight Platoon parking area, I noticed that I was the first one out. I was also the last one on scene the previous evening, as I was working on the ship until after dark. After all, ours was the oldest Huey in our company, so it sometimes required a little extra loving care. It was a UH-1 D model, which was being phased out of the fleet in favor of the newer, more powerful H models.

As some of the ships were firing up, I met Mr. Olson (a Warrant Officer), who was our AC (Aircraft Commander). He had a great amount of experience piloting this particular ship, as well as flying the lead position in our formation. Of the slicks, which were the ships that carried the troops into the landing zone (LZ), it was the oldest and weakest ship that always went in first, in the front of the five-ship V formation. This was always followed by the remaining slicks as they descended into the LZ. Mr. Olson had performed this landing hundreds of times and was superbly qualified for the job. He knew what he was doing, and he had the full faith and confidence of Capt. Leandro, our Platoon Leader. (As the 2nd Platoon Leader,

Leandro always flew his Huey at the back of our formation so he could observe everything that transpired in front of our ships.)

Our full Platoon formation consisted of nine ships. These included our five slicks (troop carriers), three gunships, and one Command and Control (C&C) ship. These ships all had their places in our formation, both for going in and coming back out of combat missions. We all got used to our places and working together to complete our missions. We had each other's backs. We had to. There was simply no other way to survive.

The morning of my first combat mission we had great weather, with clear skies and no rain in the forecast. Then again, there was never any rain in January, as it was part of the dry season. There would be no rain in the southern part of the country for several months, until the start of monsoon season in April. Once the monsoons came, there would be no letup for six months.

Our mission that day would be to fly south to refuel and then pick up several loads of South Vietnamese Army infantrymen. We were to fly them into the combat area LZ, then return later that day to extract them from the same zone. Flying into one of these regions held a lot of unknowns, and we never knew whether we would be facing enemy fire or going in unmolested. Each day and each trip was different and held its own share of surprises.

Once Mr. Olson fired up our ship and we began lifting off, our first obstacle was to clear our own revetment. A revetment was a protective L-shaped barrier constructed around each ship's parking space to provide some degree of protection against a mortar attack. It was constructed of a base of fifty-five-gallon drums, each of which was filled with concrete. Above these drums was a wall of pallet-like metal plates that extended the protection an additional three feet. It provided an effective barrier of protection around the Hueys, but it had to be avoided each time the ship lifted off from the base.

Once we lifted off the ground, the door gunner and I would check our respective sides of the ship, looking back to ensure we'd cleared the revetment.

"Clear back right," the gunner would call out, followed by my saying, "Clear back left." Once the pilot heard those confirmations, he knew we were ready to back out.

The first leg of our mission that day was to fly off in the direction of our pickup zone. After heading south for at least an hour, we landed at a base near the town of Ca Mau. Today, Ca Mau is a large city with over two hundred thousand residents. It is also the country's biggest exporter of shrimp and prawns in addition to having a pair of thermal power plants, a gas pipeline, and a major fertilizer plant. But in the early 1970s, it was a much smaller place, and it hosted a significant population of Vietcong fighters.

Once we completed the refueling, we headed off in the direction of our PZ, where we were to board our complement of South Vietnamese Army troops. The short flight from Ca Mau was only about ten minutes and culminated in a small dirt runway near a nondescript village.

As we descended into the PZ, I had my first look at the South Vietnamese troops. I was shocked. They all looked so young and unprepared for battle. Each carried an M16 and one or two clips of ammunition. Nothing else. I thought of our own infantry men going into battle and reflected on their M60s, their massive loadout of 7.62 mm ammunition, the hand grenades, the rocket launchers, and more. These young men didn't appear to have the weapons they needed to survive.

The South Vietnamese Army Infantry troops we were loading were going out in search for Vietcong guerillas in the Mekong Delta. These Vietcong, supported by the North Vietnamese government, were not uniformed. Instead they were usually dressed in black pajamas, shorts, and a T-shirt. Their equipment varied greatly. It could include anything from AK-47s to mortars and rocket launchers, and anything in-between. They fought with whatever they had and were sometimes accompanied by a few North Vietnamese "regulars" who served as advisors and trainers. Much of their equipment came by way of the Ho Chi Minh Trail.

The Vietcong employed a lot of dubious tactics throughout the war, which sometimes included conscription of prisoners into forced fighting. They would enter a village and capture the men and boys, then force them to fight against the South Vietnamese Army. If someone refused to join the fighting, their family was threatened with death, and their houses might be burned to the ground. A great many men were added to the Vietcong force in this manner, including some boys aged ten or younger. It was an ugly situation that presented the victims with little or no choice. Most joined rather than see their families and homes perish.

The detachment that embarked was entirely South Vietnamese. We really couldn't communicate with them as they spoke very broken English, and we spoke little or no Vietnamese. It wouldn't have mattered anyway once we took off, as the noise inside the ship grew exponentially, rendering any attempt at communication worthless.

As Warrior 28 and the other slicks loaded the South Vietnamese troops, the gunships and C&C ship went airborne ahead of us to prep the

LZ, then provided cover for the slicks on their final approach and landing. The C&C ship usually stayed above us to maintain tactical command and communications. They generally flew around the two thousand-foot mark while they were directing operations and monitoring the wind conditions across the area.

Heading towards the LZ with the other slicks, I tried listening to the radios to monitor what was happening up ahead. The C&C ship was talking to the gunships, which would prepare the landing zone for our arrival. This operation varied greatly from day to day, depending on the conditions and what could be seen by our gunship crews. Sometimes they might catch sight of a bunker or perhaps see some Vietcong troops along the tree lines, preparing for action. In these cases, the C&C ship directed the gunships to "go in hot," meaning they would be firing at the ground below. This might include rockets, fired down at the ground on either side, along with a continuous spray from the miniguns and handheld M60s. It was just cover fire to achieve an effect. Regardless, it accomplished its mission of keeping the enemy hunkered down as we made our own approach.

Warrior 28 was always at the head of the five slicks, as we were the oldest and weakest ship in the platoon. As we led the V formation down to the ground, the three gunships formed a protective formation around our ships, moving up our right and left flanks, then crossing over ahead of us. They could lay down an impressive barrage of cover fire, which provided some degree of comfort while we sat totally exposed, discharging our troops. While this transpired, either Mr. Olson or Capt. Leandro were communicating with our Company Commander in the C&C ship, keeping them apprised of our progress.

"We're inbound," he called up to C&C, maintaining the radio banter.

At about three hundred feet in elevation, the T-birds (Thunderbirds) threw down a white phosphorous grenade. This device was nicknamed a "WP," or Willie Peter. This grenade was not designed to detonate in the same manner as a standard weaponized round. Instead it was a "marker" grenade that discharged a steady trail of glowing white smoke for several minutes. This served as a directional beacon to the other craft coming in behind us, and it was even visible during periods of inclement weather. It was also useful because it provided an accurate assessment of the wind direction at the landing site.

A few moments later, I heard Mr. Olson suggest to the Peter pilot, "Let's lock up." This referred to a yellow lever that was located on the side of the pilot's armored seat inside the ship. When the pilot pulled that lever, his seat harness locked in place and would not move. The purpose was to hold the pilot in place in the event of an accident or if anything impacted the ship and made it jolt in one direction or another. It held the pilot firmly to his seat regardless of what happened to the ship.

I must admit that when I heard this remark by Mr. Olson, my "pucker factor" increased dramatically. It meant that my Aircraft Commander was getting ready to take hits if the area was indeed hot. You never knew what was coming your way. There were times, later on, when I could look out the front of the ship and see streams of bullets hitting the puddles in front of the fuselage. At times like that, I felt myself ducking and putting my head down. The ironic part was that I always *knew* that would do me no good if shells started whizzing through our old Huey, taking direct hits, but I still could never break the habit. I always ducked when shells came screaming by the ship.

After landing and discharging our troops, we waited for the other four slicks to unload, and then we headed back to pick up a second group of the South Vietnamese soldiers. However, as we started gaining elevation, I was startled to see that the door gunner and I were not alone in the back of the ship. A single infantry member of the first group had remained onboard, still clinging to his spot on the floor. I looked him in the eyes to attempt to read his expression. He looked terrified; abject fear was crossing his face. I believe he was paralyzed in place by his emotions.

Not knowing what to do, I quickly called Mr. Olson on the headset and reported our outbound stowaway. If anyone would know what to do about this fellow, it would be him.

Olson's response was calm and immediate. "Don't worry about him," he said in a casual voice. "His Commander will take care of him when we pick up the next load."

When we landed to pick up the second wave, the returning soldier was not treated nicely. Everyone at the pickup zone seemed to know why he was still onboard, and he was pushed around roughly and called a lot of names. Even without speaking Vietnamese, I think I could have translated much of what was said. He was pushed back through the open door of the Huey by half a dozen soldiers, then manhandled back onto the floor of the ship. I noticed that when we arrived back at the LZ, this individual did not need to walk off the ship. Instead he was jettisoned off by his comrades, becoming the first man off the Huey. He wasn't given a choice in the matter.

We quickly repeated the process, loading at the PZ and taking off for the LZ—back and forth, back and forth. It would quickly become routine in my mind, although I knew that some of those future landings and extractions would include a lot more hostile activity. I just hoped it wouldn't be anytime soon.

After making three insertion runs, we completed our work for the morning and headed back to refuel. At that point we shut down for lunch, which would last until we were called back to the LZ to retrieve those same troops and bring them back to their base. It was an extended break, perhaps two hours, during which most of us ate our C-rations along with some iced tea and anything else we could get our hands on. I think my own level of expectations on meal standards had already dropped considerably. That was a good thing, as the cuisine was never anything approaching four star (or three star, or—fill in your own number).

While we rested and took our lunch break, crew members from the different ships used the time for various purposes. Some ate, while others decided they'd rather catch an hour of sleep. Of those who enjoyed napping, some even brought their own hammocks, which they would string up inside their ship for the break. Others wandered off to talk with friends on other Huey crews or, perhaps, even to read a chapter from a favorite book. It was time to de-stress, at least until we got the signal to return to the LZ.

While this was going on, the gunships rearmed in order to have a full complement of ordnance for the afternoon extractions. Even though we hadn't experienced any enemy fire, we'd still expended rockets and M60 rounds that needed to be replaced.

It was normal for us to have work days that lasted for twelve to fourteen hours, if not longer. Very often we didn't return from a mission until 1600–1800 (4:00 p.m.–6:00 p.m.). Once we touched down and took care of immediate tasks, we'd usually head over to the mess hall and grab some dinner. At that point, once the pilot left the ship, his day was done. The same could not be said of the Crew Chief and the door gunner. There was always work to be done, and we usually had to return to the hangar following our evening meal. In the case of Rob Sandwith, our door gunner, he had to maintain the M16s and M60s along with ensuring we had a full loadout of ammunition for the following day's missions. I had my own tasks, whether they were inspections or replacing a filter or looking at some other aspect of the ship. With everything I had to handle, I sometimes did not make it back to my barracks until 10:00 p.m. It made for a short night.

One other benefit afforded to our pilots was a private room. They didn't have to tolerate a bunch of roommates who would turn lights on and off, talk after Taps, or even snore. They had their own space all to themselves. Sometimes they would use part of a room to stock their own private bar, although none of us really took advantage of drinking alcohol in our rooms or barracks. It was available, but everyone was usually too tired to partake, especially if there was any upcoming mission the following day. To remain sharp was paramount to survival.

Following our refueling, we prepared to lift off and head back to the LZ. We knew it would take us three trips to extract the South Vietnamese from the site, as it had taken us three flights to insert them earlier in the day. This would present us with more chance encounters with the enemy, more exposure to hostile fire. It was all part of the mission. There were chances and risks around each corner.

We lifted off from the fuel farm around 1300, with the C&C ship being the first one airborne, followed by the gunships. The slicks were the last ones up, flying once again in the V formation. Every time we returned to the LZ to pick up another group, we performed a "hover check" to ensure that we were able to fly and remain in formation with our new loadout. At this time, we were carrying a full load of fuel in addition to our own crew and the infantry troops. According to our technical specifications, we were limited to a certain number of passengers and crew in order to meet our ship's weight limitations. However, we also knew that the South Vietnamese natives were very small people, whereas our own troops were generally taller and beefier. Because of this, we extended our limit to ten or eleven of the South Vietnamese soldiers on each trip. We were aware that we exceeded the weight limit by a bit on each flight, but we went ahead with it anyway. If we ever failed a hover check, we would simply drop one of their soldiers back at the LZ, where he would be bumped to another flight. It worked, and we never had to leave someone behind.

Our three extraction flights ran smoothly and without incident. Looking back on it, I guess I was lucky in that I had an eventless first combat mission. It gave me the chance to ease into the role, which was so different than my original job in the hangar.

After dropping off the last of the infantry troops, we started our hour-long flight back to Soc Trang, once again flying with the other ships from our platoon. The flight gave me the chance to think about the day, my first day of real combat-mission flying. I think I had done fairly well, and we fully accomplished our mission. Just as important, I'd operated well with Mr. Olson, who acted as though he couldn't care less that it was my first mission in the air. His only concern was that I did my job so he could do his. I was even more proud of the fact that I had made this leap to Crew Chief without any formal training. I had spoken to the other Crew Chiefs and observed their work, but that was the extent of it. Neither had I ever taken a course in how to fire an M60. It was all on-the-job training, and I had performed well.

About a month later, our entire crew was moved over to Warrior 21, a much newer ship, as Warrior 28 was going in for an extensive overhaul. Warrior 21 had been a UH-1 D model that had been upgraded to an H. It was much more powerful, although it also meant that we were no longer the lead ship going into the LZ. We all adjusted to the new position and accepted it as our new routine. (But that was still a month in the future, and not in my thoughts as we arrived home over our base at Soc Trang.)

Looking back on my first combat mission, I'd call it a resounding success, although I still didn't know whether everyone had experienced the same adrenaline rush as me when coming in for their first LZ landing. I had been on the other end, watching the Hueys returning from their missions with sides riddled with bullet holes—or those ships that didn't return at all. It was very emotional going back to the barracks on some nights and seeing the empty bunks of those fellow crew members who never returned. They would remain empty for a few days, until a replacement arrived and took the same bunk. It felt strange that they never knew that same bunk had been occupied by someone else until a few days before or the reason why it was now empty.

In general, we didn't speak of these things often, as we realized that the next empty bunk could be ours. At times such as these, we just remained silent and thought about the next day and the next mission.

# 7

## LUCKY STRIKE

### Seven Helmets on the Altar

Friday, February 27, 1970: It is a date that is carved into my memory and into my soul. It will remain there forever, engraved as in granite, to the day I die.

It had been about six weeks since I'd flown my first combat mission, and things were progressing along well. I had eased into my job as a Crew Chief, and I enjoyed what I did. Working so closely with my crew, pilot Randy Olson, door gunner Rob Sandwith, and the other members of our platoon who flew with us on a daily basis, I'd developed a connection that is tough to describe to most civilians. We lived together, worked together, and formed such cohesive bonds that, at times, words were unnecessary. It was more than just knowing our jobs and having each other's back. We just seemed to sense what the others were thinking.

The same phenomena held true for other members in our 2nd Flight Platoon. We might not have flown with them on the same ship every day, but we all became friends and teammates under fire. It was the fire part that brought us all together in such a way that cemented those bonds in place and formed us into an unshakeable unit. When one of us was hurt or went down in an accident or as a result of hostile fire, we all felt it.

In the interim between the middle of January and the end of February, I had it relatively easy. We had no real close calls, and I never felt myself in harm's way, considering that we were flying combat missions in Vietnam. Luck and fate were a part of every mission, so we welcomed our eventless streak with open arms.

The schedule of activities varied for our 2nd Flight Platoon as well as the other two platoons in our company. We'd usually be running South Vietnamese troops out to different points around the Mekong Delta, while other ships in our platoon were performing other missions. One of the more routine missions in our repertoire was nighttime perimeter defense duty, which was a nighttime airborne patrol over and around our base at Soc Trang. This mission mandated that there would always be one ship airborne between the hours of 7:00 p.m. and 7:00 a.m. Those hours coincided with the national curfew that was enforced across the entire country. South Vietnam was under martial law, so no one was allowed out, whether driving or walking. If you did see someone out between those hours, they were probably the bad guys.

Perimeter defense duty involved the use of two Hueys every night. They rotated in two-hour shifts. First, one ship went up and flew from 1900 to 2100, then it returned to refuel while the other ship went airborne to follow the search pattern. Two hours later, they switched again, and they continued that way throughout the night until the curfew lifted at 0700. While airborne, the ship was literally the police, prosecutor, judge, jury, and executioner. They were "the force" in the sky, and their authority was absolute. It was quite a role, and our platoon performed it every day of the year. The Vietcong never took a day off, so neither could we.

The flight patterns of these ships actually covered a lot more ground than simply around our own base. Once they had scanned our own perimeter and ensured that it was secure from potential attack, they diverted and extended their search patterns to include the many canals that surrounded our area. Sometimes they also performed outpost "fire support," which meant that one of the many local South Vietnamese outposts was under attack by a contingent of Vietcong troops. Our Hueys were quite adept at intervening in these incursions, which they achieved with outbursts of their M60s and 50-cal guns.

Sometime around the middle of February, my own ship (Warrior 21) went into the hangar for a week-long, one-hundred-hour maintenance overhaul. During that time, I was in and out of the hangar to check on their progress, although I was not restricted to the overhaul work. I did still fly sometimes, and I found myself going out onboard Lucky Strike on some of its missions. Lucky Strike was another slick in our platoon, but it was modified for the nighttime perimeter defense missions. It carried a very large cluster light that could illuminate a good-sized patch of ground from one hundred to two hundred feet in the air. It literally turned night into day, exposing anyone hiding in the vegetation below.

When I flew with Lucky Strike, I was the sixth man on the crew. The two pilots were both Warrant Officers: the pilot, Mr. Connelly, and copilot, Mr. James Pace. In addition to the pilots, they had two Crew Chiefs, our door gunner, and then me. I was good friends with one of the Crew

Chiefs, Daniel Proctor. We were also bunkmates in our barracks; I had the top bunk, and he had the bottom. The other Crew Chief was Ron Stafford, who I believe was on his third tour in-country. The reminder of the crew was rounded out with door gunners Ron McCormick and Gary Swartz. This group was highly experienced. Most of them had been in-country for nine to twenty months, and at least two of them were nearing the end of their second or third tours. Because of their experience, our Platoon Commander (Capt. Leandro) left them alone and let them do their own thing.

When I flew with Lucky Strike, I was basically a utility man who would do whatever was asked of me. There was an extra jump seat in the back of the ship that really wasn't designated for any one purpose. They told me, "Sit in that seat, and don't touch anything." Of course, when needed, I could fire the M60s as required. With a six-man crew onboard, we could handle just about anything.

About a week after my five-day stint with Lucky Strike, I was assigned a new ship, Warrior 21, with its more powerful engine and upgraded configuration to the Huey H model. Our entire crew came over, which preserved the cohesiveness of our team while also removing me from the flights in Lucky Strike. I could have never known at the time how fateful that move would be in my life.

I was also quite familiar with the Aircraft Commander of Lucky Strike. His name was Mr. Connelly, another Warrant Officer. He was from California, a real comedian. He could perfectly imitate a British accent, which he often did when calling in to the tower. They sometimes believed they were talking to an RAF officer, which had everyone in stitches. He was also pretty intense and always gung ho.

Given that our ship was in the hangar, our pilot, Mr. Olson, was actually supposed to be flying with Connelly on the night that Lucky Strike was shot down. But fate once again intervened, this time on Olson's behalf. The morning of the fatal day, Olson learned that instead of flying that night, he was being assigned as the Convoy Commander for the day. This meant that he would ride in a Jeep, leading a bunch of trucks heading north to pick up food for the company. This convoy made the trip once each week, with Can Tho as their destination. Olson was furious that he was assigned to the convoy duty, as he wanted to become more proficient at night flying by copiloting Lucky Strike. The collateral duty ended up saving his life.

Fate. It works in strange ways.

On most nights, the chase ship assigned to fly with Lucky Strike was a slick with the call sign Super Slick. It flew above and behind, while Lucky

Strike flew the primary, low-altitude part of the mission. Lucky Strike always performed the primary ship role because it was configured for the job. It carried the cluster lights, 50-cal guns, and everything else required for the job.

Flying at night was a risky business from the get-go. Not only was the craft exposed to hostile fire from almost anywhere, but it carried a great many hazards that weren't even combat related. Trees, for example, were a particular concern. The tree lines were very dense around our base, with one tree in particular that stood above the rest like a giant. A tree versus a helicopter was no contest; the tree won every time. There was also a very tall tower with numerous supporting cables that radiated off in different directions, like a giant spider web. It was located about one mile south of the base, so we always had to keep that position in mind as well.

On the night of February 27, 1970, we were operating under our business-as-usual routine. We had our supper around 1800, then most of the door gunners and Crew Chiefs returned to their ships to perform any required maintenance and prepare our ships for the following day's mission. The atmosphere was very casual and relaxed. Our day was over, and we'd soon be turning in for the night. End of day.

I returned to the barracks around 2130, climbed into my bunk, and read for a few minutes before the lights went out. Everyone was always tired out from the exhaustive days, so the interior of our building was very quiet as the lights went out. The sound of peaceful snoring was the extent of the noise inside.

That all changed sometime after midnight, when all hell broke loose. We were all deep in slumber, all lights out, when a loud and agitated voice suddenly burst out loudly across our section of barracks. It was a Platoon Sergeant on the run through our bunk room, screaming as he went. Suddenly, all the lights went on.

*"All crews to your ships! All crews to your ships!"* the Sergeant shouted as he streaked through the door on the other end of the barracks.

Whenever someone awakens you in the middle of the night and orders everyone, at the top of their lungs, to get to their ships, you know it's not an invitation to a base picnic. We knew instantly that something very bad had happened. Most of us were already springing up from our bunks before we were fully awake.

"What's up?" called a crew mate from another bunk.

"Lucky Strike is down," replied another Crew Chief, who was also cutting through our barracks en route to the flight line. Then he, too, was gone.

As soon as I heard those words, a chill shot through my body, and I was instantly filled with a feeling of dread. I had flown on many low-level night flights with Lucky Strike, and I knew the risks that were encountered every time a ship lifted off. As I vaulted off my upper bunk, my foot touched briefly on the sheet of the lower bunk. It was empty. The bunk of Daniel Proctor, my friend and the Crew Chief of Lucky Strike, was empty. I didn't know what time it was, whether shortly after midnight or closer to dawn. But Dan was not in his bunk, and Lucky Strike was down.

I threw on my fatigues without bothering to button half the buttons. I did the same thing with my boots: I pulled them on in one quick tug without bothering to tie up the laces. Half-dressed, I sprinted out the door and across the tarmac to the flight line. As I was running, I found myself hoping, praying, that it was a mechanical problem that had forced down Lucky Strike. But in the back of my mind, I also knew that the crew of that ship were well-seasoned, excellent technicians, who were absolutely fearless and always ready for a fight. As a matter of fact, this was a crew that not only didn't fear going into bad areas, they relished it. They would fly into locations that were infested with Vietcong, ignoring the dangers, and start blasting away with everything they had. They would only leave because it was either "Time's up," or they were running low on fuel or ammo. Then, after refueling and reloading, they'd be itching to get back out and reengage. It was heroic and daring to watch, but in the back of my mind, I always wondered if they were running on an overload of adrenaline. I hoped against hope that their luck hadn't run out.

As we all arrived at our ships inside our revetments, we could hear the sounds of the T-birds departing. (T-birds are gunships from the Thunderbird Platoon, which was 3rd Platoon in our company.) Our Company Commander (Major Kilpatrick) and Platoon Leader (Capt. Leandro) were also going airborne in their own ships while we made our own preparations to follow when directed.

Within thirty seconds Mr. Olson and Rob Sandwith were both manned up and ready to go in our Warrior 21. We all had something in common: All three of us had flown with Lucky Strike many times. Olson had actually flown as copilot with Richard Connelly (Warrant Officer) on numerous occasions, as he'd been preparing to replace him as Lucky Strike's Aircraft Commander. Connelly was getting "short," meaning he was in his last one to two months in-country before returning to the safety of the States. It just couldn't end this way. More prayers.

As the scene grew increasingly more active, we strained to hear any developments over the radio. We were ordered to stay with our ships and stand by for possible troop insertions. We could hear a lot of chatter between our Commanders and the chase ship, Super Slick. As usual during the night ops, Super Slick had been flying above and behind Lucky Strike to provide cover and backup if needed. There were some nights when another ship from our company would take over for Super Slick and fill the role of the chase ship. But regardless of which ship that was, they always used the call sign Super Slick when filling in on that mission.

I can't remember how long we were on standby, listening tensely to the radio, awaiting the status of Lucky Strike and its crew. It's as though time had no meaning that night; everything happened so fast and yet so slow. All we could tell was that the situation was urgent. We could tell that from the tones of the voices of the crews above the scene. It was very "hot," with lots of firing going on from both the air and the ground. The adrenaline was flowing in waves, even for us on the ground at our base. And still, we prayed.

Then came the fateful word, the radio transmission that Lucky Strike had indeed been shot down by hostile fire. The wreckage was on the ground, burning fiercely in enemy territory. The tone of the voices on the radio turned truly frantic as they gave notice of the severity of the scene.

Shortly thereafter, another voice pierced the night, amplifying the magnitude of the disaster.

*"T-bird down. T-bird down!"* screeched the words from our radio, piercing the night.

Things were going from bad to worse. Was that a second ship that had gone down? Were two ships from our company crashed at the same location? It was tough to determine anything for certain. The term *the fog of war* has been used by various military tacticians, from Carl von Clausewitz to Sun Tzu. But until you are actually there, blinded by the unknown and surrounded by layers of conflicting reports, it's impossible to fully understand. We waited, continuing to dread the unknown.

The next reports coming from the combat scene sounded just as urgent.

*"Receiving fire. Receiving fire. Receiving fire!"* We could not identify the owner of that voice, but it could have belonged to any one of three or four ships near the scene.

Next came the voice of our Company Commander. "Let's get in there and get them out," he ordered in his controlled, gravelly voice.

"Roger that," responded our Platoon Leader, Capt. Leandro.

We continued to wait for orders to deploy as we kept our ears glued to the radio. We could hear all the radio talk with reports of "receiving fire," which was all the while punctuated by the sounds of the door gunners firing their M60s in the background. The crews in the ships knew they were taking hits from below while all this was taking place. They would have to wait until the next day to determine the extent of the damage.

We soon learned that it was T-bird 3 that had taken fire and crashed, then rolled onto its side in the hostile landscape below. Capt. Leandro bravely piloted his ship down to the ground, through the hail of enemy fire, to the gunship's crash site. His crew was able to rescue the pilot, copilot, and Crew Chief. However, the door gunner, Mark Miles, had been crushed beneath the ship when it rolled onto its side. He never had a chance.

The entire scene was one big killing zone. Major Kilpatrick, the Company Commander flying in Warrior 6, had a birds-eye view of the entire firefight, which was chaotic. He also witnessed what none of us could see, which was the crash site of Lucky Strike, the first ship to go down that night. It was still burning, with little left of the original ship. From his conversation with the chase ship, Super Slick, he determined that there could have been no survivors from the crash. The destruction had apparently been sudden, massive, and complete.

Kilpatrick was now faced with a battle decision: remain on scene and monitor the action or call off the activity and return to base. The choice was simple. There appeared to be no one else to rescue, but our ships were still exposed to enemy fire. At the same time, our ships were flying completely "darkened" (no navigations lights), thus risking the chance of midair collisions with our own ships.

There was nothing left to accomplish to account for the high level of risk. Fearing additional losses, Kilpatrick ordered all the ships back to Soc Trang. We knew it must have been bad for him to issue this order, but it was a command decision, and it was certainly the right one given the circumstances. Only Super Slick would remain on station, flying cover over the crash site.

Before the other gunships returned to base, the crewmen of one after the other vented their anger on the Vietcong troops by completely emptying their weapons loadouts on the ground below: M60s, rockets, 50-cals, grenade launchers, and even some homemade devices—in other words, the works.

Back at the base, we were all ordered to stand down and return to our barracks. I remember walking back through our barracks, passing solemnly by the empty bunks of Swartz and McCormick, knowing they would never be back. I then continued on to my own bunk area, where the empty bed of Daniel Proctor sat, also empty, beneath my own bunk. Empty. Eternally empty.

The word soon arrived in our barracks that all seven were confirmed dead: the six members of Lucky Strike as well as Mark Miles from T-bird

3. These were our platoon mates. Our team members. Our friends. The sense of loss throughout our barracks was heartbreaking. None of those men would ever be back. Even worse was the thought that, in addition to being platoon team members, they were also fathers, husbands, and sons of countless families and dependents back home. They had family members and relatives who wouldn't even learn of their deaths for at least a day or two. And only then, when the uniformed members of their service's casualty assistance team arrived at their doorstep, would they know.

I remember staring in disbelief at Daniel's empty bottom bunk as I contemplated the thought of sleep. As I stood, rooted in place, I heard the thumping rotors of the returning ships as they arrived overhead. I made a few attempts at falling asleep, although I knew it was probably fruitless. Sleep would just not come for the rest of the night, and I knew I couldn't lay there in the bunk I'd shared with my fellow Crew Chief, now gone.

Laying there was a waste of time, so I partially redressed and then returned to my ship. I couldn't fall asleep there either, but it was better than staying in my bunkroom. I lay there inside my ship for the rest of the night, thinking about the crew of Lucky Strike who had perished just hours earlier. They were all my friends, and I had flown in their ship until a week or two before that fateful night. Fate. It ran through my head over and over again. That could have easily been me onboard that ship that night. It was fate's call.

As dawn broke, I left the ship and headed over to the mess hall. In the background, I could hear the sounds of ships warming up to commence the missions of the new day. Hearing those sounds provided a somber reminder that the war waits for no one; there would be no pause or time-out to mourn the losses. We would each say our own private prayers, mourn in our own way, and then move on.

As the morning passed, the word spread across the base about the cause of the crash. According to the Aircraft Commander of the chase ship (Super Slick), they were responding to a call from a South Vietnamese outpost about twenty to twenty-five miles from Soc Trang. The outpost was under attack by a contingent of Vietcong fighters and needed fire support. The two ships were flying in at a low level to engage the enemy force when the primary ship (Lucky Strike) was struck by a B40 rocket. The Huey suddenly exploded in midair, producing a huge fireball that completely destroyed the ship. There was simply nothing left of the craft, and only burning remnants tumbled through the night air to the ground below.

Several accounts of the final minutes of Lucky Strike have been recorded by other pilots, crew members, and ground observers. But perhaps the most telling of all was that of the Aircraft Commander of Super Slick, who had been the first to call Headquarters (which was at our base in Soc Trang) to report the crash. His voice was quavering as he relayed the details of the catastrophe.

Headquarters responded by asking the AC whether there were any survivors. He only asked that question because he had not witnessed the massive fireball explosion for himself.

There was a lengthy pause while the Super Slick AC tried to pull himself together. His voice was still trembling and full of emotion when he finally responded.

"No, Sir, no one could have survived the explosion."

In the days following the shoot down of Lucky Strike, our entire company walked around in a surreal daze, much akin to a heavy fog that allows you to function while still having you doubting your own reality. Some of our men were able to put it behind them quickly—or at least hide the mental gashes that might affect their performance and judgment. Others were simply affected so deeply that it sapped their confidence and desire to continue flying. At least one Crew Chief and door gunner suddenly stepped back from their ships entirely, no longer able to sustain the mental duress of going airborne.

Personally, I never thought about backing down from my accepted mission. It wasn't that I didn't experience fear; everyone did when the bullets started flying. I think it's what I did with that fear and the adrenaline rush that accompanied it.

As Mark Twain once said in 1894, "Courage is resistance to fear, mastery of fear—not the absence of fear" (*The Tragedy of Pudd'nhead Wilson and the Comedy Those Extraordinary Twins*, chapter 12).

It was always there in the background.

A few days after the demise of Lucky Strike, a clerk showed up at the locker of Daniel Proctor, inside our barracks, with a clipboard and a pair of bolt cutters. He set three boxes to the side of the locker and then began cutting the lock off the hasp. With a very uneasy feeling inside, I watched him start to work. This guy never knew Proctor, and I felt that his approach to his personal belongings was very disrespectful.

A handful of us gathered around the clerk as he continued to pull items from the locker and toss them nonchalantly into the boxes. It was apparent that he did not care about his work; he was just cramming stuff into every corner as though he were shoveling manure into a pile. We felt we had to intervene.

"What are you doing?" I asked.

"Well, these are Proctor's belongings, his 'final effects,'" the clerk replied. "I have to get them all packed up and shipped back to his family in the States. It's part of my job."

He tried to override our request to take over the task and pack everything neatly and reverently, but he finally ceded to our demand to prepare the belongings for shipping. I'm sure his family appreciated our efforts as well.

About a month after Dan's death, I returned to my bunk to find a young soldier, freshly arrived in-country, sitting on the edge of Daniel's bunk, beside his newly issued duffel. His duffle was new-bright green, his fatigues were new-bright green, and even the expression on his face appeared to match that same bright hue. He was obviously fresh from the reception center and ignorant of everything we did. He hadn't a clue about the previous occupant of the bunk he had claimed—nor could he, and I really couldn't blame him. But I still felt uncomfortable about his presence there. So shortly thereafter, I moved into a different barracks with Rob Sandwith and Tom Wilkes. But that was still in the future, several weeks after the memorial service for the crew of Lucky Strike and for Mark Miles.

We had a few more days between the crash and the memorial service, which was held on my birthday (March 4). The empty bunks in our barracks were a constant reminder of the loss. Their deaths were mourned by everyone, including the mamasans who maintained our barracks and took care of our personal effects. On more than one occasion, I heard them quietly weeping as they cleaned and swept their way around the empty bunks and closed lockers. Permanent loss is a terrible thing to conquer, even for those who never spoke the same language as the deceased. It hit hard.

From time to time, I'd step out to the revetment of Lucky Strike, which now stood vacant and forlorn at the end of the tarmac. The quiet emptiness it painted was in stark contrast with the bustling activity that had once surrounded this area. It was so silent. If I sat there long enough, I could almost see the faces and hear the voices of the lost crew, my friends and comrades. It was impossible to describe how much I missed those guys. They were gone forever.

They conducted a memorial service a number of days following the crash. It was Wednesday evening, March 4, the day I turned twenty years of age. I thought briefly about that fact as I walked across the base to the site of the small chapel. In years past, I would be celebrating with my family and friends, with Whit by my side. Here in Vietnam, we didn't have time to celebrate birthdays. Sometimes they passed without our remembering. But this was not an ordinary birthday. This was the ultimate sadness, and we all felt it.

The service was held in memory of all seven men killed that night, including Mark Miles, who was on T-bird 3. Seven men. Looking back on it, I knew the number of soldiers who perished that night was small by comparison. I knew there were US Marines companies involved in vicious mountainside firefights where hundreds lost their lives. The day of the service (March 4), the French submarine Eurydice exploded near Cape Camarat, off the southeast coast of France in the Mediterranean, killing all fifty-seven crewmembers on board. We lost but seven. But due to our size and closeness, that meant the world to us, and on that day, we all grieved as one.

Our base chapel at Soc Trang was so small that it held but a few rows of pews. Almost the entire company, with the exception of those who were flying that night, showed up for the service. The size of the crowd meant the majority of us, including me, were forced to stand outside. I was able to gain a few glimpses of the inside, with the few rows of pews and the small altar at the front of the interior. Peering into the chapel, I saw that they had placed seven flight helmets in a line across the front of the altar. It was yet another solemn reminder of the lives lost.

There were a couple main contributors to the service that evening. Major Kilpatrick, as Company Commander, spoke for quite a while as he read a passage from the Bible. I remember hearing his voice, normally so strong and raspy, with a cutting edge that could pierce through a helmet and instantly command respect from anyone within earshot. Tonight, however, it was breaking, filled with sorrow and sadness as he fought his interior battle to continue. I wondered several times whether he would be able to make it to the end of his prepared words.

The chaplain then continued the service, quoting verse and scripture as he delivered the last words and prayers for the deceased and their loved ones. I do not remember the name of the chaplain, as it may have been the only time I met him. His words, while sorrowful, were much more composed and eloquently delivered. This was one of the main duties of the chaplain, besides performing normal weekly services, so he was better prepared for this kind of tragedy. If he felt the same degree of loss as those assembled, it didn't show, and he kept the ceremony in line until its conclusion.

As we left the chapel that evening, we walked together in small groups along the road to our barracks. Not much was said during our solemn march. Our eyes still stung from the tears, and not a soul felt like talking. While we strolled down the road, the sounds of helicopters taking off and landing roared overhead. As with the night of the crashes, it reminded me that the war never takes a day off, and the fighting never ends. We must find a time to mourn in our own way, regardless of the mission schedules, flight times, and other war-related activities that take place around the clock.

I always knew that the crew of Lucky Strike would remain with me, forever, never to be forgotten. And I was correct in my prognostication. They are all with me to this day, fifty years later.

Within a month my own ship (Warrior 21) would be selected to replace Lucky Strike on the nightly perimeter defense mission. It was a proud tradition to follow. Now it would be us who flew off each evening into the darkness, chasing the same invisible enemies who so violently ended the lives of the Lucky Strike crew. Sure, it had its dangers, but I didn't give it much thought. "Borrowing trouble from tomorrow" would gain me nothing.

I did, however, decide to embellish the nose of our ship with some symbolic nose art commemorating our predecessor. I had the words "They were Lucky Strike" painted across the nose of our ship, along with seven gold stars to symbolize the lives of those lost on that mission. It just seemed appropriate.

When we finally started flying that nocturnal mission every night, several platoon mates asked me if we would take over the call sign Lucky Strike. I told them no, explaining how that would be impossible. I, along with my entire crew, had too much respect for those who had lost their lives that night. We would never reuse the same call sign. We also never used Lucky Strike's revetment, instead leaving it vacant out of reverence for its final occupant. Maybe someone, flying another ship, would use it again someday. Hopefully, that would be after all of us currently serving in-country were gone. By then, those who remembered would have transferred away or returned home to the United States.

But never us.

**Poem written by Warrant Officer
Lloyd Drennon, helo pilot,
336th Assault Helicopter Company,
for the lost crewmembers of Lucky Strike.**

### The Chapel Bell's Last Clang

It's night outside the chapel at Soc Trang
A gentle wind stirs from the still airfield.
We all wait for the chapel bell's last clang.

Was from the heart, Amazing Grace we sang.
Silence falls, the chaplain rises, our soul's shield.
It's night outside the chapel of Soc Trang.

We began the day not fearing war's fang.
We had been wounded before but we healed.
We all wait for the chapel bell's last clang.

Some worked, some slept, at the club some sang.
While others flew and from Odins blows reeled.
It's night outside the chapel at Soc Trang.

We've tasted it; we all know it, fear's tang.
Bitter and sweet, that fruit of the battlefield.
We all wait for the chapel bell's last clang.

For the crew, we mourn, the chapel bell rang.
Taps in the darkness, no tear is concealed.
It's night outside the chapel at Soc Trang.
We all wait for the chapel bell's last clang.

# 8

# TWO BIRTHDAYS IN MARCH

There's a common expression that says, "Every man has a bullet with his name on it." The meaning of that saying is, of course, that everyone amongst us has a beginning and an end. No one gets out of this world alive, and each of our lives will eventually be terminated by some event, whether by injury, illness, or other. I once overheard a conversation, though, that put this thought into a different light. A gentleman in this exchange voiced his thoughts by saying, "I'm not worried about the bullet with my name on it. I'm worried about the one that says, 'To whom it may concern.'"

Personally, I got the meaning of this concept while I was flying Warrior 21 in March 1970. The Vietcong fighter on the ground who shot me in the back couldn't possibly have seen any part of me. I was sitting inside my ship, surrounded by walls and seats that obscured any trace of my body.

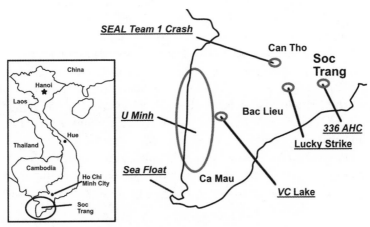

Location of U Minh Forest in Mekong Delta, Vietnam.
(Photo credit: Archie Woodworth)

"To whom it may concern."

The date was March 22, 1970, less than three weeks after my twentieth birthday. We were working in support of the South Vietnamese ARVN 21st Infantry,[2] whom we were to transport to the U Minh Forest. The U Minh Forest is a vast tract of land located on the very southwest edge of the country, where the coastline curves north and meets Thailand. The Gulf of Thailand sits to the west of this tract, while the forest itself stretches many miles north, south, and inland. Today it encompasses at least two major national parks and is home to one of the largest peat forestland areas in the world, not to mention dozens of unique and endangered species of wildlife.

We were always leery when our missions took us into the U Minh Forest. This large, dense region was notorious for being a very dangerous place. It was thoroughly infested with Vietcong fighters and North Vietnamese regulars. It was very thick and ran hundreds of miles inland. All of it was bad. It was also a 100 percent free-fire zone, which meant if you saw someone, you were to open fire and continue blasting away until you'd neutralized the threat. Additionally, it was bombed every night by B-52 bombers as well as Naval artillery. And if you crashed there or were forced to the ground, you were in deep, deep trouble. About 50 percent of our missions headed into this area, and we kept around the edges rather than venturing into the middle.

Our operations on that day followed the pattern of many others. We would first fly to the Ca Mau Airfield, where we would refuel before taking off to the PZ to pick up our load of South Vietnamese soldiers. The Ca Mau Airfield sounds like an impressive facility with lots of runways, towers, hangars, and repair facilities. In truth, it was simply a single runway with a number of fuel pumps that could refuel eight to ten ships at a time.

On many of these missions, we had only two loads of troops to ferry into battle, but for this operation, we had three, which made for a very long day. After picking up our first loadout of the South Vietnamese, we headed toward the LZ while listening to the radio chatter of the gunships who were already on scene. From their transmissions, it sounded very quiet at the drop-off point, perhaps even too quiet. We were all aware of the often-used strategy when the enemy would withhold all fire on our first insertion, hoping to lull us into a false sense of security. Then, when we returned on our next trip with our guard down, all hell would break loose. In order to

---

2. ARVN is the Army of the Republic of Vietnam. They were the ground forces of the South Vietnamese military, and they worked closely with the United States since their inception in 1955.

survive in this country, you had to be on your game 100 percent of the time. For this very reason, we went in hot, our M60s trained and firing on the tree line as we came into our landing.

We discharged our first batch of soldiers, then went back and picked up our second group, trying to make our runs as quickly as possible. We still had one more shuttle for a third group after this one was deployed.

As we approached the LZ for the second time that morning, we knew that the tactical situation had changed for the worse. There was radio talk from the other slicks, saying, "Taking fire! Taking Fire!"

We were close to landing, flaring out to touch down, when some of those guns turned on our ship. We began disembarking our troops as fast as possible, who hit the ground firing their own weapons. Inside our ship, another voice rang out: "Taking fire! Taking fire!"

This time, however, it was our own pilot, Mr. Olson, making the reports. We had to get the hell out of there as soon as possible.

Olson wasted little time in pulling us into a rapid vertical ascent, leaving the ground as quickly as possible. Even as we went airborne, the door gunner and I were firing our M60s at the ground below. We were gaining altitude with ever-increasing velocity when it hit me.

*Wham!*

It felt as though someone had slugged me in the back with a baseball bat. I didn't know what it was at first, but it hurt like hell. I involuntarily ceased firing the M60 as I tried to stabilize my body from the blow. Stars were flashing before my eyes, and I began experiencing difficulty in breathing. Time lost all meaning; seconds felt like minutes as I attempted to remain functional and upright. I quickly gave up on that idea, unbuckled my seatbelt, and dropped to the floor.

As I fell, I saw a hole in the bulkhead right behind where I'd sitting. Not good. For a few brief seconds, I thought, "This might be it. The end."

From the cockpit, I continued hearing the voices of both Olson and the other ships' pilots as they repeated their calls.

"We're taking fire. Taking fire." Then came the even more ominous words: "We're taking hits."

At this point, I keyed my own microphone and announced, "I've been hit."

Our door gunner immediately jumped over from his position on the right side of the ship to assist me. I directed him back to his gun to resume firing, as I knew the hostile fire was coming from his side. Meanwhile, Olson turned around in his seat to catch a glimpse of me laying across the floor of the ship.

"How bad were you hit?" he asked, looking for an immediate assessment.

"I'm not sure," I replied, knowing that it was impossible to determine where the bullet had entered my body and whether it had struck anything critical.

Olson then contacted Warrior 6, our Company Commander, and informed him of our situation.

"We've taken multiple hits, and Feigel's been hit," he intoned. His normally rock-steady voice registered more concern that normal. Warrior 6's response was immediate and authoritative.

"Warrior 21, break from formation and return to base and the hospital immediately."

I had to hope that the injury was not too critical, as the flight to the hospital would take us a full hour. As we gained additional altitude, I removed my flak jacket, while feeling my breathing returning to normal somewhat. I also noticed, looking forward in the ship, that we had alarms flashing on the master caution panel, indicating that vital components of the ship had been damaged.

We were just in the process of breaking away from the rest of the formation of slicks when I felt my full composure returning. I looked around my body and the floor of the ship for pools of blood. Thankfully, I didn't see any. I only felt a sharp throbbing from the middle of my back, on the right side. I felt a bit guilty about aborting our mission on account of my injury, which might have been superficial. I decided to advise our pilot to return to the mission.

"I'm not bad, I just got the wind knocked out of me. Let's rejoin the others and get our last batch in there," I said through gritted teeth. I knew I could do this.

"Are you sure?" asked Olson, hesitant to take a risk with my life.

"Yes, let's get going."

Olson then contacted Warrior 6 back and reported that my wound wasn't serious, and that we could continue with our mission.

"That's great," replied our Company Commander. "The troops in the LZ are getting hit hard, and we need to get more troops in there as soon as possible. We could use every ship we've got."

Olson immediately reversed course and headed the ship back into our formation. For some reason, he had an US Air Force Colonel flying as copilot that day. The Colonel already knew how to fly, but from what I'd heard, he was just along with us to observe tactics.

Upon landing for our refueling, I took off my shirt while our door gunner examined my wound. I asked how it looked, which he answered with a noncommittal shrug. After all, he wasn't a doctor. He was able to remove a few fragments of both bullet and shrapnel, which had been splintered off our craft by the impact of the round. But it was too swollen to do much more, and I was needed to refuel the ship anyway if we were to continue our mission.

As I leaped from the ship and prepared to begin refueling, a call rang out from the ship positioned behind us.

"Warrior 21, you are leaking fuel," he advised.

I looked beneath the ship, and sure enough, we had a small stream of fuel draining from beneath the middle of the fuselage. I relayed this information to Olson, who was sitting at the controls, staring at the master caution panel that was still flashing. He responded by taking the ship up into a low hover so I could inspect the leak and determine its source.

As the ship hovered above my head, I did the best I could to localize the fuel leak. I quickly realized that would be impossible to do. It was emanating from the "hell hole," which is a round hole located beneath the transmission that is used for inspecting the hydraulics. It is placed there to facilitate inspection and maintenance of the transmission and hydraulics, which means there's a lot in there, including a number of fuel cells. With everything contained in that one little area, and with fuel streaming slowly out, it was impossible to pinpoint the problem. To me, it meant that we had only about an hour of flight time left instead of two.

I also experienced an additional bit of queasiness as I stood below Warrior 21, knowing that the master caution panel was still sounding an alarm inside the ship. What else was wrong besides the fuel leakage that could bring us down? Had anything in our transmission been damaged? How about our hydraulic systems? Or perhaps our rotor head? It could have been any one of a dozen major issues, but we just couldn't tell. Once again, I could feel my heart racing and the adrenaline coursing through my body at 100 mph. And if our ship fell to the ground right now, I was standing directly beneath it.

I repeated my words to Olson, stating that we were "leaking fuel, but not gallons."

Olson once again reported our status to Warrior 6, repeating many of my own words to the Company Commander.

Major Kilpatrick immediately replied, "Can you make another insertion?"

Olson passed the question along to me, and I replied with a semi-confident thumbs-up. "Let's go!"

I topped off the fuel, and we headed off to rejoin the other four slicks. We immediately flew to the PZ, where we embarked with the last group of South Vietnamese infantry troops before heading back to the landing zone. This time, the area was still very hot, and other ships were taking fire. Thankfully, our ship was not on the receiving end of any of the AK-47 fire this time, and we discharged our load and got out again safely.

Once airborne, following our third insertion of the day, we were ordered to break off and head back to Soc Trang. Our day was over. As we headed east toward our base, with the rush of adrenaline wearing off, my back started hurting even worse. I was pretty certain by this time that I'd survive the injury, but it sure was making my day miserable.

I didn't have to ask Olson to park near the hangar. Both the ship and I were shot up pretty badly, and we both would require repairs. As we shut down the engine next to the hangar, we were approached by a group of familiar faces: hangar rats who had been my daily companions until two months earlier. Word traveled fast, and they were all concerned for my well-being.

"We heard you were hit?" asked one of the hangar rats.

"You OK?" queried another technician.

That's the way it was in the hangar back then, whenever we heard about a ship down or shot up or, worse yet, someone killed. Everyone was always concerned about all their mates on the other ships in the company. We all looked out for one another like a big family.

Some of the guys helped me into the company Jeep, which was ready and waiting when we landed nearby. I really didn't need the assistance, but I'm sure those men would have hand-carried me to the hospital at the other end of the base if I'd needed it. That's just the way everyone was.

At the hospital, the doctor examined my wound, which by now had swollen to the size of a grapefruit. It was still throbbing and was extremely painful to the touch. He was able to remove many of the fragments that were closer to the surface, but the swelling was preventing access to the deeper pieces. After cleaning and dressing the open wound, the doctor bandaged the injury site and gave me directions to return in a few weeks to attempt the removal of the additional shrapnel. For some reason, I never made a return visit to the physician, so the metal stayed inside my back long after I had departed the country.

From the bits and pieces of the shrapnel and bullet, it was determined that the weapon used to fire the round was an AK-47. The AK-47 was the primary assault rifle of the North Vietnamese and Vietcong fighters in the Vietnam War. It had quickly developed a reputation for its simplicity and reliability. Since its introduction in 1949, over seventy-five million pieces of the original AK-47 and its later improvements have found their way off the assembly line and into use, mostly by those in Third World countries.

Some fine investigative work also tracked down the path taken by the bullet before it buried itself in my flesh. Evidently, the round had entered our ship through the right side wall and then passed through a fuel cell. After those two penetrations, the shell was further slowed by passing through a bulkhead located behind me, which was thicker than the actual outside shell of the ship. Finally, what was left of the round passed through my flak jacket and entered my back at a point below my right side scapula.

At the time of impact, I was wearing a flak jacket that had some bulletproof protection, but most of that was located in the front part of the vest. It was a full inch up front, which included the bulletproof plate intersecting the front baffles of the garment. The less-protective materials comprising the back did stop some of the residual pieces from penetrating my back, but the rest made it through. Still, I am extremely lucky that the vast majority of the energy expended by the bullet had been absorbed by the barriers and bulkheads between me and the shooter. Otherwise, I may have ended up a statistic.

There was an expression within our platoon that if you were wounded in action but lived to fight another day, you had been granted another birthday. Evidently, I had received another birthday. "That's interesting," I thought, as I had been injured on March 22, just eighteen days after my real birth date of March 4. In essence, I now had two birthdays in March.

Our ship, Warrior 21, likewise required a full week of tender loving care to repair the internal and external damages from the hostile fire in the LZ. The ship only had three bullet holes, which was much fewer than on other occasions. But the rounds penetrated the guts of the mechanics and tore into some critical components, which took time to fix.

In a way, the holes through the exterior were some of the simpler damages to fix. Presuming that those rounds didn't damage anything on the interior, it became a simple patch job for our airframe tech. He was a short and wiry little fellow who worked in our hangar, and patching holes was almost all he did. It was an aviation support job, with the assigned MOS of 68G10/30. Primarily, he was a sheet-metal worker, and he was very skilled at his craft. He would start on the bullet hole and drill out the damage, then he'd clean up the rough edges and check inside for additional destruction. He would follow this up by applying one or more square patches, which he made up in advance. He produced these patches in various sizes and then matched them to the holes in each ship. They were then riveted to the fuselage to cover each hole until the hole was patched. He also had to inspect the ship on the side opposite the bullet hole, as these rounds often-times entered one side only to exit the other.

Looking back on the entire incident, I can see how it turned out well for both the ship and for me. Neither of us received severe hits, and we were both back in action within a week. The major damage to our ship was in the fuel cells, which could always be replaced. So it turned out that the ship itself was never in grave danger of going down. It had just been "bloodied up a bit."

The repairs were all completed quickly by the men in the hangar repair team. Meanwhile, I was very happy to be back on full-duty status before Warrior 21 went airborne again, which was a source of pride to me as Crew Chief. It was my ship, and that is where I wanted to be.

Following the events of that week, I went back into action with my crew, flying combat missions in support of the South Vietnamese infantry troops. It was long, hard work, and the memories of our missed week of duty quickly faded from our minds. But an incident that happened later in the year brought everything back into focus.

At this point, we were flying the night missions, performing the perimeter patrols in search of hostile activity near our base. We were working around the ship, making preparations to lift off for our nightly patrol, when a Jeep arrived with the Company Clerk. He hopped out of the vehicle and approached me in a professional manner.

"You're Feigel, right?" he asked, looking at me with a questioning expression.

"Yes, I'm Feigel," I confirmed. "What do you need?"

"You have to report to Battalion Headquarters tonight at 1900."

"What for?" I asked, not eager to alter our nightly mission to meet some petty administrative requirements.

"You have to attend a ceremony to receive your Purple Heart medal, along with five others," he replied. His tone of voice and demeanor left no doubt that his word was authoritative; *I was to be at that ceremony*, and there would be no discussion on the matter.

I was shocked and a bit dumbfounded.

"I'm going to receive a *what?*" I repeated.

"Your Purple Heart, for your wounds sustained in combat on March 22."

I stood there, not knowing what to say. I didn't really have words for the way I was feeling. Yes, I had been wounded in action, so, yes, I did technically meet the requirements for the prestigious award. But somehow, I just didn't feel that my own injuries added up or were worthy of the Purple Heart. My God, many men lost limbs or their eyesight or, worse yet, their lives. It just didn't seem right to me, at least at that time.

I looked back at the clerk, then at my ship, and finally at my watch. My crew was waiting. What would I say?

I can't make it," I said quickly before turning back toward the ship. "It will have to be another time."

This time it was the clerk's turn to lose his composure. "Another time?" he stuttered. "But . . . but . . . but, there is no other time. This request comes from our Battalion Colonel! He is expecting you to be there, in formation, to receive your medal."

"Sorry," I replied. "I'm flying tonight and I just can't make it." My single-sentence response was the last thing I said before climbing onboard our ship. Priorities are priorities, and my first duty was to my ship and my crew.

Shortly after we took off, I told the crew what had transpired on the ground, including the incredulous expression on the face of the clerk who learned I was turning down the orders of the Battalion Commander and the awarding of a Purple Heart. The crew had a great laugh over the matter.

"Just imagine that," said Olson, picturing the event. "I can just see the colonel standing there with one extra Purple Heart, but no one to pin it on."

✎

### After-Action Thoughts

In lieu of a medal ceremony, our battalion decided to mail the Purple Heart to my house in New York, along with the certificate. I was afraid my family would hear about me getting wounded via a communiqué from the Red Cross or, worse yet, through the grapevine, so I decided to tell them about it myself before they would hear via other means. I didn't want them getting unduly upset, thinking it was a life-threatening injury. My letter just mentioned that I had sustained a minor injury and let it go at that.

A few weeks later, the letter arrived with my Purple Heart and certificate, which my family hung on the wall. They took pictures and sent them to me, saying they were proud of my actions while expressing their hope that I would avoid incurring future injuries.

As an additional afterthought to this incident, it was years later while I was back home that I had an X-ray that revealed bits of shrapnel remaining throughout my back. They are concentrated in an area below my right scapula, along with a rib that had been jolted out of place from the impact of the hit. They remain today, along with my Purple Heart, as reminders of a very scary day in my life.

Sorry, Mother.

## 9

# OPERATING WITH THE SEALS

Depending on which accounting is cited, the origins of the US Navy SEAL program date back to 1942. Although the official title and structure of the US SEAL (sea, air, land) wasn't coined until 1962, their history includes a bevy of daring feats during World War II and, later, more regional wars.

Our 336th Assault Helicopter Company was often called to work with the elite warriors in the Delta region, although we were not fully aware of their prestigious reputation. About all we knew was that they were part of the US Navy's Special Operations Forces and that they dressed differently and carried weapons that were unique to anything we'd ever seen. I'd describe their appearance as a cross between Rambo and the Hells Angels. They were just plain cool.

The members of SEAL Team 1 didn't live with us at Soc Trang. As a matter of fact, I'm not sure they ever visited our base. They were quartered at a unique floating compound called Seafloat, which was a collection of boats, barges, and other water-borne platforms that were anchored together in the Cau Lon River in the southern end of Vietnam. Seafloat was a joint project of the United States and Vietnam that was set in place in June 1969. It was the first step in reestablishing a permanent military presence in that part of the country. The floating base remained in operation until September 1970, when the shore-based equivalent of Seafloat officially assumed all functions of the original installation.

Since the SEALs were a division of the Navy, they were supported by their own platoon of gunships. They needed this gunship support because they sometimes made contact with the enemy and found themselves greatly outnumbered. Sometimes this happened when our own gunships were deployed on another mission and could not break off to support the SEALs.

The gunships used by the Navy were the older Bell UH-1 B versions, which were "hand-me-downs" from when the Army upgraded their own fleet to the new C variants. This platoon of gunships was called the Sea Wolves, and it existed only for the time it operated in Vietnam, not before or after. Their sole mission in life was to provide support to the Brown-Water Navy patrol boats and other specialized missions, such as the SEAL activity.

The Huey B versions used by the Sea Wolves were old but still served as good gunship platforms. They weren't as capable for duty as slicks, because their smaller compartment and less-powerful engine meant they couldn't carry as many troops for insertion or extraction as our ships. For this reason, our own ships—those used by Platoons 1 and 2—served to shuttle the SEALs in and out of action while the Sea Wolves flew cover for us.

Our own T-Bird pilots conducted training for the Navy pilots, who were excellent flyers but had never provided gunship support services in the past. This training commenced when the first two Navy aviators arrived in support of Operation Game Warden, which was never explained to me, although it sounded very exciting. They were part of Navy Helicopter Combat Support Squadron 1 and were sent to Vietnam as part of an agreement between the Army and Navy to provide support of riverine operations in the Mekong Delta.

Our gunship pilots gave them training in doing reconnaissance of LZs, supporting the slicks going in for landings, performing minigun runs, using the pull-down sights for rockets, and more. It was fast-paced and took several days to get an already-proficient pilot up to speed on these tactics. They were affectionately nicknamed Water Soldiers, and they adapted themselves superbly to their new Army environment. They quickly became superb gunship pilots.

There were other differences between the Sea Wolves and our own gunships. The Sea Wolves were based out of Vung Tau, which was farther north up the eastern coast of the country. Today, Vung Tau is a bustling tourist destination with vibrant city attractions and white sand beaches. But during the war, it was fraught with dangers from Vietcong (VC) fighters in the surrounding woodlands. The Sea Wolves didn't have much of a base there, and they had no runway like we had at Soc Trang. There was just a little area with some buildings that served as hangars. Their ships were always in need of work, which their maintenance crews performed overnight just to keep them airworthy. When the crews got up in the morning, they were given a different ship to fly every day, unlike our company, where we had "our ship."

The Navy crews were also structured a bit differently from our own in that they appeared to have no Crew Chief. They still operated with crews of four men, but they used an Aircraft Commander, a copilot, and two door gunners. The supervisory and maintenance skills of the Crew Chief were instead accomplished by the night-based maintenance crew. I don't think I would have enjoyed that structure, but it seemed to work for them.

This was also the period of time when a new copilot began flying with us on a regular basis. His name was Dana Brown, and he was a Warrant Officer who was being considered for our Aircraft Commander position now that Olson was nearing the end of his tour. Brown was another excellent pilot, and he possessed the same calm, self-assured personality that was essential to survive in the job. Tall and quiet, he was a native of Tennessee, which was somewhat evident in his pronounced accent. He had a good head on his shoulders, and he got along with everyone. We all knew he'd succeed when he took over for Olson later that year. Brown's excellent piloting skills and calm demeanor served him well in the military. He ended up staying in for twenty-five years, which included service in Korea and Germany. He retired as a Chief Warrant Officer following an extremely successful career.

Our crew on Warrior 21 seemed to work with the SEALs on a fairly regular basis. Their outfit would request support through our battalion, which then posted the designated ship(s) on a daily assignment board. Sometimes our assignment would be combat assault, or other times it might be a "hash and trash" mission, which was usually just bringing in supplies to one of our outposts and then supporting them on some local lifts. But other times, it involved supporting the SEAL teams and working with the Sea Wolves to insert and then extract them from their reconnaissance missions in the Ca Mau region. My own ship provided slick services at least ten times during that summer, and it seemed like at least one of our platoon ships was working their missions on a daily basis.

Working with the SEALs was always an interesting task because they were so different from our own soldiers. They'd show up and load onto our ships wearing almost anything other than a uniform. Some wore black pants and dark T-shirts, some had bandanas and other nonmilitary apparel. As I stated earlier, they slightly resembled a group of Hells Angels, though they were quieter and more composed. They had faces that had been darkened out, and they carried a variety of really impressive weapons, none of which I had ever fired. They were tough, intimidating young men.

Something else that was memorable was that, on the ship, they had no single group Commander that was made apparent by rank device. There would be a group meeting using a map before we departed, but that would be the extent of it. Once we went airborne, their leader would set himself up next to Olson in the cockpit and kneel on the floor. From that vantage point, he would point through the cockpit windshield at the spot where he wanted Olson to land. There wasn't much talking going on, since the SEAL had no helmet or headset. It was all accomplished by pointing and sign language.

Our route on these missions was almost always the same. We'd fly down from Soc Trang and refuel at Ca Mau. Then we'd head toward Seafloat and set down on one of their three helo landing pads. This was a dedicated landing area that also had some limited refueling capability. It was big enough for three of our ships to tie down side by side. We'd then embark our SEAL team and take off with the other two Sea Wolf gunships, always flying as a group.

Our missions with the SEALs were always either one or two days long. We'd usually drop them off at dusk, then we'd fly back to Seafloat and refuel before setting down for the night. Then, after conducting our nightly postflight inspection, we'd head back to one of the barges they used for berthing and attempt to get some sleep. This was interesting because we would actually sleep in the vacant bunks of the SEALs we had just inserted into their missions. I was always interested in the unique weapons the SEALs had stowed in their bunk areas. It looked as though they each had a say over what they carried, as there were so many different firearms scattered throughout the sleeping quarters. I once heard about a SEAL who had picked up a firearm inside our bunk area and fired it at a rat that was walking across the top of a locker. What the trigger-happy SEAL neglected to consider was that there were other men whose bunks were set up just on the other side of the thin metal partition. Thankfully, no one was injured, and the firing lasted but a single round. I can't remember whether the rat survived or not.

Sleeping down in the barges was not always easy. The "bunks" were often without standard mattresses but instead topped with a woven plastic material that felt like, well, woven plastic material. It was not comfortable in the least. Some of the men opted for hammock-type arrangements, and there were even reports of some troops sleeping on top of unused body bags.

Another reason for the abundance of insomnia onboard Seafloat was the continuous, round-the-clock detonation of concussion grenades, which were constantly tossed over the sides to discourage Vietcong frogmen from penetrating our defenses. The explosions of the grenades, when combined with the whooshing of the outbound mortars, raised a cacophony of high-decibel sounds that would wake the dead. I found that I was able to sleep only when I was completely exhausted, and even then, it was interrupted at best.[3]

There were a lot of SEALs who were berthed onboard Seafloat at any given time. My guess would have been there were around twenty-five to thirty, not counting those who we'd just inserted into their mission in the Ca Mau region or the U Minh Forest. They rotated on a daily basis; not every SEAL went out on a mission every day, so we seldom saw the same crews on our ship. We got along extremely well with the SEALs onboard Seafloat, and I enjoyed their company a lot more than that of the Sea Wolf crews. (It's not that there was any hostility between our two sets of air crews, but we just didn't talk much once we walked away from our ships.)

Another thing I liked about going to Seafloat was the food. Since it was a Navy facility and a Navy galley, they obviously had Navy mess cooks and Navy food. The meals served up by the Navy always seemed to be way ahead of the rations we got back at Soc Trang, and I would have preferred to stay there all the time.

The only problem I had with laying up overnight at Seafloat was the issue of personal hygiene. It was tough to get very clean there because we never brought along our own personal bathing supplies. They had showers there, but we didn't bring along our kit bags with our soap and other essential items for cleaning. There was just too much other stuff to worry about than wash towels and toothbrushes, so we waited until we got back to our own base.

Dropping the SEALs off at their LZ was always a fascinating sight to me. We'd have a team of five or six of them embarked on Warrior 21, and there would be a second slick if there were two SEAL teams. The leader would point out to Olson where he wanted to land, and Olson would pilot our ship down to that spot, with the Sea Wolf gunships flying cover. Then, once they disembarked from our ship, they became part of the ground below. Their camouflage seemed to blend almost instantly into the darkened grassy tree line, which they approached with extreme care and deliberateness.

I once commented to one of the SEALs about the amount of ammunition they carried on their bodies. It looked like a lot, but I also wondered if, should they make contact with the enemy, it would be not enough to see them through a protracted battle. The answer I received made a lot of

3. There were rumors that the continuous explosions of the concussion grenades right next to the pontoons of various components of Seafloat damaged its watertight integrity and led to its early demise. However, there were plans in existence to replace Seafloat with a land-based equivalent from the very start of the program.

sense. He said that he carries as much ammo as he can possibly transport while still being able to wiggle his way through the jungle.

Once the SEALs reached the tree line, they seemed to melt completely into the background. We might have been able to make out their shapes if the forest had been defoliated, but that would have been our only chance. After moving at a glacial speed toward their objective, they'd split up to take individual positions to observe the enemy. This was their mission on a great many of their ventures into enemy territory. Sometimes they'd be observing the hostile troops' strengths, while other times their objective might be to gather intelligence on the presence of American or South Vietnamese prisoners of war in the area. They usually didn't share too much information with us, and we didn't ask. We just flew the ship and got them in and out, which was the only part of the mission that belonged to us.

Conducting reconnaissance in the U Minh Forest at night was always dangerous business. Our own ship never once took fire either going into or away from one of these missions. However, the SEALs were often not as lucky and did make contact with the Vietcong several times. At times like that, all hell could break loose, and we'd be called in to extract them from their concealed positions. On one particular night, two teams called in for an immediate extraction, which resulted in us scrambling three ships to pick them up and get them out of harm's way. Our own Warrior 21 headed in to pick up one team while our Platoon Leader, Capt. Leandro, circled nearby to pick up the second team. Meanwhile, we had a third ship dropping large Navy flares over the area to light up the pickup zone.

Unfortunately, we were operating at night without the support of the gunships, which, for some reason, did not accompany us on this mission. This was dangerous, and we knew we were exposed as we went in. The SEALs, meanwhile, used strobe lights to guide us into the PZ. To make matters worse, once Olson lifted off with our SEAL team and Leandro went in for the second team, the flare burned out just before he was able to land his ship. As a result, he was forced to turn on his landing lights to see where he was, which made it all the more hazardous. Once those big white lights came on, the entire world (including all the hostiles) could see your ship and know exactly what you were doing. It was an invitation for disaster, but John held his position until the last of the SEALs had climbed onboard, thus completing the extraction. He took off without any lights at all, and we got the hell out of Dodge, heading back to Seafloat.

John Leandro was always like that: accepting tough assignments when he could have easily sent someone else in to do the job. If someone was wounded and in need of help on the ground, it was common to hear John's voice on the radio in Warrior 26, saying, "I'm inbound, I've got this." That's just the way he was. Even though he was 2nd Platoon Commander, he would never send someone into a place where he wouldn't go himself. It was one of the reasons he was so respected by everyone in the company.

Thankfully, those kinds of emergency situations didn't happen often. But on at least one occasion, one of the SEAL team leaders told Leandro, "You saved our asses back there." It felt very good to hear that.

Another one of their SEAL team members told us about times when he'd be lying motionless on the ground while enemy troops returned to their encampment, often coming within a few feet of stepping on his body. He'd be prone, facedown on the ground, as they walked right by, nearly stepping on his back. At times like that, he said he got through it all by remaining lifeless on the ground and saying over and over again to himself, "I am a log. I am a log."

What impressed me even more was our regularly scheduled extractions, when we went in and picked them up sometime the following morning. In the same way they went into the forest and split up, they'd somehow managed to find one another and re-form as a group for the ride out. They often traveled great distances during the night, so we were called in to pick them up miles away from the original LZ. I imagined them treading ever so lightly through the blackened miles of swampy jungle without making a sound. They were also able to cross some pretty impressive rivers with all their gear, which is a feat that I never figured out. Then again, they were SEALs, which meant they were up to almost any task.

Another one of our SEAL team missions was to practice rappelling from our ship using ropes and then to attempt a mission insertion using this tactic. To prepare for this event, a SEAL team member brought several rappelling ropes to our ship and threaded them through the cargo tie-down rings of our cargo compartment, tying them down until completely secure.

From there we flew the SEAL team to an exercise location near the shoreline so they could exercise their newly-acquired skills until proficient. That was the way of the SEALs; they would practice and practice and practice until something became second nature and they could do it with their eyes closed. They were completely professional in every way. They had to be, as their lives might depend on it at any time.

After becoming rappelling experts, they learned (as dusk approached) that their upcoming mission had changed. Their insertion would not require rappelling. We would be able to fly in and disembark them at the LZ the same as usual. We did this with them that evening and left them to perform their recon mission without incident.

The following morning, we found ourselves in a bit of a situation. It took some time to locate the team, and when we did, they were in an area that was heavily defoliated. However, despite the fact that the leaves were gone and we could see the SEALs below, we had no way to get our ship in to make the pickup. There were a lot of tall trees still standing that rendered a landing impossible.

Luckily, the rappelling ropes were still affixed to the cargo tie-down rings, which gave us a novel idea. We quickly lowered the ropes out of both sides of the ship until they reached the troops below. The SEALs then tied loops into the bottom of both ropes that were big enough to put two feet inside. From there, it was a simple matter of conducting a "SEAL lift," picking up two team members at a time and then giving them a lift over to a nearby river bank. The bank was only a few minutes away, so it took very little time to move all six men to safety. From there, it was back to Seafloat, with another mission successfully completed.

The SEALs had already developed a number of tactics that seemed to work well in Vietnam. One of these involved us dropping them off in a deserted village that had gone back and forth a number of times between friendly and hostile forces. The village was on the outskirts of the U Minh Forest, which meant that anything was possible. Chances were pretty good that they were being observed by Vietcong spotters, who would have been watching their activity. After disembarking two teams, our ships headed out to a holding area about twenty miles away and just flew in circles for a while.

In about twenty minutes, the SEALs called us back in for an extraction, so we headed back to the village. Little did we know that we were being used as part of a ruse. It was a fake extraction all the way.

A couple of the SEALs approached our ship and signaled us by putting one finger to his lips.

"Shhh . . . keep this quiet" was the obvious message. "Now get the hell out of here and leave us to kick butt."

We didn't need to be told twice. Pretending to have completed the extraction of the two SEAL teams, we lifted off once again and headed back to the holding area. Meanwhile, the SEALs retraced their steps *covertly* into the village to wait for any curious Vietcong, who did show up a short time later.

When the enemy did appear later on, expecting to find the village abandoned, they walked straight into an ambush that had been perfectly set and executed. The two Sea Wolf gunships appeared overhead to provide extra firepower, which served to hasten the end result.

It was always a pleasure to work with the SEAL teams, as their professionalism and determination in battle seemed to make victory a foregone conclusion. They would do whatever it took to bring about success for themselves and for their teammates. Anything.

"I am a log."

# 10

# REPLACING LUCKY STRIKE

Even as I write the title to this chapter, I do so with mixed emotions. Something inside me does a gut-wrenching turn as I think about "replacing" this particular ship. Lucky Strike was something very special to all of us because it was so much more than just a ship. It was where six members of our platoon, our friends, our fellow shipmates, lost their lives. We all felt the same way about this. Not only could it have been us who lost our lives that night, but any of us would have jumped into hell for a chance to save a single one of them. However, we were never afforded the opportunity to do that, and we all grieved for their loss.

**Warrant Officer Richard J. Connelly**

**Warrant Officer James T. Pace**

**Specialist 5 Daniel V. Proctor**

**Specialist 5 Ronald W. Stafford**

**Specialist 4 Gary T. Swartz**

**Specialist 4 Ronald L. McCormick**

Their names, along with that of Specialist 4 Mark S. Miles, were commemorated on The Wall of the Vietnam War Memorial in Washington, DC. We could replace their mission with one of our own, flying their routes and performing base perimeter defense. But we could never take the place of those who had gone before us, surrendering their lives to do what they thought was right.

Throughout the month of April and into the early part of May, Olson, Sandwith, and I were flying all types of missions. Whether it was combat assault, SEAL team support, or even the ubiquitous "hash and trash" missions, it was all flying and doing what had to be done. But we also noticed that we were flying more and more night missions. It's not something we had already requested; it just started appearing on the schedule with increasing frequency.

To no one's surprise, our Company Commander (Major Kilpatrick) never designated a replacement ship for Lucky Strike to perform the nightly perimeter defense mission. The memory of Lucky Strike's fiery demise weighed heavily on his mind, as it did with all of us, and he remained gun shy about putting another crew in harm's way. Instead he decided to rotate the nightly patrols between different crews and ships of the 1st and 2nd Platoons, with a different ship taking the duty each night.

In addition to the alternating crews, the mission itself was changed to reduce the risk. The flights were shorter and were restricted to routes much closer to the base. Lucky Strike had received the lethal rocket fire while supporting a South Vietnamese outpost about twenty to twenty-five miles from Soc Trang. Free-fire zones were no longer part of our repertoire. As slicks, we simply weren't outfitted with the equipment and armament needed to take care of business like Lucky Strike had. We had no large light cluster to illuminate the ground below and no 50-cal gun to generate a truly effective aerial gunfire attack if needed. We had only our M60s, which weren't going to scare anyone. As such, the low-level river and canal patrols, the outpost fire support, and the missions into free-fire zones were above and beyond our capabilities.

But it would not remain that way for long.

As the days of April rolled past, our crew of Warrior 21 found ourselves flying almost every night, and we really enjoyed it. There were several contributing factors that came together to make this happen. The first was that Olson and I had both flown many missions with Lucky Strike, and we'd learned a lot from our ventures with their crew. We'd experienced the challenges of nighttime tactics and had learned about the many hazards of flying into hostile territory after dark. It was simultaneously exciting, exhilarating, and nerve-wracking, and we could see why the Lucky Strike crew reveled in their mission.

There was also a certain rebelliousness that precipitated our enjoying this kind of operation. Whereas the daytime missions had us flying with other ships, often accompanied by our Platoon Leader, Capt. Leandro, the nighttime missions were usually solo. It was us, alone, flying out there into the blackened sky without a backup ship nearby. We made all our own decisions and followed our own instincts. We depended on each other, the five of us inside that ship, because that's all we had. To a man, we relished the independence to accomplish our mission without interference from above.

After several weeks of us performing the night flight, it was no surprise when Olson made his appearance in Capt. Leandro's office to request a face-to-face meeting. He explained his request in simple terms. We, the crew of Warrior 21, wanted to take over Lucky Strike's mission. Our entire crew had talked it over, and that's what we wanted to do. We were convinced of it. Now all Olson had to do was to convince Leandro, who in turn had to explain it all to Major Kilpatrick, our 336th Assault Helicopter Company Commander. We didn't know how that conversation would work out.

Leandro's meeting with Major Kilpatrick went smoother than we had hoped. The Company Commander was naturally worried: He didn't want to lose another crew to hostile fire. The loss of another ship was manageable, but the cost in human life was unmeasurable. In addition to being skilled crewmembers and loyal shipmates, they were also fathers, husbands, and sons to their families back home. This only magnified the pain and suffering of the loss, so it would have been understood if Kilpatrick said no.

Thankfully, Leandro was able to convince Kilpatrick that the changeover was worth the risk. He also emphasized that our crew, as well as the way we worked, would be less perilous than that of Lucky Strike. Olson was a superb pilot with a lot of nighttime experience and knew how to take care of the ship. Additionally, we had a highly seasoned crew who were good at their jobs, and we required little or no additional training to take on the perimeter defense mission.

Additional factors also weighed on our side of the scales. First, we were not adrenaline junkies. We weren't afraid of going into potentially hazardous areas to investigate or provide support, but we also didn't get reckless either. In other words, we figured it was always better to live to fight another day rather than attempt a suicidal move against far superior firepower. That factor, along with Olson's superior skills, had saved our behinds on more than one occasion.

Finally, we also knew that should we get ourselves in over our heads, we had one of the finest gunship platoons in the entire Delta region backing us up. Those Thunderbird crews could get their ships in the air in a matter of minutes, regardless of it being day or night. They were always prepared and ready to charge in and lay down a devastating carpet of ground fire, which was very comforting to us as we began flying our night missions.

Regardless of our skill and desire, we still didn't have a ship configured to take over Lucky Strike's role, so that became our biggest challenge over the next few weeks. We needed to find a way to convert a Greyhound bus into an arms-bristling gunfighter. It was a challenge indeed, but we were up to the task.

First, we needed to find a large cluster light, which would be mounted on the starboard side of the cargo compartment. We also needed a jump seat placed directly behind the cluster light on the right side. This would be mine, and as Crew Chief, I would be operating the lights, so I took particular interest in this rig.

Next, we needed a 50-cal gun mounted, once again, on the starboard side of the ship. This would be very similar to Lucky Strike's configuration, with the "big guns" mounted on the right side. The 50-cals have been around for over one hundred years, having entered into our military service in 1921. They have been used for anti-material and antiaircraft roles, in addition to general combat assault roles. Unlike the smaller guns carried on our ships, these weapons deploy a massive round that is over 5½ inches in length and achieve a muzzle velocity exceeding three thousand feet per second. It gets the enemy's attention in a hurry.[4]

Rounding out the firepower of our ship would be a second door gunner on the port side. He would be working an M60, which was another 7.62 mm weapon that fired around six hundred rounds per minute. Its claimed maximum effective firing range was 1,200 yards, although many doubters adjusted that distance closer to 800 yards. Regardless, it paled when compared to the 50-cal gun.

In addition to the upgraded weapons, we also needed to find a light system to illuminate the ground beneath our ship as we flew at a hundred feet or less. The most commonly used system was a set of cluster lights, which was part of the Firefly system along with the 50-cal gun. These il-

---

4. A slug from a 50-cal gun travels with such force and velocity that it has been known to strike ground and ricochet as high as five hundred feet into the air. For this reason, the gun must be used very carefully when operating around other friendly aircraft.

lumination devices were an Army solution to a longstanding problem. A number of C-123 landing lights were mounted together and then affixed to a metal frame, which, in turn, was mounted onto the helo. It required an operator in the craft to manually train the light on the target, but it was effective in lighting up targets on the ground. The operator could widen out the beam or make it more narrow, as well as move it up or down. This would become part of my job, so I became pretty familiar with its operation. We found that our company supply store had at least one of these cluster flights in stock, so we acquired it and mounted it onto Warrior 21, which was now known by call sign Super Slick.

The 50-cal was a little harder to obtain. We had to have the supply store order this through the Army stock system, so it took a bit longer to get. The gun arrived completely disassembled, packed inside a bag that was packed inside a box that was packed inside a protective crate. It was Sandwith and Wilkes who had the unenviable task of unpacking all the layers, after which Sandwith discovered that all the parts were thoroughly greased over in a thick coating of Cosmoline. (This was a lubricant that was also used to keep metallic components from rusting and corroding in the high heat and humidity. It has been used by the US military as far back as the Spanish-American War.) After cleaning the components, he skillfully assembled them and ensured they were in perfect operating condition. Sandwith was an expert at anything that fired, and he could probably have reassembled the gun blindfolded.

We flew with the cluster lights for a few weeks before we learned of a Nighthawk system that was available up in Long Binh, which was located much closer to Saigon. The Nighthawk used a Xeon light with a Starlight scope and was usually deployed with a 7.62 mm minigun instead of a 50-cal. We knew that we wanted to try this system in our own ship, but we had to do some bargaining to get it.

That was no problem: We were always up to the task. We knew the folks up at the base in Long Binh and got along with them pretty well. They weren't really frontline fighters as much as they were support personnel, so they loved getting their hands on battlefield "trophies," including enemy weapons and other combat paraphernalia. They also loved their beer, so we made sure to take along a case or two whenever we flew up there. It was pure gold on the trading block. That was how we acquired our Nighthawk system, although I can't remember all the tit-for-tat details of the trade itself. Regardless, we flew back to Soc Trang with the Xeon light, the Starlight scope, and the minigun strapped firmly to the deck of our ship.

We also used the beer to barter with the Navy folks at Long Binh for their 50-cal ammunition, which was superior to ours. It wasn't that the range was any different, but rather it was the combination of rounds and how they were loaded into the ammunition belt. Whereas our Army belts were loaded with a tracer round followed by four ball-ammo rounds, their Navy belts used a tracer, followed by an armor-piercing round, followed by an incendiary, then by a ball-ammo round, and then finally back to another tracer. It was highly effective, and the incendiary round was also capable of igniting objects on impact. So we traded for their ammo using our own in addition to a few extras, whatever we happened to be carrying with us that week.

We flew back to Soc Trang carrying all the fruits of our trading labor, but then we faced the task of getting it all prepped and installed into our ship. This wasn't an easy task, as some of the components needed to be modified and rewired before being fitted into place. Thankfully, we had a good man to do this: a machinist who was assigned to our company. He was in an enviable position; he had very little to do. His MOS was to machine parts for our ships, but there were very few parts that were produced by hand like that. Most of our parts were ordered through the supply system and were ready to install. So this technician was a bit like the proverbial Maytag repairman. He was so bored that he even accompanied us on our missions at times, serving as a "door gunner in training." So he volunteered to fill some spare time by wiring and installing our Nighthawk system into Warrior 21.

We moved the 50-cal gun to the port side, installed the minigun with the Xeon light and Starlight scope to the starboard side, and we were ready for business. In fact, it wasn't long before we discovered that the Xeon light (which resembled a laser beam) and the Nighthawk system were actually superior to the cluster lights and Firefly system in the Mekong Delta region. The Xeon light was a monster, with a six-million candlepower beam that would blind you in a heartbeat. This became our preferred configuration for the remainder of our nighttime missions. We'd use the Starlight scope (on top of the Xeon mount) to look for hostiles, then flip on the Xeon light to engage with the miniguns, which Sandwith would fire and target the tracers to the spot where the light played on the ground. It was highly effective and highly lethal.

As we became more and more experienced in running the nighttime perimeter defense missions, our reputation as a ship and a crew grew. We were good at our jobs and took pride in our ship, and that reputation spread across our platoon and then throughout our company. We were asked on several occasions whether we were going to adopt the call sign Lucky Strike, as we were now firmly entrenched in its old mission. Whenever we received that question, our entire crew answered in a single voice.

"No."

That would never happen. We used the call sign Super Slick, and we would stay with that call sign. No one would ever use Lucky Strike again, least of all us. We had too much enduring respect for that ship and crew to claim it for ourselves. We simply didn't feel worthy of the title, much the same that some ball players have their uniform number retired. As far as we were concerned, Lucky Strike was permanently retired.

We also never used Lucky Strike's revetment, which was located right next to ours, out on the flight line. They had both been placed there in order to enable quick departures when necessary. But no one ever used Lucky Strike's revetment again. Instead it sat unused, empty, and unnaturally silent, as though the space itself was a memorial to the ship lost. It became a solemn place, especially for me. Sometimes when the activity level was low, I would walk over to their revetment and just look inside, my head down and hands clasped. On some of those occasions, I could sense the presence of the crew. Strike's crew. My friends. Standing by their ship with their adrenaline coursing through their veins, preparing to get back out for their next two-hour shift. Their images and voices faded away as I turned back toward my own ship and crew. I missed those guys.

We had one more turn of good luck as we escalated our base perimeter mission to a full-time pursuit. With our new loadout of weapons, including the minigun on the starboard side and the 50-cal on the port, it was obvious we needed another door gunner. It was close to the end of May, and we had just had a US Cavalry Company assigned to our base, with all their own personnel and equipment.

They were called Dark Horse, C Troop, 16th Air Cavalry Company, and they arrived at Soc Trang from somewhere up north. They had a full complement of ships, including cobras, loaches, and slicks, although they were in the process of getting rid of their slicks. The "loach," designated as OH-6 Cayuse, was a very small scouting helicopter that was supposed to fly low and fast and spot the enemy hiding in the grass and foliage. Once they'd made contact, they would then call in the cobras, which would follow up with the big guns and rockets to engage the hostiles. The problem with loaches was their tiny size and susceptibility to being shot down, which happened often. Being a crewmember on a loach was considered to be one of the more dangerous assignments in the aviation community.

The Dark Horse Company also had an infantry group attached to them so that if their loaches made contact with the enemy, the slicks would stand down with the infantry and wait to be called to the scene by the scouts and cobras. They were a tough bunch of soldiers with a great reputation for not backing down from a fight. But they, too, were on the chopping block, as the Cavalry was getting rid of both the slicks and the US infantry troops. The entire Delta region was being handled by the Army of the Republic of Vietnam (ARVN) troops.

The Cavalry's reduction in force left their infantry troops without a job. Those who were being asked to reemploy were given a choice. They could either locate to an infantry job with another company, or they could find an opening as a gunner with our own 336th Assault Helicopter Company. The choice was up to them.

The Dark Horse Company had an infantryman by the name of Tom Wilkes, who was now out of a job. We had heard of him and had spoken with him a few times, and he impressed us with his seriousness and approach to duty. He was another weapons expert who was well-versed in ground fighting, which is a skill we lacked as an air crew. We figured that if we ever went down, he'd be a good man to have along for defense. We pursued him as hard as we could, trying to convince him to become part of Super Slick's crew.

For Wilkes, the choice was easy. As he himself has said, "I was given a choice. I could go crawling around on my belly in the jungle with 40 lbs. on my back through ninety-degree heat, slopping through the mud while getting shot at. Or I could ride along in a helicopter with a mounted gun, carrying nothing on my back with a nice breeze blowing through my hair, but still getting shot at. The choice wasn't hard to make."

After a short period of deliberating, Tom Wilkes joined the crew of Super Slick and became the port-side gunner, tending the 50-cal gun. He was a great addition to the crew, and we were always thankful to have him along for the ride.

With the addition of Wilkes and the Nighthawk system, we were now completely outfitted with all the resources we needed to perform the base perimeter mission, which we held on to for several months. No crew or unit is ever permanent in the military. There are too many people who transfer between units and bases and hit their end-of-tour dates to ever achieve much continuity, especially if the unit in question has more than a few people. We experienced the same kind of transitory existence: Olson would be going home soon (to be replaced by Dana Brown), and Sandwith would be departing to join the Cavalry scouts' unit sometime in August.

But while we were together, we formed a team and a bond that would last far beyond our days in the Mekong Delta. They still exist today, a full half a century later.

I have thought about these bonds many times over the years, particularly when I stood looking into Lucky Strike's vacant revetment. These are things that cannot be explained to those who have never been there and who have never entrusted their lives to their shipmates under fire.

Somewhere, I suspect that the crew of Lucky Strike is still watching us, their bonds as strong as ever.

# 11

# FIRST CONFIRMED KILL

## The Scar on My Soul

So much happens in the life of a soldier as he makes the difficult transition from civilian to warrior. Starting as a young and impressionable high school student, he is cast into a stressful boot camp scenario, where the main purpose is breaking down the child and turning him into a man capable of fighting a war. So much focus is placed on obedience, on taking orders and following routines, and on going above and beyond and doing whatever it takes to accomplish the mission.

Another part of basic training is weapons familiarization, with hours dedicated to cleaning and disassembling, cleaning again, and then reassembling until you could literally do it blindfolded. It becomes second nature. You become one with your weapon: it becomes a "best friend." Then come the hours spent on the practice range, firing at target after target at different distances until you can hit your mark dead center from almost any range. You have to. Your life might depend on it someday.

But firing at a target is a very artificial arrangement. It is basically a rectangular piece of paper featuring a series of concentric black circles, each surrounding the smaller ones inside. The target doesn't run or jump or talk or laugh. It has no friends, no family, and no feelings. Even more important, it doesn't bleed or suffer when hit. It just displays a neat little hole that says,

"Nice shot. You get eight points for this hit."

Shooting at another human being, regardless of their race or nationality (or any of the other plethora of distinguishing characteristics), is an entirely different proposition. To see a person standing before you, whether running away, hiding, or performing any other activity, and then to take his or her life is a very unnatural act. A great many soldiers in Vietnam and other wars found it impossible to do, and they never fired their weapon in battle. Some of them would have preferred to perish themselves than to live with the memory and knowledge of taking a life. This was the internal strife I faced when cast into this situation for the first time.

It was April of 1970, and I had been flying for four months. Since I first went airborne in January, I had flown many different types of missions, including combat assault (CA), SEAL support, outpost fire support, base perimeter flights, and more. With all of these missions, we were constantly engaged with the enemy. It was their ground and their terrain, so contact was expected. It was the norm rather than the exception.

Most of the time, the views we got were best described as fleeting glimpses. They seldom stopped to wave to our ship as we passed overhead. We never saw signs that read, "Welcome Americans! Enemy bunkers one mile ahead!" That just didn't happen. The few times we caught sight of the Vietcong, they were usually running for a bunker, clump of trees, or anything that would obscure the view or provide protection.

This evasion became very frustrating to many of our crews and gunners throughout the country, which must have resulted in numerous random outbursts that weren't actually directed at a specific target. Horrific events—for example, the My Lai Massacre—have been attributed to American forces receiving fire from invisible foes whom we could never engage. They were like ghosts who emerged from hiding for only enough time to shoot and kill before vanishing back into the landscape.

From our own perch on Warrior 21, we had the means to spot and engage hostile troops as they sprinted from one hiding spot to another. The Mekong Delta was flat, and it didn't offer the same thick jungle foliage as much of the country up north. The rice paddies and flat muddy terrain did contain "islands" of trees in places, as well as vegetation that formed borders between the paddies, but much of it was open land without an abundance of places to hide. This kind of open terrain often favored the troops in the air, and we took full advantage of that fact.

Oftentimes, the degree of danger associated with a mission depended upon how well prepared the enemy was to see us. For some reason, the combat assault missions were the worst. Those were big operations that involved a lot of ships, and it somehow seemed as though the plans for the mission would leak out. We'd arrive on scene at the scheduled time of day only to find a lot of enemy guns in place and ready to oppose us. However, when we deployed on a small "hash and trash" mission to support Lt. Ahearn's post, it was usually fairly quiet. I think it's because we were usually a single craft with a small crew, and news hadn't yet circulated about our visit.

On the day of this particular incident, we were performing an outpost support mission for an outpost near Tuan Tue, which was north of our base by twenty to twenty-five miles. An Army Special Forces Officer, Lt. William Ahearn, who led a Mobile Advisory Team (MAT), was the only American stationed at this post. The rest of the troops located there were all members of an elite team of South Vietnamese infantry. They were all special forces: the best of the best. It was hazardous duty, both for Ahearn as well as the native troops stationed at the post.

I worried about Lt. Ahearn a lot. They were often attacked, usually by Vietcong forces that greatly outnumbered their own. They always had to have their guard up and be ready to fight or run depending on the tactical scenario of the hour. I couldn't imagine being placed in that scenario, as he was a small force facing a large and well-armed enemy. It was a precarious and apparently unbalanced setup from the get-go.

Working with Lt. Ahearn was always an interesting and challenging mission. Often times, we'd arrive, carrying ammunition, supplies, and other requested items. Ahearn himself would appear with a stack of maps, each annotated with markings and notes about the suspected presence of hostile troops in the area. After providing lunch to our entire crew, we'd talk about the tactical picture, and he'd then ask us if we'd like to go check out one of the areas "up close and personal."

At that point, we'd usually load Ahearn and a small group of five or six of his South Vietnamese Special Forces troops onboard Warrior 21 and take off for a recon flight. I know that none of these incursions was approved of by our company, but we headed off into the surrounding area anyway, dropping the infantry men off to investigate their quarry. It was usually pretty hairy stuff, and they often engaged enemy troops or went after Vietcong bunkers or other emplacements. I often wondered what would have happened had our own Company Commander found out about these excursions. I suspect that Olson would have been called before Capt. Leandro and told not to do that anymore. Then with a wink, Leandro would have dismissed him, and that would have been the end of it.

The area where Ahearn wanted us to take them on this particular day was "bad guy" country. As a matter of fact, it was quite close to that spot where Lucky Strike had been shot down, so we knew there were enemy in the vicinity. It was a free-fire zone; if we saw unknown fighters below, we would assume they were hostile and automatically engage.

Almost anyplace we took Ahearn and his group of South Vietnamese Green Berets (equivalent) was dangerous. They never seemed to mind going into areas where there were most certainly concentrations of Vietcong

fighters present. Sometimes we'd drop them off right near the enemy bunkers, and they'd either fire Mk 79 grenade launchers into the entrance or
jump in themselves. I remember looking out of the ship on one of these
occasions and not only seeing the footprint of an enemy soldier, but it was
one that was *still filling up with ground water*, which meant that the maker
of the footprint had been there only a moment earlier. It was scary stuff.

We inserted their complement off in a clearing and then took off into
a low circular holding pattern about one hundred to two hundred feet
above them. In a short while, they called in that they were receiving fire
from a tree line about fifty yards in front of them and asked me to "say
hello" with a few bursts from the 50-cal. I responded with a burst of shells
into the same tree line, after which the fire ceased completely.

The 50-cal gun often had that effect. I remember one occasion where
Major Kilpatrick called upon me to fire some rounds at a bunker that was a
good half a mile back into the woods. I complied with a lengthy outburst,
hoping that I had done enough damage to interfere with their resistance.
A later inspection showed that it had blown several large holes through the
roof and compromised the structural integrity of the entire bunker. Power.
Just tons of penetrating, destructive, lethal power.

It wasn't too often that I had the duty of firing the 50-cal gun, as I
wasn't the door gunner. But on this particular day, Sandwith wasn't with
us, and I happened to draw the lucky straw. I never minded this, as I actually enjoyed shooting the 50-cal gun. Almost everyone did. Unlike the
minigun, the M16s, or even the M60, the 50-cal was heavy stuff. It made
you feel like the king; it carried everything before it. The 50-cal, especially
the armor-piercing rounds, could burrow through thirty inches of dirt
and take out the enemy as they hid in their bunkers. It could even snap
branches off of trees! As I said, it was heavy stuff.

So there we were, circling in our ship as we awaited Ahearn and his
men taking care of their business below, when I caught movement out of
the corner of my eye. They were two Vietcong soldiers running across an
open-water rice paddy, racing to reach an island-like clump of trees that
was perhaps fifteen to twenty feet in diameter.

"I've got two running at six o'clock," I called out over my headset.

Six o'clock meant that they were directly behind our ship, probably
hoping that we wouldn't see them, as we were all facing the other direction. But any good door gunner (or other air crew member) would always
keep one eye trained in back of the ship. The enemy often waited until we
had passed over before moving or firing at our tail. They weren't stupid—
insufficiently armed at times, but not stupid.

Olson responded to my report by immediately swinging the ship to the right, which brought the two runners into full view from my starboard door position. They were now clearly in my sights.

"Bust 'em, Feigel!" I heard Olson scream through my headset. He would hold his position until I had engaged.

I responded by opening up with the 50-cal, directing my fire upon the lead runner. They were running through water that sat on top of a muddy flat, so they couldn't move too quickly. That coupled with the fact that they were less than one hundred feet away meant that I couldn't miss. The first one fell to the ground almost immediately and was dead before his body hit the water.

I half expected the second soldier to stop running and try to help his comrade, but that didn't happen. He continued his race for the trees, hoping to save himself. I retrained my gun on the second VC soldier and walked the trail of tracer rounds up his path. He, too, fell immediately, his now lifeless body thrown to the ground by the overwhelming impact force of the massive round. I knew right away there was no chance that either could have survived. I made a mental note of the date and time, recognizing it as my first confirmed kill.

"Great shooting," yelled Olson over the headset. I don't believe I responded to his remark. I was too absorbed with my own thoughts to engage in conversation.

I must admit that I didn't know what to think of it at the moment. I guess I didn't think anything at the time. Ahearn confirmed the kills to us when we picked him up. A *confirmed kill* meant that we had physical evidence—as in, a body to show for it. This was important to the higher-ups, as they were responsible for calling in a body count for the day. That report started at our company level before being passed up the chain to the battalion, and so on, before it landed on a desk somewhere in the Pentagon. I strongly suspected that the count of "bad guys" killed on any given day got inflated by a few bodies at each level of that chain, although I certainly couldn't prove it.

Knowing that I had ended the lives of two VC infantry troops that afternoon had me immediately questioning myself as a person, as a soldier, and as a follower of the Roman Catholic faith. They were the enemy, for sure. They may have even been the same men who shot down Lucky Strike, I thought (very unlikely, but possible). All I was doing was getting revenge on the death of my friends and fellow platoon mates. After all, they surely would have shot at me, given the chance. This was war, and in war, people die.

Even being the one firing the 50-cal that day was chance. Any one of us in the back of the ship could have been manning the gun, but on that day in particular, I had just announced, "I got it." And that was it. I was a pretty good shot with most of the weapons we had onboard, including the 50-cal. But that was the first time that I got to see the direct result of my accuracy. Two "targets," two men, were dead.

In retrospect, I realize it shouldn't have mattered whether we witnessed their demise or not. For all the times we'd engaged the enemy with all our weapons, in daytime or at night, we knew we were making kills all the time. We just couldn't observe them dying, which made it easier. For all the times we'd fired down with our M60s and miniguns and M16s, it would have been pure folly to speculate that we didn't hit someone at least some of the time. It was the same when I dropped my homemade C4 bombs out the side doors onto enemy bunkers and encampments. These incendiary devices were made by inserting three to four sticks of C4 high explosives into an empty 7.62 mm ammo can and then fixing up a fuse and detonator device. Once again, we know it killed anyone within a twenty- to twenty-five-foot radius. But we never saw the bodies fly. This was different.

Within a few minutes of shooting the two Vietcong infantry, we extracted Lt. Ahearn and his men and dropped them back off at their post. I remember that my hands were still quivering with the adrenaline pumping through my body. My eyes were completely dry from not blinking, and it felt as though a strong electrical current were passing through me from head to toe. It was something I'd never experienced before, and even though they would not be my last kills, I would never feel quite this way again.

Everyone was different in how they handled killing the enemy. B-52 pilots must have known that they killed hundreds of people in a single run, yet the attack was conducted from a high altitude and thus wasn't personal. We had also heard stories of crews from other companies where men actually enjoyed killing. They looked forward to it. When no enemy was present, they would open up on livestock: water buffalo, pigs, and goats, whose only crime was to be in the wrong place at the wrong time. I often wondered what those men thought when they were alone or going to sleep or, later in life, attending church with their families. Maybe they didn't feel anything. Maybe they were just emotionally absent at the time of the action. I didn't know and didn't ask. I only worried about myself and my own emotions, and making it one day at a time until I could return home.

When we got back to the base, everyone seemed to know about our action and my confirmed kills. A number of the men from the company congratulated me and seemed impressed. For a while I did feel some pride, like getting the first notch in my gun belt. I would now gain some respect of sorts from the crews of the other ships.

Little did I know how that kill stays with you.

*"Thou shalt not kill."* As a Roman Catholic, I found the words of the fifth commandment engraved into my mind and soul. We were always taught that this applied mainly to the taking of an innocent life. Killing an unjust aggressor to preserve your own life is still killing, but it isn't considered murder or immoral. But regardless, it was yet one more factor that had me questioning my own actions on that day and those that followed. It shouldn't have counted as murder, since this was war. But every soldier remembers his first kill, and he always will.

In my letters home to my family and to Whit, I never once mentioned the kill. I likewise abstained from discussing future engagements where we caused the death of enemy soldiers, whether I had a personal hand in the matter or not. I instead focused my correspondence on more mundane topics, such as my crewmates, the weather, the food, and so forth. It was good enough. They didn't need to hear the gory details, and I didn't want them to associate me with the killing. It would have ended the little bit of innocence they still attached to me from my high school persona. That was the way I wanted it.

In the years since I left Vietnam and reentered the civilian world, I've watched myself and my platoon mates become overcome by the lifelong effects of post-traumatic stress disorder (PTSD). Not all of us experienced all of the symptoms. But the nightmares, the sleepless nights, the flashbacks, the uneasiness, the numbness, and emotional absence, all of these and more have appeared in a relentless march that has cut us off from a normal existence. Many of my comrades have required extensive therapy, while others have lost their ability to experience a normal range of emotions, thus interfering with marriages and other family relations.

In my own case, I still see those two soldiers running through the field on that summer day, fifty years ago. Their images are still razor sharp as I view them through the crosshairs of the 50-cal gun sights just before pulling the trigger. I see this image even though I know the 50-cal had no crosshairs, but it is there in my mind. I see it every day, and it haunts me to my very core.

The roomful of therapists to whom I've spoken over the years have prescribed a long list of prescription drugs to help me deal with the sleepless nights and other symptoms. I haven't enjoyed the side effects, so I've dealt with them by substituting a nightly over-the-counter drug to overcome the insomnia. Sometimes it helps a bit; other times, it doesn't. There are some problems a pill can help to resolve. Others symptoms are more difficult to handle.

A scar on the soul is more permanent, and it cannot be healed with medications.

So the television is often turned on in my bedroom, the images of a movie or sitcom flickering through the nighttime hours as I await the coming of dawn. Time passes slowly as I mindlessly watch the screen, not really paying any attention. There are times I do drift off to sleep, although the television continues to broadcast the show to no one in particular.

At times like that, my mind wanders back to Vietnam, to that fateful day, to that moment I will never forget for as long as I live.

I still see those two men, still alive, still running across the field. It is always summer, and they are always caught in the crosshairs.

# 12

## WHIT

## Another Casualty of the War

Seven.

If a seven-page letter sounds like a lot, it probably is. It's tough to fill up that much stationery with normal, everyday details about the weather, meals, and accountings of which system checks you've performed on any given day. It's even harder to do if you write on a fairly regular basis. You just run out of things to say after a while.

Unless you're in love.

When I arrived in Vietnam for my one-year tour of duty, I was most certainly in love. Whit and I had been inseparable for the past year, and the thought of being apart was painful at best. Cell phones were still decades in the making, and even landline phones were expensive as well as few and far between. We had no international phone service on our base. As much as I would have loved to have heard her voice, it was impossible. So we wrote.

I tried to be a faithful letter writer both to Whit as well as to my family. This meant getting off at least one letter every week, although I probably sent a few more to Whit than to my mother and father, which was to be expected. Then again, what was I supposed to say in these letters? That I had cheated death for yet another day? That our crew had shot up an entire platoon of Vietcong soldiers as they fled their burning bunker? Or maybe that we'd stood by as our friends in Lucky Strike had taken a rocket to their ship and had exploded in midair, then crashed into the ground with no survivors?

No, they would never hear about any of that. It was bad enough they listened to the nightly news and saw all the horrible scenes and the soaring body count. They didn't need to hear the additional episodes of Warrior 21. It was better they imagined I was part of a resupply crew that picked up and delivered groceries.

I also tried to remain as upbeat in my letters as possible. I always ended the ones to Whit with the same lines: "I love you more today than yesterday. But not as much as tomorrow." It was an old song written by Spiral Staircase, then later performed by Chicago and other artists. It had been "our song" back in high school, and we used those words often to express our feelings for each other.

Six or five.

When I transferred from hangar duty to the Crew Chief job, the stress level tripled. I was no longer protected by a metal building inside a large, well-guarded base. I was now flying out over hostile territory, where the bad guys had guns and shot back. I began to notice the changes in myself: the laughs were fewer and further in between, and I felt a level of anxiety that had not troubled me in the past.

The letters I wrote to Whit may have been a bit shorter: maybe five or six pages instead of seven. I don't recall whether the level of emotion was still as high, but there were plenty of other things on my mind by this time. Anyway, many of the same topics still appeared in our correspondence. We still talked about the life we would have together when I returned home. We also kept a daily countdown calendar with the number of days left until I returned home. We both knew at all times how much time remained before that final set of orders would take me back to the States.

Whit's letters to me usually followed the same formula. She spoke of her work and what our families and friends were doing, adding who had passed along a hello to include with her letter. She'd tell me about her visits to my family and what was going on around town. She always signed her letters in her large, flamboyant handwriting, with stylized letters that were punctuated with drawn flowers or peace signs. She really was a hippie, through and through.

I usually read her letters in private, when I had a chance to get off by myself. Oftentimes, this was in my bunk room, where I could relax if even for a few minutes. It was also where I had an eight-by-ten-inch photograph of Whit framed by my bedside. My parents had Whit make that for me shortly before I left. I may have had another picture or two of her with me, but I cannot even remember. The more time elapsed, the more of myself I lost in the war.

Four or three.

My days were now more mechanical; I felt myself operating in "automatic mode." Even though I was now in the second half of my year in-country, my self-analyzed level of depression crept higher. My letters to Whit were now less frequent, and their length was reduced to three or four pages at the most. I no longer knew what to say. What more could I write? The words just wouldn't come. Her letters to me were growing shorter and less frequent as well. We were definitely growing apart, and I think we both realized it.

My overall feeling of detachedness did not apply just to Whit. My letters home were also getting sparse, and I hoped my parents realized that my lack of correspondence was due to the war and nothing more. It is a common phenomenon, but usually only those who have experienced the nonstop anxiety of living in a war zone are capable of understanding. They probably knew that I was still alive, but not much more.

It was at times such as these that I climbed even further into my own shell. I communicated with my shipmates and fellow platoon members, but even that was on a limited basis. I met a lot of the new arrivals as they were flown onto our base, but I tended to avoid making any new friends. It was better that way. I didn't want to go through the pain of becoming close with someone, only to lose them the following month to a crash or a bullet. It just hurt too much, and it wasn't worth the emotional drain.

Two, one, or zero.

The work and responsibility started to weigh on me more and more each week. As Crew Chief of Warrior 21, I was responsible for everything on that ship. The pilots walked away after we landed, and the gunner was responsible for everything that shot projectiles. The rest was up to me, and I did not take this responsibility lightly. Once we shut down, I checked everything and then performed the maintenance that was required for that time and mileage. I then checked my work once, twice, and again once more. After all, my crew's lives were in my hands.

My letters to Whit were now down to an impersonal page or two, providing only the skimpiest of details. I knew that I dared not send her a photograph of myself "today." It was a sad and scary sight, especially when I compared them to the "before" picture I'd had taken the week I arrived in-country. In those photos I looked entirely different. I was standing tall and upright, and I looked proud of who I was and what I was doing. And serving to differentiate the early photographs even more, I was actually smiling for the camera.

Not anymore.

When I studied my current photographs, I saw that I didn't look like the same person. The difference was obvious. I looked pained, and I was standing in a hunched position. My body ached every day from the exertions of the job and felt old despite my physical age. My face was etched with lines and bore the thousand-yard stare that is so often seen on frontline troops. It looked like an expression of pure exhaustion. No smiles. They couldn't stand up to all the death and destruction. Living in a Third World country wasn't helping me either.

By the time I transferred to another unit (still in the future), the letters had dwindled to almost nothing. The spigot of emotion had been shut off. Whit continued to send the occasional letter to support me emotionally, and she never sent me a Dear John letter. But I think we both knew it was over between us. The thoughts of a lifetime together were fading away like a ghost in the wind.

Our relationship was yet another casualty of the war.

# 13

# BATTLE AT VC LAKE

*Note*: **This chapter is written about the events involving a May 12, 1970, battle with Vietcong fighters in the area surrounding VC Lake. It has been drawn from the remarks and observations of three members of the 336th Assault Helicopter Company who were on the scene at different times of that day and following evening. These three individuals—a pilot and 2nd Platoon Leader (Capt. John Leandro), a Crew Chief (myself), and a door gunner (Spec Sady Caicedo)—were all on different ships, thus offering unique and varied accounts of the action.**

VC Lake. It's a small and very shallow body of water located in the Mekong Delta, southwest of Ca Mau. I'm sure it has a more official name on the local Vietnamese maps. But to us, it was just VC Lake.

The place didn't have a good reputation. It got its nickname from the fact that it was infested with VC fighters and had been used as an ambush site for some time. It was later determined to have been used as the Headquarters of the North Vietnamese Army's (NVA) 95th Regiment, although that was unknown to us at the time. We had operated in that vicinity in the past, and it was never fun. The place had about the same reputation as the U Minh Forest: there were lots of bad guys, so it was a free-fire zone.

For us, the day of May 12, 1970, started out as most others. We were on the schedule to perform the night flight mission along with a sister ship from the 121st Assault Helicopter Company. It would be a routine night of alternating two-hour shifts: two hours of flying, then two hours on the ground. Since it was our turn to take the first shift, Sandwith and I were sitting in our revetment, making preparation for the night's activities. Everything was as usual, with nothing out of the ordinary.

That didn't last long.

Everything stopped as we saw Olson running toward our ship with a copilot in tow, trying to keep pace with our Aircraft Commander. That was never a good sign. If our AC was sprinting when nothing appeared wrong, then something was definitely wrong. Seriously wrong.

Sandwith and I didn't wait for instructions. Without a word, I ran to unhook the blades while our gunner quickly finished the last of his weapons preps.

"Throw some flares in the ship," yelled Olson as he launched himself through the starboard side door without seeming to take a step up. I had seldom seen him in such a rush.

I complied by throwing some extra flares into the back as the engine was spooling up.

"We got a ship down," he called out, turning his head in my direction.

So much for our routine night flight. Everything would be changing, and we'd be flying into a firefight somewhere, which was about all we knew. I wasn't even sure I'd seen this copilot before. I don't believe he'd ever flown with us on any prior missions. It was probably someone Olson had just grabbed on his way out the door. I put on my helmet and then checked with Sandwith to see if he was ready for liftoff. As I did so, I could feel my heart racing and the adrenaline starting to pump through my body. I knew that this was where we earned our pay.

"Are we ready to go?" called Olson, already set to work the controls for liftoff.

"Yes, Sir," I replied.

Olson then called the tower and started pulling pitch. It all happened in a matter of minutes. As soon as we'd pulled to a hover and cleared the revetment, we turned and pointed our nose toward Ca Mau, which would be our first stop before the high-speed transit to VC Lake.

As we flew, we monitored the urgent radio transmissions from the operating area. There was a lot going on, and we could tell there was a lot more taking place than a simple rescue of a shoot-down. There appeared to be a major ground battle in progress with a lot of support ships in the air. As we picked up more bits of radio talk, we heard that there was a ship burning on the ground, although we did not yet know which ship that was. I felt my adrenaline pick up even more. So much death and destruction.

By the time we arrived at Ca Mau, it was completely dark outside. We would have to pick up a lot of ammo that had been on Leandro's ship while also taking the opportunity to top off our fuel. This was going to be a long night.

## FLIGHT OF CAPT. JOHN LEANDRO

Capt. John Leandro, 2nd Platoon Commander, had been operating out of Ca Mau that same day. The ARVN troops had been operating in the area of VC Lake for a couple of days and had been meeting stiff resistance. Intel had provided reports of North Vietnamese regulars supporting the Vietcong, and the level of hostile fire seemed to back that up. They had received reports from the ARVN that their troops were in real trouble and were in dire need of ammunition.

As we headed out from Ca Mau, we were flying along with Warrior 23, which was piloted by Warrant Officer Steven Seeman and Chief Warrant Officer David Gallion. Also onboard were Crew Chief James Milne and door gunner Sady Caicedo. They were in the lead, while I was flying off their left wing, slightly behind them. (I always flew tail—last one in, last one out.)

The C&C ship, which was piloted by our Operations Officer, Capt. Stan Coss (call sign Warrior 3), gave us instructions to reach the LZ. We were to proceed straight ahead until we intercepted a canal, where we would turn and follow the canal until we could locate the area to land. At that point we were to turn ninety degrees into the LZ and set down.

Warrior 23 accidentally overshot the turn, so I asked them to pick up my wing. Once they came back up on my left side, I turned back toward the LZ and saw C&C drop a smoke grenade. Immediately, I reported the sighting.

"This is 26, inbound," I reported over the radio. "I got your smoke."

I said this because I thought he was marking the LZ. It turned out he was marking something far more sinister. The accidental miscommunication cost us dearly.

"Negative," came the response from C&C (Warrior 3). "You are to make a high, steep approach to the LZ."

We were in a tight turn toward what we thought was the LZ when this transmission came in, and were ready to follow C&C's directions for our descent.

Both of our ships were carrying a lot of ammo as we approached the LZ. At some point my copilot, Lt. Jack Bagley, pointed out a green smoke to me at our one o'clock position. I called it back to our W3 (Warrior 3) and reported, "I've got smoke." We then started into a very steep, almost vertical approach to the area of the smoke, following it right down toward the ground.

Very suddenly, we began taking a tremendous amount of machine-gun fire. I looked about twenty yards or so in front of the green smoke and saw a machine gun. It wasn't a 51-cal, but it looked to be equivalent to our 7.62 mm, which was plenty deadly. It was mounted on wheels on either side and had a metal plate across the front. I could also see two VC soldiers, one behind the gun, while his assistant knelt beside him, feeding the ammo belt into the weapon.

Bedlam!

Tracers and other rounds were screaming all around our ship, some hitting us, while others passed by so closely we could hear them whistle. By now we were down to about fifty to seventy-five feet above the ground. Suddenly, one of the gun ships that was covering us yelled out over the radio.

"We've lost one," he screamed, his voice raised in panic.

I kicked the aircraft over to the left just in time to see Warrior 23 dive into the ground. It is something I will never forget. There was so much going on at the moment that time seemed to slow down to almost a complete standstill. For a moment, it resembled a stop-action film, slowed to the point where we could see every frame as it displayed on a giant screen before advancing to the next still shot. Each frame appeared in agonizing detail as it flashed before us—a mechanical behemoth dying a painful death. I watched the nose assembly on the ship crumble as the ship keeled over in midair. Next, the blades struck the ground, and a small ball of fire erupted in the cargo hold. I knew it was a matter of a few seconds, but it felt like it played out over a lifetime.

I didn't have time to make a report, grieve, or to even think. Things were happening too quickly. The next hint of disaster came over my headset in the form of a shriek. It was from my Crew Chief.

"I'm hit! I'm hit!" he said, repeating himself with urgency. But unfortunately, he had his foot on top of the floor-mic button, which meant that I couldn't talk to anyone. It was unintentional on his part, and I couldn't blame him for panicking. However, there was nothing else I could do but rotate in my seat and yell back at him.

"Shut up!" I screamed, which startled the hell out of him. He also immediately took his foot off the floor-mic button, which allowed me to use the radio once again. It also didn't help that this was not my regular Crew Chief, who was with me on 99 percent of my missions. My Crew Chief was with the ship I regularly flew, as it was in for maintenance. So this ship was another one in my platoon that I'd selected on very short notice, and the crew chief was attached to that particular ship. I really didn't know him very well, although, as the 2nd Platoon Leader, I was familiar with just about everyone (but some better than others).

Not knowing the extent of my Crew Chief's injuries, I broke off and turned immediately back to Ca Mau. I had to head there first to get the Crew Chief evaluated, which was my highest priority. I radioed ahead that he had been hit and requested immediate medical help. I also wanted to get to Ca Mau because we were overloaded with so much ammo, and we needed to empty out the aircraft.

Once we landed, I climbed into the back and found that the Crew Chief had been shot through the hand. It was bloody, but it didn't appear to be life-threatening, which was a relief. I had heard that there was an American doctor with CORDS in the village,[5] which turned out to be true. The doctor met us at the airfield and tended to the wound. He was able to patch it up and stop the bleeding, which would hold him over until we reached a hospital. He also shot him up with morphine, which would help with the pain for a little while.

Unloading the boxes of ammo turned out to be an interesting experience. As crews from other ships pulled more and more boxes out of the cargo hold, the extent of the damage from hostile fire became ever more apparent. It appeared as though at least forty to fifty rounds had passed right through the boxes, each doing some damage, but none hitting a primer. I can only imagine what would have happened if one of those rounds had impacted a Mk79 grenade primer. I can't be sure, but the result might have been one very loud *kaboom!*

Once we had unloaded the ship and the doctor had treated the Crew Chief's wound, we took off again, this time for Binh Thuy. They had a major medical evacuation hospital up there that could take care of just about any emergency medical procedures, and they could stabilize almost any wounds before the patient could be moved to Saigon and then out of the country. I knew they'd be able to take care of the Crew Chief's hand, which would require surgery that day. I walked him into the facility while Bagly kept the rotors on the helo turning, as we'd be lifting off again in a matter of minutes. I never saw the Crew Chief again, as he never returned to our base at Soc Trang. But at least I know he survived—at the cost of a couple of fingers, but this was a better fate than many of our wounded. In

---

5. CORDS was the Civil Operations & Rural Development Support program. It helped to build relationships with Vietnamese villages and communities by assisting with American civilian medical and governmental resources.

war time they use big bullets, and many aren't lucky enough to walk into a hospital under their own power.

From the hospital in Binh Thuy, we flew back to Soc Trang, landing on the very last of my physical and emotional reserves. It was very late, and we were all exhausted. I wandered into the Operations Office, which was located in a building next to the runway. Stan Coss was in there, just making some notes and wrapping up from the day. We looked at each other, blinked wearily for a few seconds, and both blurted out,

"What the hell happened today?"

War is a funny thing that has a huge range of effects on different people. It pulls a veil of mist down over reality so that no one seems to know what to do or how to react. It had been an exceedingly long day, and we had lost a ship and a number of crewmates. And in a matter of hours, it would start all over again.

## FLIGHT OF WARRANT OFFICER RANDY OLSON, WITH CREW CHIEF TOM FEIGEL

We already knew that our main mission of the night was to get ammo into the hands of the ARVN while they could still withstand the VC attack. It sounded as though they were outnumbered and in danger of being overrun. Having witnessed the sparseness of their ammo belts and magazines while dropping them in numerous LZs, I could attest to that fact. They usually looked painfully unprepared and underarmed for significant combat.

So we quickly refueled and loaded the ammo from Leandro's ship onto our own before lifting off.

We could tell a lot about the fierceness of the battle just by looking at the ammo boxes that had come from Leandro's ship. The boxes containing the munitions were shot to hell. Considering the number of hits on the boxes, it was nothing short of a miracle that there hadn't been an explosion that took the ship down with it. Strange things happen sometimes in war.

The call for help from the operating area also included an urgent request for immediate medevac support. Apparently, the ARVN platoon had experienced a lot of casualties and needed our ships to evacuate the injured out of harm's way. Unfortunately, that meant that we had to put ourselves in that same path of destruction, which elevated our level of stress once again.

The next leg of the flight would take us directly into the teeth of the battle, VC Lake. It was sometime around then that we learned the identity of the downed ship. It was Warrior 23 that had been shot down. This was a craft from 2nd Platoon, and I knew most of their crew well. I felt my adrenaline pick up even more.

I found myself wondering, Was the crash a shoot-down, or had they experienced a mechanical failure but were able to land themselves? Did part of the crew survive? Did any of them survive? It was painful to think of, especially coming so close on the heels of Lucky Strike.

So much death and destruction.

As we approached the area around VC Lake, the level of radio chatter increased even more. I could always tell how controlled or uncontrolled a scene was by the tone of the voices on the radio, and this one was way out of control. The only really calm voice was Maj. Kilpatrick, our Company Commander. Even though his voice was raspy as always, he sounded calm and collected, which is why so many people enjoyed serving with him. He always seemed to have things under control, even in the worst of situations.

The action was so intense in the area around the lake that we could see the tracer fire from fifteen to twenty miles away. What we couldn't see was a majority of the ships, which were flying without lights. It didn't make sense to announce your presence with lights, which were sure to draw enemy fire. We did know that the gunships were circling somewhere around one thousand feet, while Kilpatrick was up there at maybe one thousand feet higher (at two thousand feet). We also had a C47 gunship circling way up there around five thousand feet, ready to spray minigun fire if needed. The C47 was the first in a series of fixed-wing gunships during the Vietnam War. This craft was actually a specially modified DC3 that was operated by the US Air Force. It flew out of Bien Hoa, near Saigon. Somehow, it had earned the nickname Puff the Magic Dragon. Its mission was to provide heavier firepower than possible from light and medium ground-attack aircraft. It had a series of three 7.62 mm miniguns that fired through rear windows and a cargo door on the left side of the aircraft. But we never operated *with* it. It just showed up from time to time when the action really got intense. And it was now very intense.

As we started closing in, we began seeing not only more tracer fire but also more muzzle flashes as well. It looked like the Fourth of July but without quite as many colors. This was obviously a serious firefight that would go on for many more hours, perhaps into the next day. Then Maj. Kilpatrick's raspy voice came over the radio.

"Make your approach from the south," he told Olson. "Keep the burning ship to your right. Your drop zone will be just west of the downed ship. Watch for a strobe as you go in."

Having received his instructions, Olson then told us to stay on our toes. He hadn't needed to say that. This was one of those situations where every fiber and sense in your body is fully ramped up to the max. You can feel the adrenaline flowing and your heart pumping in overdrive. We were painfully aware that anything could happen at any moment as we started our descent to the drop zone.

Our descent must have been very rapid, but it seemed to take forever. We were painfully exposed although running without lights. We couldn't afford to turn on anything that would give away our location to the enemy gunners. We were completely blackened to appear as one with the sky.

We eased down into the dark landscape below while Olson kept the burning ship to our right. As the ground came into view, we observed that it was marshland, which was covered by a heavy layer of very tall grass. This meant there was no way we could land, as we didn't know what was beneath the vegetation. It would have been too risky for landing, unloading, and possibly even getting out of there after unloading the ammo and taking on wounded. So right away, Olson knew that his hovering skills would be tested to the max over the coming minutes.

As we continued our descent, the strobe light suddenly appeared, acting like a beacon for our touchdown (although without our actually setting down). Olson flew the ship toward the strobe flashes, then finally pulled into a low hover. We could see the ARVN troops on the ground right below our skids. We were now holding at around three feet above the muddy ground, which was as low as Olson could take us.

Now it was my turn.

I was already standing next to the starboard side door with the first box of ammo in my hands. These were heavy boxes, perhaps 25–30 lbs. each. Each box had a pair of rope handles attached to the topsides to make the handling easier. But as I stood there, looking down at the faces of the ARVN soldiers as they reached up to accept the first parcel, I realized that this method would not work expeditiously. We had a massive amount to unload, and we were surrounded by hostile troops who wanted to shoot us and disable our ship. Speed was essential.

I turned back around and grabbed the next box of ammo with only one hand. That box didn't get handed to anyone. The ARVN troops stepped back as I flung the box from the ship onto the ground, not waiting for anyone to take it from me. Once the ground troops saw that I was throwing the boxes off instead of handing them down, they gave me a wide berth so as not to get hit. Then I grabbed the next box and flung that. Then the next. Then the next. I became a box-flinging machine: Turn, grab, fling. Turn, grab, fling. Turn, grab, fling. As I was doing this, I was aware of the fact that these were very heavy boxes that I was tossing off our ship effortlessly, using only one hand. As a matter of fact, I was amazed with my own strength even as I recognized it being due solely to the adrenaline of the moment.

Throughout the ammo off-load process, there was yet another super-human feat underway, although that was coming from the cockpit. Some-how, for as long as the off-loading continued, our pilot kept the ship in a rock-solid hover about three feet off the ground. So there we were, completely darkened and without any other lights around us, surrounded by different heights of vegetation, and Olson held us right in place without wavering either in height above the ground or in a forward-to-back mo-tion. It was as though we were sitting on a carnival ride that was fastened to the ground on a pole. It was that solid. It was an incredible display of skill for which he would later be recognized.

Once all the ammo boxes had been off-loaded, it was time to shift over to our medevac mission, which would be equally as taxing as the previous task. From my elevated platform on the back of the ship, I saw an ARVN soldier holding up a man's body, using his arms around the other soldier's torso. I really wasn't trained in moving or lifting injured personnel, so I just bent forward and put my hands beneath the motionless form and dragged him into the back of my ship. Turning back to the ground troops, I saw that another soldier had taken the first one's place, and he, too, was holding up a wounded member. So I repeated my motions: lean forward, hands under armpit, and drag onboard. I placed this inert form next to the first one and then turned back to the crowd. I was not surprised to see yet another wounded soldier being passed up for loading. As a matter of fact, a line had formed of similar couples that extended some distance back from the ship. There were so many wounded.

For what felt like hours, I continued the process of pulling injured ARVN Infantry troops onto our ship. At a certain point, I had to actually stack them on top of one another; there were that many. I lost count of how many there were. It was just a process that became almost mechanical: Lift, pull, stack. Lift, pull, stack. Repeat, repeat, repeat.

In addition to the wounded, I saw that there were many dead on the ground. My mind became numbed to the whole situation. It had to. There was too much hurt to think about. Many of the bodies on our ship were silent and motionless. At a certain point, I started slipping and sliding on the floor of the ship. Blood can be a very slippery substance, and our floor was covered in it. I also had blood on my hands and arms, face, and flight suits. It was everywhere and could not be escaped. It was pure chaos.

Something else of concern was that we were now totally overweight for liftoff. I didn't know if we were going to be able to lift out of our hover or whether we'd have to offload a few of the injured. I only hoped we could make it with everyone.

I was about to key my mic to talk with Olson up front when one more ARVN soldier appeared in front of me. I didn't know what he wanted, but with a trace of a smile and a nod, he handed me up a captured AK-47. It was as though he were saying thank you. I didn't know what to say, but I accepted the gift and tucked it under my seat in a single motion. Then he vanished back into the night.

We had already stayed on station for too long, and I wanted nothing more than to get us the hell out of there.

"Let's go," I hollered into my mic.

Olson didn't need to be told twice. To this day, I cannot determine how he held our ship in that motionless hover for so long without any illumination. It was a superhuman feat that cannot be adequately described. There aren't enough superlatives to put it in words. After checking his surroundings, he immediately pulled us up into a ten-foot hover. Even as he did so, I could feel the ship straining, with our pilot struggling to control the lateral movement caused by the excess weight. He then did a tail rotor 180 to reverse our heading, and we were on our way, still flying dark.

As we rose up from the drop zone, Maj. Kilpatrick's voice came over the radio again.

"Twenty-one, you're taking fire," our Company Commander called into our headsets. "Max climb! Max climb!"

He didn't need to tell us. Regardless, we couldn't climb too quickly, since our ship was so overloaded. We could see the tracers streak by and could hear the occasional shell strike our ship. Yet it didn't appear that the gunners on the ground had a good fix on our ship. Instead they were spraying the whole area where they *thought* we might be, since they couldn't see us in the darkness. Most of the hits on our craft were striking our tail section, thankfully, rather than in our cockpit or cargo area. So we were making a successful exit from the operating area without any major damage.

In any case, we had already decided not to fire from our ship for fear of disclosing our location. Muzzle flashes or tracers from our guns would definitely be seen by everyone on the ground, which was just not worth the risk. It was more important to remain hidden from view so we could live to fight another day. As it was, we were lucky to have been able to get off the ground with all those wounded onboard. For a while I thought we were going to have to make a return trip to pick up an additional load.

Thankfully, that never happened, so we were able to take our one load of wounded ARVN Infantry soldiers to their hospital facility and then return to Soc Trang. It was late, and we had already lost one ship that day. It appeared as though we would live to fight another day.

## FLIGHT OF SPEC 4 SADY CAICEDO, DOOR GUNNER FROM WARRIOR 23.

**Spec 4 Sady Caicedo was the only surviving member of Warrior 23, which crashed on the afternoon of May 12, 1970.**

We were returning to our base at Soc Trang when we received a call asking us to help an ARVN Infantry Platoon that was being overrun by VC soldiers in the area around VC Lake. Our pilot, Mr. Galion, accepted the mission, which involved picking up a lot of ammunition and transferring it to the operating area.

We were flying in Warrior 23 and were accompanied by our Platoon Leader, Capt. Leandro, who was flying in Warrior 26. We flew up to the area near VC Lake together, and we were preparing to descend to the LZ when things suddenly got very hot. Both our ships started receiving a massive amount of machine-gun fire, so I opened up with my gun in return.

I was on the right side of the ship when, suddenly, we went into a severe bank to the left that was so tight that all I could see was the sky out the starboard side door. It was obvious that we were going down. I quickly grabbed my monkey strap and pulled it as tight as I could to ensure that I would remain in place on impact.

The next thing I knew, we were on the ground, all of us stuck inside a burning ship. Everything was happening so fast that much of the events seem like a blur. I had also been slammed to the ground, so I probably suffered some head trauma at the same time.

The first thing I remember about starting my egress after the ship smashed into the ground was that I was able to unbuckle myself and then pull my body out the cargo door. This was in spite of the fact that I had multiple fractures, burns, and other wounds. As I moved to rescue myself from the ship, I noticed that no one else was moving.

Once I was able to get out through the cargo door, I moved around to the right cockpit door and grabbed onto the door handle, trying to open it so I could pull the pilot out before he perished in the flames. As soon as I put my hand on the metal of the handle, I had to let it go, as it was red hot. The one to two seconds of contact with the flaming-hot metal severely scorched my hand with second- and third-degree burns. My height did not permit me to see much inside the cockpit, but I was able to see the helmet of the pilot on the right side. I could not see anyone moving inside, which meant I was probably the only crew member to survive the crash.

The next thing I remember was that my legs went numb and I fell to the ground, not knowing that my pelvis was fractured. I had burns on my waist, knees, face, and hands. But I knew that I had to get away from the burning ship, so I commenced crawling toward a canal, which I eventually reached. I climbed into the canal and almost drowned due to the extra weight of my heavily armored chicken plate and my helmet. I was able to get the chicken plate off, but when I tried removing the helmet, even more skin started separating from my forehead, so I decided to leave the helmet on.

I also noticed that I had lost all feeling from the waist down, which I later learned was due to the compression of numerous vertebrae during the crash. It must have been even worse than I remembered, although most of it was a blur even back then.

I remember being rescued from the canal by a team of ARVN troops who were shouting repeatedly, "GI, don't shoot!" There was a US Special Forces soldier there who was leading the ARVN team, and they pulled me out of the canal and laid me on the ground. The entire area was hot, with lots of firing as the VC attempted to overrun our position. So I lay there next to the US Special Operations (SPECOPS) fighters while they repulsed the attacks. There was nothing else I could do while waiting to be extracted from the scene. The SPECOPS leader looked exactly like Jesus Christ to me, and I remember thinking to myself that I must be in good hands!

Getting me out of the immediate combat area was really touch-and-go. The first ship's attempt to pick me up had to be aborted due to heavy, high-powered machine-gun fire. The SPECOPS leader told me to get ready, they were going to have to throw me into the next ship that could get close to us. I'm not sure what that ship was, but I think it was a gunship from the Thunderbirds Platoon.

Once we finally cleared the area, I was taken to a field hospital for diagnosis and X-rays. I was awake for part of it—that is, until they put me on a stretcher, after which I believe I was moved to a medevac hospital in Binh Thuy. There a team of nurses cut off my uniform and boots, and then I was placed on an X-ray table. I was totally naked and very, very cold. At that point I passed out, probably from shock, and didn't awaken for part of a day. From there, it was on to Saigon and then eventually to the Camp Zama Hospital, which is southwest of Tokyo, where the staff worked some miracles on my various burns and fractures.

I was then transferred to the Saint Albans Navy Hospital in Brooklyn, NY, where I was discharged from military duty, although I still required extensive rehabilitation in a VA hospital.

To this day, I do not remember who risked their life to land in that nightmare of a landing zone and rescue me on that fateful day. Originally, I was told it was Capt. Leandro in Warrior 26, but he has denied it was his ship. Regardless, it was one of my brothers in our company who braved the hailstorm of gunfire to save my life, and for that I will always be eternally grateful.

⌁

**Spec 4 Sady Caicedo served this tour of duty despite the fact that he was not an American citizen at the time of his Army service. Originally from Ecuador, he was a legal resident of the United States. As a legal resident, he had the same obligations to serve in the military as any other US citizen. He was drafted, and he reported to the Army as instructed.**

**During basic training, Caicedo submitted a form stating that he volunteered to serve in Vietnam. His dedication to serve his country was documented in his service record.**

**For his injuries and his brave actions on the day of the crash, Caicedo was awarded the Purple Heart, the Air Medal, and the Distinguished Flying Cross.**

⌁

## ADDITIONAL THOUGHTS ON THE MISSION
## FROM CREW CHIEF TOM FEIGEL

As we were flying back to Soc Trang, we received confirmation that it was Warrior 23 that had been shot down. We also learned that both pilots and the Crew Chief were dead. It appeared that only the door gunner, Sady Caicedo, had made it off alive, although with extensive injuries.

In retrospect, I think one of the only reasons we were able to save so many of the injured ARVN troops at VC Lake was due to the incredibly skilled abilities of Randy Olson. Without his superior capabilities in holding a rock-solid hover for such an extended period of time in total blackout conditions, none of that would have been possible. For his skill and bravery on that nighttime mission, Olson was awarded the Distinguished Flying Cross. It was most certainly warranted.

My final memory from this episode was very unpleasant, and it remains with me to this day. Following that mission, we had to complete an extensive cleaning of our ship, Warrior 21. Many of the dead and wounded we'd transported to the hospital that horrific night had bled extensively onto the floor of the ship. Much of that blood had congealed and needed to be washed off with bucket after bucket of hot water, which also turned red from the sticky residue.

But even that wasn't enough. Much of the dried-on gore required scrubbing, which we tackled with brushes and cloth and anything else we could get our hands on. It was messy, dirty work, made all the worse by the very nature of the stains.

But it wasn't until later that day that I discovered the worst part of the detail. I was involved in some other bit of manual labor when I discovered that each one of my fingernails was caked with a dark film of dried-on blood, trapped beneath the nails. I made a few quick attempts to wash and scrub them and then to scrape the residual material from beneath the exposed surfaces. However, none of those techniques worked fully, and I resigned myself to the fact that only time would wear away the blood stains from that fateful night.

Over the next week or so, the residual blood did work its way free until it was finally gone from view. Unfortunately, the memories of that night and of those we left behind will be with me forever.

# *14*

# CAMBODIAN INCURSION

Most Americans would not have suspected that Cambodia had played a factor in the Vietnam War. If one were to say that role was *active*, they'd be correct. Yet the very fact that these two countries share a common border that is 720 miles in length, with the Vietcong sometimes using Cambodian territory in concert with parts of the Ho Chi Minh Trail to move supplies, was an invitation to conflict.

The background history of the development of these two countries (Cambodia and Vietnam) is too long and detailed to fall within the confines of this book. Suffice it to say that for the past millennia, the two nations have witnessed countless periods of war and peace, with leaders and peoples who never enjoyed a mutual trust. Governments and borders have shifted constantly, while larger foreign nations (i.e., China and France) have attempted to intervene. Thus, it was no surprise to our government when the armies of North Vietnam and its sponsored Vietcong forces began using Cambodia as a safe haven for personnel and supplies.

For those of us who were fighting in the IV Corps region of the Mekong Delta, it's something we never thought about very much. We got pretty close to the Cambodian border while transporting our ARVN Infantry troops to the U Minh Forest, but we never flew west from there. We never had a mission that crossed the border, and we certainly weren't authorized to head in that direction. It wasn't part of our war.

The first indication of anything out of the ordinary took place on April 22, 1970.[6] It was the end of the dry season, just before the start of the monsoons, so the temperature was well up into the nineties. Our daily

---

6. This was also the date on which the US Marines launched Operation Beacon Star, using two battalions to attempt to locate and destroy a battalion of Vietcong up in Thua Thien and Quang Tri provinces. These were located much further north, in the II Corps territory.

schedules and missions were tracking along as always, with no indication that anything out of the ordinary was planned. It was business as usual.

That afternoon, our Company Clerk alerted us that we had a company-wide assembly, an all-hands formation at 1900 hours. Attendance was mandatory; no one was excused. This was unusual, as company formations were very rare. But no explanations were offered. We were just told to be there.

Our curiosity was further aroused that evening when our Company Executive Officer appeared at the formation and announced that all flight operations were being put on hold until further notice. All combat assault missions were to cease. Also, all company ships were to be inspected, and any repairs were to be completed as soon as possible. Every ship was to be ready for flight operations by the last day of the month. And that's all he said before ending the formation. There were no explanations, no other comments, and no questions. Formation was over.

Needless to say, we walked away wondering what was going on. Was the war ending? (That was not very probable.) Was this some kind of a safety stand-down? (This also was not very likely.) So we were left to believe that there was some upcoming operation that was very big and required all of our ships

Whatever it was must have been very, very big.

As of the date of the formation on April 22, we had about five ships in the hangar that were in the process of being inspected and repaired. These were quickly repaired and made air-worthy. Flying hours were tightly restricted; only emergency usage was permitted. We then learned through the grapevine that this was the directive not only for our company but throughout the entire country.

We didn't have to wait long for an explanation. A week later, on April 30, we were called to another company formation, where the upcoming operation was disclosed. Our company would be joining forces with almost every other helicopter company in Vietnam to cross over the border into Cambodia and strike at enemy sanctuaries that had set up camp on the other side of the demarcation line between those two countries. It would be "the mother" of all helicopter assault missions. If that wasn't enough to get your blood pumping, nothing would.

Our company's mission was quite specific. We were to fly to the cement factory near the Seven Sisters, which was a mountain range very close to the border. There we would refuel before picking up our ARVN Infantry soldiers from the 21st ARVN Division. From there, we would cross the border into Cambodia to a predetermined LZ. We were restricted to a nineteen-mile incursion and were to go no further.

We didn't know what to expect, as we were on new ground. None of us had ever flown in Cambodian airspace before, so we didn't know whether there would be any defensive positions in place or not. What would the LZs look like? Were the Cambodians (or Vietcong) expecting our arrival? There were lots of questions but no answers.

It turned out to be a very long day. The flight was an hour in and an hour back, and we made four or five incursions that day. It involved a lot of refueling logistics, and for our pilots, it represented a lot of stick time. Yet for all that air time, there were few or no surprises. They were just routine in-and-out shuttles with our ARVN troops, nothing more.

As we transported our South Vietnamese counterparts into the country, we had a laundry list of things for which we were supposed to be searching. Our search-and-destroy mission included finding any enemy hospitals, barracks, warehouses, supply depots, training facilities, and more. Some of the facilities we encountered contained caches of weapons with tons of ammunition. Others housed massive stockpiles of food and other supplies.

So many of these supplies and stockpiles had been moved down the Ho Chi Minh Trail from North Vietnamese territory. This trail, which had been under continuous improvement by the North Vietnamese government, had been in existence for over a decade. Its recognized origins dated back to 1959, although parts of it may have been carved into the ground years earlier. It is also important to understand that this "trail" was not just a north-to-south path that extended six hundred miles though Laos and Cambodia, as is sometimes thought. It was actually more of a web of trails, or a trail "network," that extended over twelve thousand miles and multiple borders of North and South Vietnam, Laos, and Cambodia. It included trails, simple roads, bridges, and tunnels, and it was often impossible to detect from the air.

Our efforts to destroy the supplies and stores in Cambodia were not new. In 1965 President Johnson had used the air force to deploy millions of tons of explosives to demolish parts of the Ho Chi Minh Trail throughout Laos and Cambodia, and Nixon had later attacked by using both air and ground forces. So our incursion into Cambodia was basically an extension of earlier activities.

One other mission assigned to us that week was to keep an eye out for American prisoners of war (POW) being held in POW camps across the border. This topic (POWs in Cambodia) is a hugely divisive subject that has been discussed and debated for years, with each side claiming to have documentation proving their arguments. To the best of my knowledge, none of the ships deployed from our company visually sighted any signs of POW detention camps on the other side of the border, although we did find plenty of other facilities and supplies.

We conducted basically the same operation twice that week: dropping the ARVN troops off in Cambodia, then picking them up again about a week later. We were pleasantly surprised in the insertion stage when we encountered no hostile activity at all. We had our Thunderbird gunships along with us in case we needed to employ gunfire support, but thankfully, we never received fire. It seemed as though the Vietnamese forces who were operating in Cambodian territory simply were not ready for us to come across the border. There were few if any defensive fortifications in place.

One thing that will always stick in my mind was the number of helicopters involved in the operation. It seemed like thousands of ships, although I know it could not have been so many. They were stacked up in the sky, with long tails of ships following in pursuit of our own. It reminded me in no small way of a huge flock of geese, with massive V-shaped flocks following behind. It was that impressive.

To those of us deployed in Vietnam, we knew this was a necessary evil that had to be undertaken. The enemy was smart, and they had countless soldiers bringing weapons and ammo down the Ho Chi Minh Trail through Laos and Cambodia. They also knew that we were not authorized to venture into these countries on foot, although we did conduct numerous B52 strikes on the Trail in Cambodia. Regardless, our government had our full support behind these strikes. We actually thought they should have been longer and more aggressive.

Meanwhile, back in the States, Nixon kept a tight lid on the movement of troops into Cambodia. Not even Secretary of State William Rogers or Defense Secretary Melvin Laird were informed about the incursion until it was announced to the American public on April 30.

Once Nixon announced the invasion to the American public on April 30, the country erupted in a negative uproar. The reaction in the US to the incursions was immediate and widespread. It was viewed as a full-scale invasion. Protests broke out on over four hundred college campuses across the country, sometimes involving over three thousand students and causing significant damage to school buildings and other facilities. On May 2, four students were killed by National Guard troops at Kent State University in Ohio. Soon over four million students were protesting across the country.

Our company's mission into Cambodia lasted a little more than a week. It was only seven days later that we returned to extract the ARVN troops from their prearranged LZs, which once again required us to make four to five trips across the border to fully extract all their troops. Once again, the gunships had little or nothing to do, as we received no hostile fire throughout our mission.

It was most interesting to see the items carried out by the ARVN troops. They brought out a lot of weapons, including the AK-47 rifles and the earlier Soviet SKS carbines, both which used the 7.62 mm cartridges. There were also small arms of Chinese origin, as well as some leftover French MAT-49 submachine guns that dated back to 1949. And with those weapons, they brought out ammunition. Lots of ammunition. It just went to show the extent to which the North Vietnamese and Vietcong exploited the soft Cambodian border to the west.

Other less offensive items were carried out of the country as well. A ship from one of our sister companies at Soc Trang brought back a Honda 90 motorcycle. I don't know what they intended to do with this bike, because we weren't allowed to carry war "trophies" back to the States. Perhaps they intended to use it as transportation around our own base at Soc Trang. But it was in good shape, and it weighed less than 200 lbs., so they stowed it on their ship for the ride back to our base.

One other thing we brought back was an entire locker full of North Vietnamese currency. The currency used by the country of North Vietnam has generally been the VND (dong). It officially came into being in 1978, although the dong has actually been used in different forms since the 1940s. The exchange rate has varied greatly over the years, so we didn't have a clue about the value of the locker stash we found. For us, it was more of an interest thing than anything else. It was freshly minted and wrapped, ready for use. (Perhaps it was to pay the VC troops? We never did get an explanation.) I still have some of that currency today, a souvenir of my time in-country.

For us, the return trip with the ARVN troops onboard was completely satisfying, as they had accomplished all their goals without suffering any killed or wounded. In most places, it appeared as though the enemy had simply picked up and run, leaving everything behind. They were so surprised by our presence across the border that they never attempted to mount a defense.

To a man, the ARVN Infantry troops we assisted were extremely pleased. They had landed a huge blow to the VC troops in Cambodia and had wiped out years of their work in a single week. They called their operation Toan Thang, or Complete Victory.

As we wrapped up our operations from the week, we knew that Nixon would be taking a huge political hit back home. The war itself was unpopular, and our president (who had promised to end the war) had done an apparent 180 degree turn and escalated the conflict instead. But we knew it was the right thing to do. I only wish it hadn't cost the lives of four innocent students to achieve.

*Super Slick parked inside revetment at Soc Trang, 1970. Photo taken by Tom Feigel.*

*Tom Feigel working near the hangar in Soc Trang, with Spec 4 Toomey. Photo by Rob Sandwith.*

*Tom Feigel on Super Slick with Firefly cluster lights. Photo taken in May 1970 by Rob Sandwith.*

*Warrant Officer Dana Brown standing next to the minigun on Warrior 21. Photo taken at Soc Trang in September 1970 by Rob Sandwith.*

*(Left to right) Spec 4 Tom Wilkes, CWO2 Randy Olson, and Spec 5 Mike Sullivan. Photo taken by Tom Feigel in 1970.*

*Unidentified US Navy SEALs by Super Slick, loading up for a mission of SEAL Team 1. Photo taken at Sea Float in 1970. Photo by Tom Wilkes.*

*Unidentified US Navy SEALs by Super Slick, loading up for a mission of SEAL Team 1. Photo taken at Sea Float in 1970. Photo by Tom Wilkes.*

*Tom Wilkes, behind twin M60 machine guns with lights, Rob Sandwith in the background left. Photo taken at Soc Trang by Tom Feigel in 1970.*

*Feigel standing next to Super Slick at Soc Trang.*
*Photo taken by Randy Olson.*

*Spec 4 Tom Wilkes next to Super Slick, with arm in a cast*
*after a fifty-five-gallon drum had fallen on him. Photo by*
*Tom Feigel.*

*View of unnamed Vietnamese village over the top of 50-cal gun and ammo clip. Photo by Tom Feigel in 1970.*

# THE UNITED STATES OF AMERICA

TO ALL WHO SHALL SEE THESE PRESENTS, GREETING:
THIS IS TO CERTIFY THAT
THE PRESIDENT OF THE UNITED STATES OF AMERICA
HAS AWARDED THE

## PURPLE HEART

ESTABLISHED BY GENERAL GEORGE WASHINGTON
AT NEWBURGH, NEW YORK, AUGUST 7, 1782
TO

SPECIALIST FOUR THOMAS K. FEIGEL, UNITED STATES ARMY

FOR WOUNDS RECEIVED
IN ACTION

ON 22 MARCH 1970 IN THE REPUBLIC OF VIETNAM

GIVEN UNDER MY HAND IN THE CITY OF WASHINGTON
THIS    NINETEENTH    DAY OF    JULY    19 70

*Citation for Spec 4 Tom Feigel's Purple Heart, awarded July 10, 1970. (Scan by Tom Feigel of original certificate.)*

# 15

## CRASH OF THE SEAL SHIP

### Another Unnecessary Loss

By the time early summer rolled around, I had worked with SEALs a lot. Usually, it was in conjunction with a visit to Seafloat and then on to some reconnaissance mission in the Delta. But regardless of the location, I always had a childlike admiration of these incredible warriors. Dressed like street people in nonmilitary apparel, they seemed to be able to handle anything with their small, professional teams. I could not ever imagine having to fight them myself. Close-in combat was what they did, and they seemed to love it.

On this particular day, we had no idea we would have anything to do with a group of SEALs in any way. It was a normal kind of day, and as dusk approached, we went through our preparation to get underway for another night of flight ops. We flew every night of the week seven days a week, with no breaks. The enemy never took a break, so neither could we.

Yet this would end up being very different: It was probably one of the worst nights in our tour in Vietnam. It might have even competed with the loss of Lucky Strike, as we were personally on the scene for the viewing. That kind of thing wears you down quickly. It ages you beyond your years and stays with you forever, no matter how long you live.

As dusk approached and we made our preparations to lift off, we were told that a ship was down north of Soc Trang. Once we got the word, we thought we'd take off as soon as possible in order to take advantage of the fading daylight. Unfortunately, that was not the case.

"Hold off on liftoff until further notice," instructed the Operations Office. Although we didn't understand the reasoning, we sat in our revetment and awaited permission to depart.

We finally received the command to lift off and proceed to the area of the downed ship, although by now, it was completely dark. It made no sense. With no daylight available, it would make it much more difficult to locate a downed aircraft, and it would necessitate the use of our search lights. This was something we didn't want to do if possible, as we'd be advertising our presence to anyone on the ground. Then again, we were tasked with this mission because we were probably the best-equipped ship in the entire Delta region to undertake this kind of search and rescue at night.

As soon as we cleared the revetment, we headed north in the direction where witnesses had seen the ship go down. It was not from our platoon or even from our company. Instead it was from the 162nd Assault Helicopter Company, out of Can Tho. The ship was overdue for its arrival back at Can Tho, which set off the first alarms that something might have been amiss. The delay for sending us out was due to a weather flare-up in the area; other ships were available but were holding off until there was a break in the storm.

As we headed northeast toward the suspected area of the downed ship, it was obvious that Olson was pushing our Warrior 21 (now call sign Super Slick) as hard as he could. Our ship had an advertised cruise speed of 125 mph, although its actual max speed was around 100 mph. In order to achieve that speed, Olson had to manipulate the controls by pushing the cyclic stick forward and pulling up on the collective, which tipped the nose of the ship down and pushed us forward as fast as we could travel. There were multiple reasons for his haste, the first being that we didn't want the crew to spend the entire night in a hostile area. There would probably be injured among them, so time was of the essence to save every possible life. There might also be enemy troops in the area, so we wanted to get there before they did.

One problem we encountered was that we were given very limited details about the precise location of the crash. A general area was provided, but that was about it. So we didn't have much to go on, and we knew that as we were in transit. We figured that we'd probably see signs of a crash before we encountered the ship itself. Sometimes, all that's visible is a bunch of broken branches and other vegetation that can only be seen in good light and from the right angle. It wasn't very promising, and I had my doubts about ever finding them.

It didn't take us long to arrive in the general search area, where we commenced flying a low-level search pattern with our high-powered lights scouring the ground. Back and forth, back and forth, we combed the ground in a row-by-row search pattern, which also exposed us to every bad guy for miles around.

For quite a while, we proceeded using our bright Xeon light, but that didn't seem to be doing the job. So Olson took our ship down even lower, to a point about five feet off the ground. He then began using our ship's light that he controlled from the cockpit. It worked a bit like the swivel light inside a police car and was very maneuverable. Olson was also very good at using that light, and he could pinpoint the beam wherever he wanted while still flying the craft.

We didn't see anything at first, so we kept up our search, which had to be slow and methodical if we were to have any chance of sighting the downed ship. All the while, we knew that we were a sitting duck to anyone on the ground with any small-arms weapons. We were that low to the ground, and everyone could see us. Yet we couldn't leave without trying; they most certainly would have done the same thing for us if the tables were turned.

We were certain that we were in the right area, yet we weren't sighting it. We were on the verge of asking ourselves whether we'd have to return the next morning when I suddenly spotted an unnatural form on the ground, just outside of the area illuminated by the ship's light.

"Over there . . . at one o'clock!" I called out to Olson.

He spun the ship to look in the direction I had requested, and within seconds, the remains of the ship came into view.

Total annihilation.

As soon as we were able to approach the wreckage and get a good view, we knew there would be no survivors. We flew directly over the remains of the ship, then performed a quick recon of the area surrounding the crash scene, as we were suspecting a possible ambush. The area was a wet, marshy flat that was still awash from the monsoon rains. The muddy soil had some standing water on top of the muck in places and didn't appear to offer an inviting landing spot next to the wreckage.

Next, we flew back to the wreckage and descended into a three-foot hover. We checked the bodies for signs of life, but in this case, we knew it was useless. The ship had slammed into the ground with such force that it had actually collapsed upon itself. The roof of the ship was now laying on top of the cargo hold floor. Meanwhile, we spotted a number of bodies that had been scattered in a circular pattern around the ship. We flew in a tight pattern that took us over each of the bodies, our search light illuminating their lifeless forms. Each body was surrounded by a water-filled crater that was formed when their bodies had hit the ground.

The force with which each passenger had impacted the wet surface indicated that the ship had either been shot down or had experienced a catastrophic mechanical failure that had caused a free fall from a high altitude.

There were twelve bodies. Twelve souls. More death and destruction. More fathers and husbands and sons not returning home. It was becoming unbearable to witness. Maybe next time it would be my turn.

Since there wasn't much else for us to do, and we had already located the wrecked ship, we got on the radio and called in for the medevac ships to come in and retrieve the bodies.[7] We then flew a holding pattern, circling in the skies above as we awaited their arrival. Once they appeared on the scene, we guided them down to the ground to help them pinpoint the sight of the wreckage.

"OK, thanks. We got it now," they called over the radio.

They then set their ship down in the wet marsh, which, thankfully, was absent of any tall grass or other vegetation.

At that point, we departed to return to Soc Trang even though the medevac helos had no gun ship flying cover for them, which I thought to be unusual. After all, we knew that just the presence of a Red Cross symbol on the side of a ship didn't guarantee their safety.

The flight back to Soc Trang was one of the most silent and somber interludes in my entire tour in Vietnam. We had done all that we could, having not been involved in the events leading up to the crash. But the result was still the same: twelve more dead bodies. All of us had hoped that we'd arrive on scene and see crew members on the ground, standing next to their ship and waving up at us. But it was not to be. The sight of that ship, collapsed upon itself after slamming into the ground with such force, was a genuine and gut-wrenching catastrophe. To see the lifeless forms of the deceased crew and SEALs, who were killed instantly upon impact, is a sight that will stay with each of us forever.

During our flight back to base, so many disturbing images kept floating through my mind. Being close enough to the bodies to see their faces—the vacant expressions of death, seeing nothing, but still looking out expectantly onto the ground around their corpses—it bothered me. A lot. I could even see the copilot, still strapped into his seat, with his hand still on the collective. Even though the ship had no rotors, they had flown that aircraft right down to the ground. They never gave up, despite the fact that they were probably plummeting at a couple hundred miles per hour at the moment of impact. It was gruesome.

---

7. Medevac ships also had the nickname of Dustoffs, and were clearly identified by the presence of the Red Cross symbol painted on the sides.

Who knows what was going through their minds as the ground rushed up at them at an ever-increasing velocity? Did any of them jump out? The ship, which was quickly spinning due to the tail rotor still cycling, probably had ejected several of them out the cargo doors since passengers in the back are not belted in like the pilots. At least some of them were probably sitting on the floor when the ship went into its spin. I know that I often had this discussion with other Crew Chiefs: Would you stay inside a plunging helicopter, or would you jump? From above a certain altitude, it wouldn't make a difference. This was one of those times. They were all dead no matter what they had tried.

For about the eighth time in that last hour, I thought again about the lives of not only the deceased but those family members back home who would forever be affected by this disaster. They wouldn't even find out about it for another day or so, even as the remains were flown out of the crash site and prepared for the final trip home.

It was not much of a homecoming.

We arrived back at Soc Trang and refueled the ship prior to setting down for the night inside our revetment. Each of us had our standard checklist of tasks to perform as we readied the ship for the night. And all the while, as we went about our work, there remained a cathedral silence over our chores and preparations. No one said a word to anyone. I know that each of us felt the same; there was nothing left to say.

We were about ready to call it a night and return to our barracks when another call came in. The medevac ships had completed their first runs and then returned to wrap up their work when they discovered they couldn't find the crash site again. They were requesting our assistance to return to the site and re-find it once more.

Great. It was late, we were tired as well as being emotionally spent. But there really wasn't much else we could do. So we went through our preparations yet again and lifted off for the crash scene. It didn't take us long to rediscover, although none of us wanted to see the downed ship again. I was having nightmares about it, and I hadn't even been to sleep yet. At least it appeared as though the medevac crews had already removed a few of the bodies.

Once the medevac ships arrived on the scene, we decided to remain overhead and fly cover for them while they performed the rest of their recovery operations. I could only imagine that their duty was worse than ours that evening, so providing them with some protection was the least we could do. At the conclusion of that detail, we had another completely silent flight back to Soc Trang, where we could finally shut down for the night.

The following day, we finally got word on what had happened to the ship from the 162nd Assault Helicopter Company. Evidently, the ship had been operating in the area around Ca Mau when it took fire from a VC machine-gun position. They suspected that they had taken multiple hits throughout the craft, which was backed up by observers' reports. Rather than shut down to investigate any damage, they flew on to Seafloat as they'd previously planned. There they performed a "hot" refuel, which means they never shut down the main engines before pumping the fuel. (Most crews did hot refueling on a regular basis. On Super Slick, 99 percent of our refueling was done hot.)

The ship refueled in spite of the fact that it had evidently lost altitude after taking the initial fire, but it had then regained its capabilities and flown normally en route to Seafloat. The ship probably shouldn't have been permitted to continue on after landing on the river-based helipad, but they had chosen to do so in spite of the warning signs.

What was truly unfortunate was that, had the crew shut down the ship for refueling, they'd have found (with even a quick, cursory inspection) the extent of the damage to the exterior fuselage and, even worse, to the rotors and rotor head assemblies. There were unsubstantiated reports that several bullet holes had been spotted through the bottom of the helo when it landed on Seafloat. At least one individual reportedly pointed out the damage to the Crew Chief and suggested that they shut the engine off and conduct an inspection of the ship's mechanical integrity. However, according to this accounting, the Crew Chief said that was impossible if they were to keep on schedule. The seven US Navy SEALs who boarded were also trying to get to Saigon as soon as possible and were in favor of an immediate departure.[8] Some of those SEALs were heading home on end-of-tour orders, while others were simply traveling to Saigon for a few days of rest and relaxation (R&R).

There was also one other passenger on the ship that day who has remained somewhat of a mystery. There was a Vietnamese woman, perhaps in her thirties or forties, who'd boarded the ship at Seafloat. No one knew who she was, and no one asked. Some people have since speculated that she was a prisoner, while others have said she had connections with the CIA. It is very doubtful that she was a prisoner, as she would have been handcuffed or otherwise restrained in some way. Also, based on her apparel, she was probably of some importance. She had on the standard black "pa-

---

8. There are multiple reports about the extent of damage to the craft as well as to the exact sequence of events that had led to the crash. This book does not pretend to present an authoritative correct accounting of these proceedings but instead mentions commentary from various sources.

jama" pants, but her shirt or blouse was a flowy long white gown with the long white tails that sweep down to the ground. It was the kind of thing that only women of some stature could afford to wear (thus my speculation about her social status or importance). Regardless, I saw her body on the ground as well, and I noticed her immediately because of her clothing and the fact that she was the only female body around the wreckage.

The next leg of the flight was supposed to take them to Can Tho, but they never arrived at their destination. According to the account of another pilot who'd been flying parallel missions with the downed ship, there was an extreme storm in the area that forced him to fly out to the coast and around the storm. The pilot of this ship ended up flying a "hash and trash" mission up the coastline to Ha Tien. Unfortunately, Warrant Officer Moore had decided to attempt take a direct route through the storm.

These environmental factors may have been a contributing factor to the mast bumping that brought down the ship. *Mast bumping* is a condition in which the spinning rotor system tilts too far forward and breaks the mast, which causes the blades to disconnect from the aircraft. Once the rotors detach from the ship, it immediately plummets to the ground without any means of slowing the descent. The military has found that over 99 percent of personnel on ships experiencing mast bumping are killed in the ensuing crash. This summarizes what had happened to the ship transporting the SEALs to Can Tho on that fateful day.

The post–incident investigation estimates that the ship was at 1,500 feet in elevation when the rotors detached, after which the ship fell like a stone into the marshy ground below. It was falling in a spinning motion, with the engine and the tail rotor still operating. When the ship impacted the ground, it struck with both vertical and circular momentum, which could have explained the positioning of the bodies around the wreckage.

The remains of the ship were brought back to Soc Trang, where they conducted a thorough postcrash forensic investigation. However, there were so many potential explanations for the accident and the wreckage was in such poor shape that it was impossible to point to a conclusive explanation for the crash. The ship never did explode or burn, so that didn't interfere with the investigation. However, there wasn't a single piece of the craft that wasn't broken, bent, or completely crushed. There really wasn't much left to investigate, as it was impossible to determine what was damaged during the crash itself versus what had existed prior to the impact and might have been a contributing factor.

Several theories were offered as possible explanations. These included the rotor blade failure and mast bumping, a possible pitch control link failure, and serious damage to multiple components of various propulsion systems caused by a hailstorm of enemy rounds penetrating the ship. It was impossible to determine which of these factors—or perhaps a combination of several—had brought down the ship.

Another of the maintenance pilots alluded to the fact that the ship had an incorrectly installed horizontal stabilizer bar installed before the crash, which might have played a hand in the casualty. As was already mentioned, it would be impossible to determine whether any of these issues entered into the equation of what caused the demise of the ship. They are all just possibilities that came to mind as we wrestled with the total destruction of the ship.

In all, twelve people lost their lives that night: four crew members, seven SEALs, and one civilian, who we believe was a female Vietnamese person of some importance, although her identity has never been positively confirmed.

Looking back on that night, I have so many thoughts that come to mind and so many vivid memories that still haunt me and reappear as nightly ghosts in my dreams. I can still see down to the ground and view the corpses of the deceased, tossed about the ground as so many rag dolls. The lights were bright enough to bring their expressions to life, even though their lives had already been snuffed out in the course of a violent crash that lasted but a second.

To me, there is a huge contrast between what I thought, what I saw, and what I remember. They say that truly horrible circumstances often act like an eraser on your mind. The brain protects itself by either altering a memory or wiping it out entirely. (One witness to the horrors of the World Trade Center collapse in 2001 stated that he didn't see people jumping off the top of the tower building. He saw a series of cows tumbling through the air and smashing into the concrete below—an obvious attempt of the brain to block the horrifying images.)

I found it interesting that I can still, to this day, see the faces of the deceased on the ground. I can still remember the positions of the bodies, broken, shattered, and slammed into the turf in such unnatural positions that they resembled department store mannequins that had been tossed into a garbage dumpster. And I remember the remains of the ship that had been pancaked into a two-dimensional shape, the roof of the ship now flattened against the floor in a single, compact layer. I shudder to think what the medevac crew found inside that crushed layer of metal.

On top of all these seemingly vivid memories, which I can still see with incredible clarity, there are parts of this night that are totally gone. Perhaps it is the fifty years that have elapsed since this episode, or maybe it is my own mind playing tricks on me, but much of this evening simply does not remain with me. It has been removed, erased. And perhaps that is a good thing. There are so many things like this that I would rather not remember.

The ultimate irony in this story, of course, was that the SEALs, who risked their lives on a daily basis as they countered the Vietcong presence against the greatest of odds, would lose their lives to a preventive mechanical failure. Somehow it just didn't seem fair.

**Those who lost their lives in the helo crash on June 23, 1970**

*Crew Members*:

**Warrant Officer Lawrence Michael Moore**

**Warrant Officer Daniel John Hallows**

**Specialist 5 Dennis James Dillon**

**PFC James Warren Lenz**

*Passengers and/or Other Participants*:

**SN Thomas Richard Brown (Navy SEAL)**

**SN John Joseph Donnelly III (Navy SEAL)**

**SM3 John Stewart Durlin (Navy SEAL)**

**FN Toby Arthur Thomas (Navy SEAL)**

**HM2 Harold Lee Linville (Navy SEAL)**

**BM3 James Raymond Gore (Navy SEAL)**

**MM2 Richard John Solano (Navy SEAL)**

**Plus one unknown civilian**

# 16

## MEDEVAC REUNION
## FORTY-FIVE YEARS LATER

This chapter is written about the rescue of a US Navy SEAL who operated out of Seafloat and who was transported into some of the combat zones of the Mekong Delta by the 336th Assault Helicopter Company. The focus of this story is about the rescue of Navy SEAL, EN3 Ray Smith, as told through the eyes of Capt. John Leandro, 2nd Platoon Leader. Smith was gracious enough to share some of the emails exchanged with Capt. Leandro forty-five years after the incident.

While writing this book, we debated whether to include it or not, as it is somewhat outside the flow of the other chapters. However, as Leandro said, "This is one of the few feel-good stories in this compendium," and for this reason, we have included it in this book.

⌦

June 12, 1970.
I really can't remember what mission we were flying that day. All I remember was that I was piloting my own ship, Warrior 26, and that we were sitting on the ground in Ca Mau. It was early afternoon, and I believe we had already refueled and were awaiting liftoff for the next leg of our transit when we got a call on the radio. It was an emergency medevac for a member of a SEAL team who we had inserted into a hot zone somewhere north of Ca Mau.

We could usually determine from the tone of voice on a radio call whether it was a routine versus a genuine emergency call. This one sounded pretty bad, so it drew our immediate attention. Someone needed to get in and pick up this wounded warrior—and quick.

"I got it," I announced in reply to the radio transmission.

I was used to flying medevac missions, and I felt personally responsible for the fate of this US Navy SEAL. It was always possible to send one of the other pilots from my platoon into harm's way, but I didn't like doing that. I was the Platoon Leader, which meant that I wouldn't send one of my pilots anyplace where I wouldn't go myself.

As we approached the area of operations (AO) for the extraction, we were told to hold off at first, as the entire area was extremely hot. The SEALs were encountering a lot of hostile fire, and our ship probably would have received significant damage or even been shot down. So they attempted to secure the area as best they could before we went in for the rescue.

The other SEALs on the team were able to drag the injured team member across a rice paddy and onto a rice dyke. This was a raised, solid berm that served to contain the watery rice paddy and keep it separated from the next rice field. The only problem was that the dyke was too narrow for me to set the ship down on two skids. I had to put the right skid on the solid ground of the dyke, while the other skid was suspended over the paddy. In essence, I was performing a hover with one skid on the ground. It wasn't an ideal position for loading wounded personnel, but it's all we had at the time.

The area surrounding the rice dyke was still hot, and we knew it wouldn't be long before we started receiving enemy fire ourselves. As soon as I had set our right skid down on the berm and stabilized the ship, two other SEALs threw their injured teammate into the back of the cargo area and then dove in themselves.

"Go, go, go!" I heard my Crew Chief, Dale Cram, screaming through the headset. He was as concerned about our exposed position as me, and we wasted no time in lifting off and getting out of there. Time was of the essence for multiple reasons, as we knew the SEAL's injuries were substantial.

The next thing I heard over the headset was my Crew Chief providing a grim assessment of the SEAL's condition.

"He's bleeding out," he called out, keeping his eyes on the injured man.

Thankfully, one of the SEALs was their team medic, so he was able to tend to the wounds as best he could. But the back of a Huey helicopter is a far cry from an operating room, so there was very little that could be done on the ride to the hospital. From what I was told, the wounded man's color was terrible, and the bleeding was uncontrollable. There didn't appear to be much hope that this SEAL was going to survive.

In the cockpit we just hoped and prayed that he'd make it to the hospital. That's about all we could do besides fly as fast as the ship would take us.

The flight from the pickup to the hospital at Binh Thuy took us around thirty minutes, which was pretty good time. We landed, and they immediately offloaded the injured SEAL and got him into the hospital. He was still alive as they were removing him from the ship, which gave us all a sliver of hope. But we had to depart immediately for the return flight, so we never heard how he did once he was admitted to the facility. I only knew that if he was to survive, he would need significant surgery—and quickly.

After making our urgent stop at the hospital, we flew back to Can Tho, where we would get the ship cleaned. The entire bottom of the craft was covered in blood, which had congealed into a jelly-like layer of deep crimson. It required some high-powered-water-jet action from a firefighting pump to blast the blood out of the ship. It was messy work, and the water that poured from the cargo bay was all tinted in different blood-colored shades. It was even worse to think that all this blood had come from one person, making it seem even more impossible that he hadn't perished.

Looking back on the experience, I think it stood out because we very seldom medevacked Americans from the field. Usually, it was South Vietnamese troops from the ARVN. So it was very different from that perspective.

When I originally looked at the injured SEAL and saw the extent of his wounds, I thought it was a sunken chest wound. I later heard that the bullet had entered through the arm, but then traveled into the neck, where it passed though part of the carotid artery. This accounted for the massive amount of bleeding and should probably have been fatal. An emergency surgery was performed on the spot by a surgeon who may not have even waited for an anesthetic. Time was that critical.

Once we had wrapped up our end of the rescue, I literally forgot about the injured SEAL, as well as the medevac mission. There was so much else to do, and we ventured into harm's way on a daily basis. It was impossible to keep track of every mission and every soldier, SEAL, or ARVN troop. And you quickly learned not to care too much about any one individual, as you never knew how long they were going to last in this country. Life was ephemeral for just about everyone in Vietnam, including helicopter Platoon Leaders.

⤛

Fast forward to the year 2007. The Vietnam War had been over for thirty-four years, and my stay in that country had ended even earlier. I was sitting in my home in Raeford, North Carolina, just surfing the web, when a thought popped into my mind.

I wonder if that guy survived?

I was thinking, of course, about the wounded SEAL whom I'd flown to the hospital in Binh Thuy that day back in June of 1970. I rather doubted it, based upon the comments of my Crew Chief and the amount of blood we'd scoured from the floor of our ship. I hadn't heard anything further about it, although the evidence suggested that he wouldn't have made it.

I then found a US Navy website about the Seawolves Helo Platoon that seemed to be active with ex-service members who had served with that unit. I wasn't sure of which SEAL team it was or any other specifics, so I just listed some general information, including dates and places. It didn't take long to post, but I was mildly interested to see whether anyone online would recall the incident and perhaps know the fate of the SEAL.

Nothing.

As I expected, no one answered my posting, which wasn't a surprise, as it had transpired so long ago. Thirty-seven years is a very long time. And even if someone did know the answer, what were the chances they would read my post so many years after the fact?

Fast-forward another eight years. It was then April 2015. Retired SEAL Ray Smith, living in Chicago, was doing some research online for his son's homework assignment. Having served in Vietnam himself, Smith didn't usually discuss the war, as it brought back many painful memories. But in this case, he just needed to find some information on helicopters in Vietnam, so he ventured onto this particular website.

Slowly, he perused the various articles, then began reading some of the postings that readers had placed on the website. His curiosity about the subjects had him reading more and more of the comments, which took him back a number of years. Then, out of the blue, one posting stopped him dead in his tracks.

It couldn't be. But it was. The words in the posting from 2007 jumped off the page and brought everything back in excruciating detail. It was about him. He knew he had to respond.

A few days later, John Leandro was seated at his own computer in North Carolina when the email arrived. It was from someone whose name he didn't recognize: Ray Smith. The writer simply wanted to know whether Leandro had found out about the SEAL he had sought out back in 2007. Was he from Golf Platoon, SEAL Team 1? Also, had he medevacked that SEAL to Binh Thuy?

Leandro responded that he didn't know to what platoon the SEAL belonged but that he was part of the unit that was stationed on Seafloat, south of Ca Mau. He also said that, yes, he had flown him and his two team members to Binh Thuy. He then asked the writer whether he had any information on the SEAL and whether he had survived.

The next email from the writer to Leandro was everything he'd dreamed of hearing.

"I have some good news; I am the SEAL. I am alive thanks to you. I needed to be sure, yes, you took me to Binh Thuy."

The email went on to discuss how his teammates had dragged him across the rice paddies and formed a perimeter around him to keep him alive until the medevac helo arrived. It also discussed how the fierce enemy fire had kept the rescue ship away but that they had eventually braved the fire and made it through to the pickup area.

Leandro and Smith began corresponding and eventually decided that they'd have to meet. The whole thing seemed like a matter of fate, just as so many other things about these people in this war. Even the fact that Ray Smith was browsing the same website some eight years later and came upon Leandro's posting was nothing short of a miraculous coincidence. The world is filled with amazing twists of fate, and this was just one more.

Ray Smith had evidently returned to the United States and, after recovering, had graduated from San Diego State with a degree in engineering. He'd started his own company and distinguished himself as an innovator and recipient of two dozen patents.

On June 12, 2015, Ray Smith and his wife pulled into Capt. Leandro's driveway in Raeford, North Carolina. It was forty-five years to the day since Leandro had set one skid on the rice dyke and risked everything to pick up a seriously wound SEAL.

A serious case of fate.

Leandro and Smith have remained in contact, bonded by the events of a half-century ago. These kinds of connections, of friendships, are probably not unique in our military, but the stories are always much more rewarding when they have a happy ending. This one, thankfully, does.

As a short postscript to this story, Smith mentioned that he had never received his Purple Heart for his wounds during the war. After his conversations with Leandro, he spoke with US Navy officials, who reviewed his case and pledged to correct the situation. As a result of this unfortunate case of "forgotten honor," Ray Smith Jr. was invited to a formal ceremony at the Naval Special Warfare Center in Coronado, California, on October 7, 2021. There he was honored in a ceremony in which he was presented with the Purple Heart by Capt. Bradley Geary, Commanding Officer of Basic Training Command. Smith was simultaneously presented with the Naval Special Warfare pin (often referred to as the "Trident"). This pin was approved just weeks after Smith was wounded, so he'd never received the device.

Accompanying Smith at the ceremony was John Leandro, who had played such a critical role in transporting him to the hospital, thus saving his life. The ceremony, which took place fifty-one years after the action, was attended by a great many members of the US Special Forces Command as well as by the classes of US Navy personnel in the SEAL training pipeline.

*Ray Smith Jr. receives his Purple Heart from Capt. Bradley Geary, Commanding Officer, Basic Training Command at Naval Special Warfare Center, Coronado, CA, in October 2021. (Official Navy Photo.)*

*Ray Smith Jr. makes remarks from the podium during his Purple Heart ceremony at Naval Special Warfare Center in October 2021. John Leandro looks on (left). (Official Navy Photo.)*

# 17

# FOURTH OF JULY

## The Good and the Bad

The Fourth of July is a massive holiday in the United States, celebrated by hundreds of millions of Americans. On this most patriotic day, Americans will consume over 150 million hot dogs, purchase 68 million cases of beer, and spend over $1 billion on fireworks (which also accounts for over 230 fireworks-related injuries). It's also known that fireworks (on a smaller scale) were used in the United States as far back as 1777, even though the Fourth of July was never recognized as a federal holiday until 1870.[9]

In Vietnam none of this stuff mattered. Sure, we had calendars, and we knew the date. It's possible that the base mess hall also served up some kind of a special meal, as they did on Thanksgiving (turkey) and Christmas. But this was wartime routine, where we arose at the same time every day and conducted wartime-related activities. There really wasn't time for festivities, nor was it ever advisable to let our guard down. After all, our enemies had calendars too, and they were just as familiar with our holidays as anyone.

The idea of a Fourth of July celebration wasn't really anyone's brainstorm, per se. It just germinated as a result of a conversation and slowly took form after that.

It was in the afternoon of a workday, perhaps two to three days before the Fourth, and three of us were working on the ship. Wilkes, Sandwith, and I were going about our endless tasks that were part of maintaining a helicopter and its components, weaponry, and systems. These chores were extensive and detailed but also very routine. We performed them every day of the week until we could complete them with our eyes closed. Wilkes

---

9. John Adams wrote in a letter to Abigail, his wife, that he wanted Independence Day to be celebrated with "Illuminations," among other festivities (penned July 3, 1776).

and Sandwith took apart all the guns and cleaned each one of them in meticulous detail. They had the miniguns, the M16s, the M60s, the 50-cals, the .38 or .45 pistols carried by the pilots, and on and on.

As Crew Chief, I had my own list, which included inspections for loose bearings, replacing bearings that were worn, cleaning filters for the engine, and more. It was detailed work, but not at such a level that would require complete concentration and silence. We could certainly talk while we worked, which was commonplace in our revetment during our afternoon maintenance sessions.

On this particular day, the three of us were comparing notes about our hometowns. Rob Sandwith came from Friday Harbor, Washington, which is on San Juan Island in the waterways off the northwest corner of the state. Tom Wilkes, meanwhile, hailed from Danbury, Connecticut, which is nestled up against the border of New York, on the southwest side of the state. These compared in size and population with my own hometown of Webster, NY, which is a suburb of Rochester. All three had the look and feel of small-town America: places where you knew your neighbors and were part of a close-knit community.

As we talked about the similarities of our home towns, our conversation gravitated toward the Fourth of July and what we did back home to celebrate with our families. We spoke of the parades, the picnics, the hot dogs, and, of course, the annual firework displays that served as the culmination of each of our holiday celebrations. There was a certain tone to our discussion that expressed a longing for that kind of an event, even there in Vietnam. It felt like we were all thinking and dreaming of the same thing: a Fourth of July fireworks show for our base at Soc Trang.

Once one of us proposed the idea, it just started to grow. First, one of us suggested shooting magazines of solid tracer rounds through our M16s. That certainly sounded like fun! Then someone else proposed firing off some hand flares, just to add color and brilliance to the display. This was followed by the idea of releasing white phosphorous ("Willie Peter") grenades, then concussion grenades, and then incendiary grenades to leave a trail of sparks. One idea built on the last, and it just continued to grow in size and scope. We were enthralled with the concept and determined to make this party happen.

To this day, there are parts of the fireworks party preparations that I cannot recall, including how it became publicized across the base. I believe that Tom Wilkes told some of the Cavalry personnel, and from there, it just spread. The guys in our own company learned about it from our conversations in the barracks, and the news leapt from platoon to platoon, with everyone talking about it in the day or two leading up to the Fourth. It gave people something fun to look forward to, and the anticipation seemed to grow by the hour.

One thing I do remember about the event was that we did *not* ask permission from anyone up the chain of command. We just decided to go ahead with it. Our pilot, Mr. Olson, never objected to the idea but instead passively complied with it. Dana Brown, who was flying with us more and more as copilot, also seemed to be OK with the idea. So it would be our regular crew of five flying along on Super Slick, the fireworks ship.

As dusk approached that evening, we got all our ammo loaded into the ship, which was a bit of an extra load. We would need all of our regular loadout for our nightly perimeter mission, plus our fireworks display rounds. And we did want to provide a great showing for our audience, which would hopefully include most of our base.

We were encouraged beforehand by the seating arrangements that had been set up by the northern-perimeter fence of the base. It was still afternoon, and yet row after row of chairs had already been carried into position by would-be spectators, hoping to claim a prime viewing position for the show. It was obvious that most of the base would be there, which made us even more proud of our idea. This thing would be big.

We lifted off right on schedule. As we did, we called Guardian Angel (the call sign for the base night officer) and requested permission to test fire weapons on the northern perimeter of the base.

"Roger, Super Slick, approved," replied the official.

That's all we needed as we moved into position, our rotors thumping as we passed over the improvised spectator stands. Then we opened fire.

The display was awesome, whether viewed from the air or from the ground. We made at least four or five passes along the entire length of the fence, firing guns, miniguns, hand flares, and more. It was a great time and a great show, a way for everyone to celebrate the Fourth and experience a feel-good pause. It probably lasted about thirty minutes, with us firing everything but the kitchen sink to the north from our base.

"We fired so many tracer rounds that we completely burned out the barrels on some of our guns," said door gunner Tom Wilkes.

For days following the show, people told us how much they enjoyed the event. We also heard a few people wondering what any nearby VC might have thought. (Perhaps they thought it the mother-of-all offensive attacks?) It was an amusing thought, although the presence of all tracer shell bursts probably didn't fool anyone.

We also thought that we might catch hell for putting on such a show without running the idea up the chain of command or getting permission from the Battalion Commander. But once again, there wasn't a peep heard about it. Not from Major Kilpatrick. Not from the Battalion Colonel. Nothing. We believe that the higher-ups just thought, "What the hell, it's the Fourth of July. Let them have their fun." It's quite possible that some of them may have been in the seats enjoying the show.

⌇

Once the fireworks show was over, we found ourselves faced once again with our daily dose of reality. As always, we had our nightly perimeter defense mission to fly, and it was just about that time. We had arranged to be the second ship up in our alternating flight schedule, but because we'd been putting on the show for the past hour, it was now our turn. So we shifted gears from shooting off tracer rounds to immediately focusing on the real-world mission.

Unfortunately, this would turn out to be anything but an ordinary night. Sometimes fate, that ever-present, lurking factor, appears in the form of the hunter, always ready to strike and take you down. It can happen in the blink of an eye, out of nowhere. And, in fact, it usually does.

On this particular night, July 4, 1970, we were flying about twenty miles north of Soc Trang, conducting reconnaissance over an area that had contained VC bunkers. Although we had cleared those bunkers a few months earlier, there was evidence that enemy troops had since reoccupied them or, at least, were making use of them once again.

In order to get them to abandon the structures, we began using harassing fire from our ship, with Sandwith firing down with the miniguns. We were flying fairly low, and our lights were illuminating the targets for him to draw a good bead on the targets. Things were going well.

Suddenly—and for no apparent reason—Sandwith stopped firing, and I could see his hands release from the handles on the minigun.

"Why are you stopping?" called out Olson, puzzled at the break in the action.

Sandwith did not reply. He briefly reached up again to the handles on his gun, only to immediately release them again and bend over as if in pain.

Unlike Olson, I hadn't bothered asking Sandwith why he wasn't firing, but I did know something was wrong. Before attempting to resume shooting the minigun, he had reached over and grabbed at his leg. So instinctively, I leaned over and put my hand on his knee, where I instantly felt the presence of a thick fluid. I immediately recognized it as blood.

"He's been hit," I called up to the cockpit.

It was kind of an odd, eerie report, as I don't recall Sandwith saying anything himself. Also, we didn't hear anything unusual, as we might have if some enemy fire had hit the ship. It was as though a single round had appeared out of nowhere, passed through the open door, and struck our door gunner.

Olson immediately broke out of our flight pattern and banked our ship hard to port. We went to full speed en route back to Soc Trang and the hospital. Inside the darkened ship, I could see Sandwith was in a lot of pain. It appeared as though it was only one round that had passed through his right leg, but a single round from an AK-47 carries a lot of firepower, and there had been nothing to absorb any of the energy prior to impact. It must have hurt one helluva a lot. Additionally, if the bullet had passed through an artery, it could cause a massive loss of blood, resulting in shock and life-threatening implications. We had to move fast.

As we approached Soc Trang, Olson was on the radio talking to the tower, getting permission to land. Heading inbound, he spoke to the Air Controller and asked for permission to land next to the hospital building. The AC granted permission and then contacted the hospital to alert them that we were inbound with an injury.

Our "hospital" at Soc Trang really wasn't a full-fledged medical facility equipped to handle major traumas. It was more closely related to a MASH (Mobile Army Surgical Hospital) unit, although it was an actual brick-and-mortar building rather than a tent. But still, this level of injury was beyond the kind of first aid treatments they normally provided, so we knew Sandwith would probably have to be transported someplace else before he was done.

As we pulled into a hover next to the hospital, Wilkes and I got Sandwith out of his helmet and flak jacket, then maneuvered him out from behind his gun. Next, we rigged up the gurney and lifted him onto it. We then jumped from the cargo bay and lifted him out, ready to be rolled into the building. Several hospital medics were already by our side, ready to move him into the facility. There was a lot of care and concern, as Sandwith was in considerable pain. There was also a lot of blood on his uniform pants, which had turned a dark crimson red.

Once Sandwith had been moved into the hospital, we climbed back onboard our ship, which had never been shut down. Olson then flew us back to our revetment, where we conducted our final end-of-mission tasks before shutting down the engines. Dawn was breaking as we were getting off the ship. I did a thorough inspection of our slick from top to bottom without coming across a single bullet hole. But there was yet another puddle of blood on the floor of the ship beneath where Sandwith had been sitting. This confirmed my suspicions that Sandwith must have been struck by a single round that had passed through the open door before hitting his leg. It was unusual, but it had happened before to other crew members in the past.

Cleaning up congealed puddles of blood was becoming a routine operation on our ship.

The following morning, all of us visited Sandwith in the hospital before visiting the mess hall. He was lying down on a hospital bed, his leg heavily bandaged and padded. He was obviously a bit more comfortable than he'd been the previous evening, as I'm sure they had him sedated with painkillers for the transit to the larger hospital in Can Tho.

Later that morning, Sandwith was loaded onto another slick and transferred to the Third Surgical Unit in Can Tho. There they were better suited to perform the necessary surgery to repair as much of the damage as possible. However, he was still up there for three to four weeks as his wound healed and he worked his way back into action.

In his absence, we located and trained a substitute door gunner who could stand in on the night flight missions. I don't remember who that individual was, but until he was prepared to fully perform the job, our Super Slick was restricted to purely base defense missions, which meant endless circling over the base perimeter. It was boring and monotonous although probably much safer than our routes twenty miles beyond the fences.

In a bit of a coincidence, Tom Wilkes was injured just a week after Sandwith, although his accident wasn't caused by an enemy round. Wilkes was in the process of firing off a hand flare when he struck the wrong point with the flare tube against his thigh. The flare ignited, severely burning his leg.

Another trip to the hospital.

The hospital staff examined Wilkes and said that he, too, would have to be transferred to the larger facility in Can Tho. But this presented us with a genuine problem. We were a night ops ship with plenty of fire power but no one left to fire the guns. This obviously negated our value and completely eliminated our ability to perform our mission.

I was left with no choice but to go and find replacement gunners to join our crew. That shouldn't have been a problem, as there were plenty of gunners in our company who were more than capable of doing the job.

But our ship had lost two door gunners in the past week, which meant that we were developing a reputation as a high-risk unit. It shouldn't have been the case, but it was. As I walked around the barracks, looking for gunners to address, I sensed them moving away from me as fast as possible. Bodies were slipping out back doors, diving into toilet stalls, and doing anything else possible to make themselves invisible.

Meanwhile, up in the surgical unit in Can Tho, an unlikely reunion was taking place. Sandwith was sitting in a wheelchair in a hallway when Wilkes was brought in with his burn wound.

"What the heck are you doing here?" asked Sandwith, amazed to see his ship mate close by in the same facility.

"Well it sure isn't to visit you," Wilkes replied. They got a good laugh out of the surprise, although both of them would have preferred to be meeting on different terms. Wilkes ended up staying in Can Tho for five days before returning to our ship.

Looking back on the whole week, it was representative of much of our time there. There were good, bad, and ugly events that happened on most missions and most weeks. In between the long hours and uncomfortable conditions, we still found ways to laugh and have our moments of fun. The Fourth of July show was a great time that was enjoyed by all, even if the day was brought to a terrible end by Sandwith's injury. Still, it was a joy to know that we were able provide entertainment and make people smile, if even for thirty minutes on a July evening.

This story also has an interesting afterthought attached to the narrative. Many years after the war, Rob Sandwith had to submit a claim to the US Veterans Affairs Department (VA) for medical services. He was having a hard time getting his claim through the system, which he mentioned to me during a phone call. (We had maintained contact since we'd returned to the US after the war.) They would provide the services, but there was a lengthy waiting period before his case would be handled.

"That's not a problem for you," I explained. "All you have to do is attach a copy of your Purple Heart to the forms, and they'll move you to the front of the line."

"That would be great if I had a Purple Heart," he replied.

"They never gave you a Purple Heart? You were shot by the enemy in Vietnam!" I was incredulous at the oversight.

"Nope, never got one," he answered. "And I still have part of the bullet in my leg!"

It wasn't the first time I'd run into that over the years, and it wouldn't be the last. I decided right there that I would help Sandwith get his due recognition. I promptly sat down and wrote a letter to the VA in which I summarized the events of the evening of July 4, 1970, and the injuries sustained by our door gunner. It was addressed "To whom it may concern," but it evidently found its way through the system. Rob was eventually moved to the front of the line, and the VA was able to conduct the appropriate research and channel the letter to the right people to prompt the awarding of his Purple Heart.

It was just about three years ago, circa 2017, when Rob Sandwith received his Purple Heart in the mail. There was no one there to present the medal—no family members there to watch it get pinned on and no one there to shake his hand and thank him for his service. It was just an envelope from the US Army with a medal and a citation.

It is unfortunate that this kind of omission happens much more often than we would like to admit. Wars and conflicts are fought in a frenetic procession of crises that often don't permit the powers that be to stop and document every act of bravery, achievement, or injury. So many of our servicemen have returned home at the end of their enlistments without the full recognition they deserve. Then again, for those who don't return at all, no amount of recognition can ever serve to call out their full measure of devotion and service to our country.

# *18*

# AGENT ORANGE

## How OCD Saved My Life

O n its website, the National Institute of Mental Health (n.d.) defines obsessive-compulsive disorder (OCD) as "a long-lasting disorder in which a person experiences uncontrollable and reoccurring thoughts (obsessions) engages in repetitive behaviors (compulsions), or both." It goes on to state that the symptoms can interfere with various aspects of life, including work, school, and personal relationships.

These statements are probably true, although as someone who has lived with OCD since childhood, I'm not complaining. Not one bit. Because in Vietnam, my OCD definitely saved my life.

My experience with OCD dates back to a very early age. As long as I can remember, I've been obsessed with cleanliness. If I was working on a project in the garage or somewhere on my car, I always had a rag in hand, cleaning as I went.[10] While outside mowing the lawn, I had to make sure that every row of grass was cut perfectly parallel to the previous row and that each row was perfectly uniform in width to the last. I kept my bedroom, my car, and all of my clothes in the same condition. Nothing could be out of order.

I had OCD, no doubt about it.

Once I got to Vietnam, I realized that having this affliction was definitely a good thing. This was especially so for the role of Crew Chief, where attention to detail and repeating the same processes over and over again with no variation were key to attaining the zero-defect approach to mechanical maintenance perfection. Day after day, I know I drove Sandwith and Wilkes crazy by my insistence that they clean and wax the ship

---

10. The ghostwriter of this book has visited Feigel at his home and was astonished to see a gleaming layer of polished aluminum diamond plate around the walls of his garage. It had a mirror finish and was cleaner than any plate found in a high-end restaurant.

until it was absolutely perfect. They must have been reluctant to take it to that level and certainly felt that the nonstop cleanings were a waste of time. But personally, I knew that by cleaning a surface until there was no dirt remaining, I could identify cracks, leaks, or loose hardware that otherwise would have escaped my attention. So cleanliness was not a "nice to have" feature; it was mandatory every day, every mission.

What the rest of the crew probably never knew was that I was much tougher on myself than on anyone else. If I was ever replacing a component, I would never, *ever* take a break until the job was complete and the new replacement was fully installed. Likewise, I would never leave hardware loose, even for the shortest increment of time. It was just not in my wheelhouse to do so. Everything had to be completed and secured before I could turn my back on it.

This self-imposed regimen was also manifested on my preflight and postflight inspection processes, especially the preflight examination. I always insisted that the pilot accompany me on a preflight walk-around inspection of the entire ship, looking at the entire exterior and major systems that could be observed from the outside. Often, Olson or Brown would try to convince me that "it's all good," although I would never accept their assurances.

On one occasion, the two of them (pilot and copilot) tried to pull a fast one on me. They both got to the revetment before me and performed a preflight inspection on their own, without my presence to go along. They wanted to see if I would accept their assessment of a "Crew Chief-less" inspection. As soon as I arrived, they informed me that it was done, and they were "all set to go."

"Nope," I shook my head. "We are doing a preflight right now, you two and me."

They disagreed, and we went back and forth a couple of times. Finally, after sticking to my guns, they agreed to perform another full preflight inspection, as I had demanded. We did the preflight as I had insisted. They knew me too well.

This part of my routine, performing a thorough preflight check, may not have been as much OCD related as it was having it drilled into me while learning to fly back in New York. My father taught me to look over everything thoroughly before going "wheels up."

"Better to catch it on the ground" was one of his favorite aviation axioms. It had caught on with me and become part of my mindset that I'd brought to Vietnam.

I still remember one incident that really drove home my level of OCD and put it on display for my entire crew. We were performing a "hash and trash" mission and were coming in on an angled descent to land next to an outpost. From a distance, I could tell that the ground was wet and very muddy, which was sure to leave a thick coating of the wet soil on the skids. As Olson brought the ship down to a low hover, I told him that I had just painted the skids the previous night and asked him if he could please not land in the mud. He obliged me by maneuvering the ship sideways until it was over a small concrete pad before touching down. Even as he was feathering the controls to remain in a hover while sliding sideways, I could imagine what the copilot was thinking.

Despite my OCD tendencies, which I pretty much kept to myself, I had developed a decent reputation as a skilled and hard-charging Crew Chief who was willing to accept just about any mission. I especially enjoyed the unique operations, including the SEAL insertions, the sniffer flights, the nighttime base perimeter assignments, and so forth. We were a great team, and I loved the thrill of going out and getting the job done with this group of professionals. Because of this reputation, I was probably at the top of the list when our company officers were looking for an experienced Crew Chief to lead a new kind of mission.

With this in mind, I found it wasn't much of a surprise when our Platoon Sergeant showed up at our revetment one evening as we were preparing for another night mission. He approached me directly with his offer.

"Hey Feigel, how would you like to crew the defoliant ship?" he asked.

He was simply passing along a question from the higher-up, and I knew that I could turn it down if I didn't want the job. But I decided that I would at least go out and look at the ship, if nothing more than for interest's sake.

"Sounds interesting," I said. "Tell me a little more about it."

"Well, it's set up a bit like an old-fashioned crop duster," he started. "It's configured to carry defoliant chemicals, and it flies along right at the treetop level. It uses special equipment to spray this stuff into the trees and brush that surround the canals and rivers, which eventually makes the leaves fall off. After that, we can see the enemy troops a lot better since they can't hide behind the vegetation anymore."

The Sergeant went on to describe how the defoliant ship is escorted by two gunships, whose job it is to provide cover in case anyone on the ground starts firing up at the defoliant ship. It sounded kind of interesting, and my rebellious side was emerging once again to talk myself into accepting the job.

"Where is this ship?" I asked.

"It's at the other end of the field," he replied. "Hop in the truck, and I'll run you over there to take a look."

As we drove along the airfield road and the ship came into view, I got my first view of the defoliant ship. (I'm sure it had a different, more official name, but that's all I remember from our conversation.) The closer we got, the more detail came into view, and none of it was good.

"You've got to be kidding me!" was all I could think.

The entire ship looked like a Rube Goldberg contraption, something that you screwed together in someone's backyard over the course of a weekend. It looked to be very crude in construction, totally unsafe, and obviously not of military issue. Two pipes, each with lines of holes drilled through them, extended out on either side from the cargo area. Each of these were held in place by an array of jerry-rigged cables. Meanwhile, two fifty-five-gallon drums, which presumably held the defoliant chemicals, were stashed away in the cargo area. Those were semi-secured with seatbelts, whose holds looked tenuous at best. There was also a gasoline-powered pump on the floor that didn't appear to be held in place by anything.

I approached the final few feet to the ship hesitantly, trying to believe my own eyes as to whether this thing was for real. The theory of operation was simple; I didn't require a tour or an explanation. Once the ship was airborne and over the area to be sprayed, the Crew Chief would fire up the pump, which would force the defoliant chemicals into the pipes. From there it would spray out through the pattern of holes and disperse onto the jungle below.

Several observations came to mind as I was looking over this mess. The first was that the entire ship was covered with the defoliant chemical, from the front of the cockpit to the back end of the tail. It was likewise painted inside and out with the substance. It was literally dripping from the tail boom.

The more I looked, the worse it got. It was obvious that the forceful wind from the blades had cascaded the chemicals absolutely everywhere. Even the area where the ship was parked was drenched in a circular pattern of the fluid. As I walked around, I could literally feel my feet sticking to the ground and making an audible sound every time I lifted a foot from the tarmac. It was everywhere: on the floors, the walls, everywhere. What a mess.

As I silently paced around the goop-covered ship, getting more and more appalled at the entire scene, I spotted the ship's Crew Chief and door gunner as they went about their daily routine. They were actively filling the fifty-five-gallon drums inside the cargo bay, chattering away as though they didn't have a care in the world. Watching them perform their daily routine, surrounded by all those toxic chemicals, I thought, "Gee, that could be me."

No.

With each passing minute, the OCD alarm in my mind flashed brighter and brighter. It was now in full overload, and I couldn't remain on-site a moment longer. I needed to be out of there immediately.

The Platoon Sergeant had remained close by my side as I performed my walk-around, and he seemed to sense that I had arrived at a decision.

"So what do you think?" he asked, his own shoes making sticky, sucking sounds each time he lifted his feet. "Should I tell the Company Commander that you'll be flying the missions?"

I knew I had to be direct, forceful, and perhaps overly blunt in my response.

"Sarge, I don't want to disappoint anyone, but there's no way in hell I'm going to crew that ship. That's one god-awful mess that I'm not going to clean up."

"No way?"

"No way."

So the Sergeant drove me back to my own ship's revetment still in need of a Crew Chief.

In retrospect, I'm not even sure that my OCD came into play with my decision. The defoliant helo was such a mess and so infused with chemicals that I think I would have turned down the mission even without being obsessive-compulsive. It just didn't look like a healthy environment for anyone, much less a finicky clean freak like me.

All of us would end up having direct or indirect contact with Agent Orange before departing the country. Olson had actually copiloted a defoliant mission in his early days in Soc Trang in which the helo had crashed, although everyone in the crew survived. Still, they were all completely drenched in Agent Orange.

I also recall flying over the U Minh Forest, which was heavily defoliated from years of Agent Orange use. The dead trees would catch fire and send up thick plumes of smoke as we flew overhead, which meant that we were all inhaling the dioxin-laden residue.

Flying over one of those regions, where C-130 aircraft were used to spray large areas, is a bit of a shock. To witness the altered landscape where all foliage has been removed is difficult to imagine. The entire earth is brown, including the shrubs and smaller plants, right down to the roots. Tall, lifeless trees are toppled to the ground from the mere touch of our rotor wash. Meanwhile, pools of groundwater collect in shallow depressions, each a different color of the spectrum. With the stick-like trees and dried-out brush, it resembled a lifeless moonscape in haunting detail.

⋙

**The following is a contribution by Warrant Randy Olson, Aircraft Commander, Warrior 21 (call sign Super Slick), of his sole experience flying the defoliant ship over the forests surrounding Soc Trang.**

I had a single mission flying a ship that was configured to deploy the Agent Orange compound out of Soc Trang. The date was November 11, 1969, and we were flying a D model Huey, which was older than the H models we used later. I was flying as the copilot on this mission, as I was not yet an Aircraft Commander. One thing that was different about this defoliation mission was that it required us to carry an extra supply of the chemical. As a result of the size of the targeted area, we lifted off with four of the fifty-five-gallon drums instead of the normal two, which created weight and balance issues with the ship. We'd loaded up the ship on a dike between rice patties rather than at an airfield.

I also remember this flight because we had a Colonel who went up with us as a passenger. He was riding in the back, mainly to acquire enough hours to qualify for his Air Medal. This was a bit comical to any pilot who flew every day, as these aerial awards were given for every twenty-five hours of flying in direct combat support (CA) flights in a combat zone. Other missions (i.e., resupply) also qualified for the same medal, although fifty hours of flight were required to earn the same award. Some of our higher-tenured pilots left Vietnam with quite a few of these medals.

As soon as we lifted off, we experienced a load shift that rendered the ship extremely unstable. We reached about one hundred feet in altitude when the ship became almost impossible to fly, and it came down hard. The crash destroyed the aircraft, but luckily, no one onboard was injured. We received enemy mortar fire while sitting on the ground and were eventually pulled out a couple hours later.

The worst part about our landing was the resulting discharge of the fifty-five-gallon drums. They erupted in a cascade of the defoliant that splattered all over the entire interior of the ship's cargo bay and cockpit. We had Agent Orange dripping off of everything from the front of the ship to the tail. All of us inside the ship were drenched with the stuff. I'm sure, by now, the Colonel must have thought that his Air Medal just wasn't worth the effort.

Although I wasn't overly concerned at the time, everything I was wearing was thoroughly infiltrated with the compound. My flight suit was completely saturated, which would have been bad enough. But the deadly fluid had so permeated my clothing that it began to drip down my legs and drain into my boots. We were able to completely clean the flight suit (at least I believe we did if we didn't replace it), but I was stuck with the boots, which carried the residue forever. I wore those boots until they completely disintegrated some time later.

In retrospect, I believe I was extremely lucky. Today, some fifty years after the incident, I am still perfectly healthy with no ill effects from the dousing. Perhaps it's because that was my only experience with Agent Orange; I never flew another defoliant mission the entire time I was over there. But I also credit having good genetics and the luck of having fate on my side.

Sadly, in the years since Vietnam, more and more information has come to light about Agent Orange and its deadly effects. Everyone knows of its use as a seriously effective chemical defoliant that can be applied in aerosol form to remove the herbivorous cover in almost any setting. It was in use years before the Vietnam War, applied by the British forces in the Malayan Emergency of 1948–1960. The US then used it to remove foliage in Vietnam from 1961 until 1971.

Contrary to popular opinion, Agent Orange was not named after the color of the chemical itself. (It was colorless while being deployed, although some witnesses claim to have seen a "reddish-brown fog in the air.") Instead it received its moniker from the color of the markings found on the fifty-five-gallon drums in which it was stored. There are other versions (mixtures) of the defoliant, too, called Agent White, Agent Blue, Agent Purple, Agent Green, and Agent Pink.[11] Of these variants, Agent Orange was the strongest and most lethal.

---

11. Much more of this information can be found on the history.com web page on Vietnam history.

Combined, the US sprayed more than twenty million gallons of these defoliants in Vietnam, Cambodia, and Laos. In addition to hitting their targets, which were usually canals, rivers, and roadways, they also found their way onto rice paddies and farmlands. Dubbed Operation Ranch Hand, it was used across 4.5 million acres of Vietnam to destroy not only forest vegetation but also food and crops that might be used by the Vietcong and North Vietnamese.

It is doubtful that anyone knew the full scope of the illnesses, diseases, and birth defects that would arise as a result of the spraying. Dioxin (which is one of the main active ingredients in all the forms of the defoliants) has proven to be a long-lasting and lethal carcinogen that is even capable of passing down its aftereffects to following generations. Before its full carcinogenic characteristics were recognized, Agent Orange was tested and stored at numerous locations across the United States. Unfortunately, dioxin can remain in the soil for decades and can cause health issues even in trace amounts. Various forms of cancer, heart disease, diabetes, severe skin conditions, and more are included on the list of diseases linked to its use. Birth defects also appear at higher rates among the children of those exposed to the chemicals, although studies testing this theory have not been verified.

Still, when I look back on those days, I am profoundly glad that I declined the Agent Orange Mission. It is one time in my life that I can honestly say I was happy to have that affliction, even if I didn't know what it was called.

⚬⚬⚬

**The sad truth about Agent Orange and its potency was that many of us were affected years after the war, even if we were not directly involved in the spraying. It was inescapable, as it was sprayed in the wide swaths of territory in which we all had to operate. I myself developed type 2 diabetes, which I know was in reaction to breathing in the aerosol compounds in the Mekong Delta.**

**Many of the pilots and crew members with whom I operated have developed different diseases and symptoms as well. A good friend and fellow Crew Chief, Victor Mantano from Albuquerque, passed away from cancer in 2017. He and I had arrived in Vietnam at the same time, and we'd developed a close friendship. We were surprised to learn years later that we both worked for Xerox in different capacities. I got to see him on a job site a couple years**

before he passed away, and he was convinced that his illness was linked back to his exposure to Agent Orange.

The government has since provided treatment and compensation for those struck by diseases caused by these chemical defoliants. Unfortunately, these payments cannot bring back to life those who risked everything to serve in this traumatic war.

## 19

# THE MORAL COMPASS

## To Shoot or Not to Shoot

The strains of combat and their observable effect on service members is almost impossible to measure. It is also difficult to anticipate the forthcoming actions of any one individual when he is placed in a situation where he believes his life—or the lives of his fellow combatants—is in imminent danger. These uncertainties represent a nightmare for a Battlefield Commander, as the consequences are so drastic in a time of war, when each of his troops already has a finger positioned on a trigger with the adversary squarely sighted in the crosshairs.

This chapter focuses on a series of events where we, as helicopter crew members with weapons at the ready, were forced to decide on whether to engage the enemy or to stand by and allow them to pass. Each case was different from the others in factors including location, timing, appearance, and behavior of persons unknown who were caught in the searchlight's beam. They also tested the moral compass of each us inside Super Slick as we walked the delicate balance beam between self-preservation and doing the right thing.

Each one of these situations represented a difficult choice, especially since we were flying the nighttime perimeter defense patrols that were, by their very nature, different than flying daytime combat assault missions. We weren't flying with a bevy of other slicks, inserting and extracting troops with a layer of protective gunships overhead to provide cover. We were out there by ourselves, at night, with no one to serve as a backup if we got into a jam. Heck, we didn't even have another set of eyes to give us an opinion. We were it, the sole authority and "eye in the sky."

Nighttime flights were also different from those flown in the daylight hours. Everyone knew that the nights belonged to the Vietcong. This was when they would move their weapons and supplies in sampans up and down the endless miles of canals and rivers in the Delta region.[12] Our job was to patrol these territories at night using search lights, flares, and starlight scopes. It was a war zone with a declared curfew, which meant that no one was permitted out from dusk until dawn. That included walking, driving, or anything else. Anyone seen violating this curfew was assumed to be the enemy. Since another part of our mission was to enforce the curfew, this meant that some life-or-death decisions were often entrusted to the collective judgment of our crew.

As I've mentioned already in this book, we were the police, the judge, the jury, and the executioner all rolled up into one unit. It's a job that none of us took lightly, and that judgment was tested on a regular basis.

## BOY IN THE ROAD

On one particular nighttime patrol, we were flying down a road that led out of the city of Soc Trang. We were flying only a few feet above the road, while Olson had the ship's spotlight on to illuminate any details below. While cruising at such a low level, nothing really escaped our eyes, and we could even see the individual ruts in the road as they flickered beneath our skids. Olson could control the beam of the light by moving a knob that was mounted into the cyclic stick. He could direct the light up and down, right and left, with a simple twist of his finger.

We traversed up the road at a slow-to-moderate speed when suddenly, out of nowhere, we all saw a human form flash by in the light pattern. It happened so fast and the body was in such a prostrate posture that we all thought it might be imaginary.

"Did you see that?" asked Olson over our headsets.

"Yes," we all answered in unison.

Olson immediately doubled back while we all shared a common thought. Was this some kind of a setup? It was a common tactic of the enemy to place an object or person in plain sight just to lure in a ship like this and then to open fire when the ship would touch down.

We next conducted a series of high-speed reconnaissance passes over the body just to see if it would move. It didn't. Whoever it was, he or she was lying facedown in the road, arms splayed out from his or her sides and hands empty. We also noticed that there didn't appear to be any weapons

---

12. The Mekong River alone measures over 1,200 miles in length, although it originates in China and flows through a number of other countries before draining into the South China Sea.

anywhere in sight, which bode well for us. As a matter of fact, the entire area didn't appear to be conducive for an ambush of any kind. The road lay in a wide-open area, and the tree line was at least a mile away, making it difficult for anyone to conceal themselves from our searchlight.

Next, Olson decided to use the forceful downdraft from the rotors to turn the form over. He came in fast, approaching the body at high speed before flaring the ship hard, which produced a large volume of air forward. Still, the body did not roll over, although we could see a conscious effort on behalf of the form to resist the flipping. So now we knew that whoever it was, he or she was most certainly alive. But we didn't know why he or she was out there, breaking curfew, laying in the middle of the road. He or she was weaponless—or at least appeared to be without a weapon of any form. It was a genuine mystery.

We landed on the road about twenty-five yards away from the body, with all our lights trained on the form. Once down, our door gunner on that night (who was from the infantry) volunteered to leave the ship and investigate the individual. None of us were certain as to the wisdom of that move, as the opportunity for an ambush or booby trap was well documented in this area. All too often we had lost troops who foolishly decided to risk their cover in exchange for a VC flag or other war prize. It just wasn't worth it.

We all held our breath as our gunner approached the form in the road. Each of us had our fingers on the triggers of our respective weapons, ready to commence fire if the threat materialized. The closer he got, the slower and more cautious his approach—slower, slower, until he was right upon him in the middle of the pavement. He tentatively reached out and touched the leg of the body.

That got a reaction. The body sprung to life, jumping up into a standing position. It startled every one of us and made our trigger fingers squeeze just a little tighter against our weapons. It appeared to be a boy, and he started walking away from us down the road. This was highly unusual, so we decided to call Guardian Angel, our night officer at Soc Trang, to request the local authorities for some assistance.

Guardian Angel called the local Soc Trang city police (we called them the "white mice"), who appeared shortly thereafter in a Jeep with every possible light on. They used all their lights to make sure we knew who they were and didn't confuse them with a VC vehicle.

Upon investigating, the police determined that the boy was a thirteen-year-old local kid who had accidentally found himself out after curfew. When he saw us approaching in our ship, he had panicked and lain down in the road, playing possum and hoping that we wouldn't see him or evaluate him to be a threat.

Summarizing the incident, I'll say he was very lucky because we could have justifiably opened fire on him, being out after dark and violating curfew. But we made a judgment call, which included evaluating the factors of the area (wide open with no tree cover), the possibility of threat (no weapons), and the timing (early in the evening). This judgment call ended up favorably for all hands, and the boy returned home OK.

## NEAR-FATAL WEDDING

A similar kind of incident took place on a different night that once again tested our judgment and mettle. It was still before midnight, and we were out doing a general reconnaissance mission. We weren't looking for anything in particular, except for signs of the "bad guys" up to no good. In the distance we saw a lot of lights that had illuminated a swath of ground. This was unusual, as almost no one wanted to be seen after the curfew had started. These people, whoever they were, didn't seem to care in the least whether they were visible or not. These lights were bright.

As we made our approach, we could see a lot of people in formal attire gathered around a decorated patch of ground. It didn't take much evaluation on our part to determine that a wedding was taking place, which we did not want to disturb. We backed our ship slowly out of the area and continued on with our patrol.

Later on that night (probably in the early morning hours), we approached the same area once again and noticed that all those lights were out. We had expected that, as the wedding had likely ended earlier in the night. However, we also spotted two sets of lights traveling down a road, away from the site of the original gathering. This fell into a different category of suspicious, so we dropped down farther and moved in for a closer look.

We closed to within a couple hundred yards and were able to determine that the lights belonged to a pair of Honda 90s. These iconic motorbikes are not high-powered, and they weren't moving along at a high rate of speed or performing any evasive maneuvers. They were just plodding ahead down the middle of the road as if it were daylight. Once again, we trained our own ship's lights on the pair of vehicles to get a better view of the riders.

Each bike held a pair of passengers, including a man and a woman (husband and wife) in the same formal attire. It was pretty obvious that they were riding away from the wedding that we had spotted earlier. Perhaps they were even part of the official wedding party itself. That part would have been OK except for one thing: It was well after curfew (closer to dawn), and these couples were clearly ignoring the local regulations. We knew that ignoring this violation would not suffice. We had to do something (nonlethal, of course) to get across our message.

"Feigel, do we have any CS (tear gas) onboard?" asked Olson from the cockpit.

"Yes, we do," I replied while looking for the specially loaded grenades.

Olson then called the Soc Trang control tower to ask for the wind direction and speed. We needed this information to efficiently deploy the gas on the correct side of the road to maximize the effect.

Once we had all the information we needed, we maneuvered into place and pulled the pins on the two grenades, lobbing them into the path of the oncoming bikes. It was a windless night, so we didn't have to do much calculating. The cans landed right on target and were already spewing out clouds of the noxious fumes when the motorcycles drove into the plume. One of the bikes immediately swerved off the road, while the other appeared to attempt to drive through the gas. It was simply a message, which said, "You're not supposed to be out here now, and if you persist, this can get worse." We think our message was received, and hopefully, they would not break curfew in the future.

These kinds of incidents always started out as question marks until we could figure out the situation and determine that there was no hostile intent involved of any kind. At that point we could just do our part to enforce the curfew and then proceed on our way. It was great when we weren't faced with the dilemma of potentially firing on a civilian or noncombatant individual.

## THREE CIVILIANS IN THE SAMPAN

The last case in this collection is a vastly different scenario than the previous two. It involved a trio of individuals in suspicious circumstances who chose to run rather than remain in the open to be seen. It called into play our knowledge of behavioral patterns and also our varying levels of experience in dealing with potentially hostile (and nonhostile) players. This one did not end as well as the others.

This patrol took place after Olson had departed on his end-of-tour orders, so we were flying with a different pilot. We didn't yet have a permanent Aircraft Commander, so we were using a rotating collection of designated pilots to fly Super Slick. We all wanted the final selection to be Warrant Officer Dana Brown, as he had flown with us a lot, and we were used to his abilities and demeanor. But on this particular mission, I cannot remember who was in the pilot's seat. (I can't remember who was copilot either.)

For that matter, almost all the crew members were substitutes on that mission. This sometimes happened whether due to illness, orders, or some other function. But at times, you found yourself flying with crew members you barely knew, which made communications more difficult as Crew Chief. When flying with your own crew, words were often unnecessary. Every person knew their job and was familiar with my expectations. I liked it that way, although that was not the case on this mission.

We had already spent most of this mission patrolling a number of the canals in the area. It was getting close to the end of our shift, around 0400, and we were in the middle of shifting our focus from one canal to the next. This required a hard bank to port, which we executed while I maintained my eye on the waterway.

Suddenly, the search light spotted three men in a sampan, which we lit up brighter than day. As soon as we pulled into a hover above the watercraft, one of the passengers jumped out and sprinted to a hooch that was located alongside the canal.[13] Meanwhile, the other two passengers attempted in vain to cover themselves with various materials, all to no avail.

We happened to have a chase ship above us that night, so we used them to contact Guardian Angel and provide them with our location, along with other details of the situation. We wanted them to know what was happening, but we also knew that this was not a hostile area. We were pretty close to town, and the VC did not represent an ongoing threat at this location.

As we hovered in place over the sampan, I found myself thinking that we were a sitting duck in our current location. We were down low, stationary, with lights on. If anyone were around with a weapon, we'd make an easy target. I also noticed that the two figures below did not appear to be carrying any weapons. The VC almost always had at least one AK-47 along for protection.

"I don't see any weapons," I called up to the pilot.

---

13. A *hooch* is a word used to describe any kind of small, crude structure that is used for shelter or storage in Vietnam. They are often constructed of wood and plant material harvested from the immediate vicinity.

He didn't respond. I found myself wishing once again that either Olson or Brown was in the front seat.

As we hovered a bit longer awaiting clearance to fire, several thoughts were running through my head. I kept thinking that this was not "bad guy territory." I knew this area and had flown across it many times over the past few months. Additionally, I now had flown hundreds of hours at night and had developed a keen sixth sense about dangerous situations, and this just didn't fit the norm of a VC operation.

Additionally, the canal area was densely populated, with hooches lining the banks of the waterway. This was not the kind of place where the VC normally conducted their operations. That thought kept driving home in my mind.

Suddenly, one of the two remaining passengers in the sampan jumped up and ran into the same hooch as the first runner. It may have been in response to his inability to hide on the craft, but I'm sure he was just looking for cover that was unavailable on the little boat.

"We've got people running down here," our AC called loudly into the radio.

This expression was often used to infer that we had bad guys running for cover, which is how Guardian Angel at Soc Trang interpreted the transmission. Up until now, we were standing by for clearance to fire, but our pilot's call to Guardian Angel ended all that. It was the tipping point that forced the Operations Officer's hand. The response was immediate.

"Super Slick, you are cleared to fire," he said, giving the clearance order.

I will remember that radio transmission for the rest of my life.

Within seconds our 50-cal came to life, firing straight down on the sampan. The small wooden boat instantly disintegrated into a thousand pieces. It was as though a giant's foot had landed on top of a small wooden matchbox. Parts of it flew everywhere, the main body of the craft instantly breaking into shapeless shards of wood that spread across the water's surface. The sole remaining passenger was dead within a second of the gunfire burst, thrown lifeless into the bottom of the boat. He probably never knew what hit him, it all happened so fast.

Once the sampan had been obliterated by the fire of the 50-cal, the gunner turned the weapon on the hooch where the two passengers had taken cover. I cannot begin to guess how many rounds were pumped through that flimsy structure, but I'm sure it was way more than necessary. The roof of the hooch (as well as the rest of the building) fragmented into a pile of splinters. Absolutely nothing had a prayer of surviving that intensity of heavy fire.

After what felt like an unduly extended amount of time, we broke off our engagement and continued our patrol. We all had excessive amounts of adrenaline surging through our systems, although in this case, it didn't feel good. I had a very bad feeling about what had just transpired. Over the past months, I had been in numerous firefights, including some really bizarre situations, but for some reason, this one just didn't feel right. My gut feeling was telling me that we had made a bad decision and engaged nonhostile civilians who had simply been at the wrong place at the wrong time.

Living and operating in a combat zone for extended periods of time exposes you to a lot of sights that your mind doesn't want to see. Over the course of the year, I had seen so much death and destruction, and I was getting weary of it. I was definitely getting burned out, and I found myself questioning my own judgment, as well as the collective judgment. (This was tough to determine on this particular mission, as almost our entire crew were substitutes.)

The next morning, we received the word. We had killed three civilians. I knew it before we were even told. It was simply a confirmation of what my gut had told me the night before. I cursed myself for not taking more of a stand, especially with substitute, less-experienced gunners onboard. I also felt badly about not being more forceful with the Aircraft Commander and convincing him to listen to my opinion. But it was too late now; the people on the ground and in the sampan were already dead. This would remain as another scar on my soul that I will never forget.

Perhaps something that bothered me just as much was that there was no official reprimand to me or anyone on our crew. No disciplinary action was announced, and the subject wasn't even mentioned on the battalion, company, or platoon level. We were expected to just continue on with our missions, business as usual.

Meanwhile, back at the canal, three civilians lay dead, their bodies shredded by heavy gunfire from an unseen force that never fully investigated prior to opening fire. I thought a lot about the Vietnamese family members weeping as they performed their traditional funeral rites, mourning their losses without ever knowing why it had happened.

I also wondered about the families in the surrounding hooches who listened to the gunfire and heard the agonized screams emanating from right next door. Those hooches were so small and tightly spaced that the residents of adjoining structures must have thought that their turn was next. I imagined the cries of the children as they huddled next to their parents, terrified and not knowing whether their own lives would be snuffed out in the next burst of fire. The proximity of the hooches along the canal was such that a misdirected round aimed at the intended target would most certainly strike another. I tried not to think about it and prayed that the other residents had survived the firestorm without injury.

I realized that in war, sometimes things happen. In modern warfare, we lose people to blue-on-blue engagements, where we fire upon our own personnel, aircraft, and ships. It happens. The fog of war that we speak of so commonly means that we almost never see clearly to observe the whole battle space. We receive fire from enemy fighters who sometimes are ghosts that we can't see. We lose our friends to these phantom bullets, and it becomes frustrating beyond words. It sometimes leads to us firing first and then asking questions later. It becomes a form of revenge and can lead to catastrophic events such as the My Lai massacre.

To this day, I wonder if those three civilians would still be alive had Olson or Brown been piloting our ship that night. I believe that either one would have reacted with more calm, cool, and collective thoughts and responses.

If only. Once again, fate had played its hand.

# 20

# OUR OWN BRAND OF
# VIETNAMIZATION

One aspect of our lives in Vietnam toward the end of my tour was *Vietnamization*, which was defined as a program to "expand, equip, and train South Vietnamese forces and assign them to an ever-increasing combat role, at the same time [be] steadily reducing the number of U.S. combat troops" (Term coined by US Dept. of Defense, under Sec. of Defense Melvin Laird). It was something that we didn't deal with on a frequent basis, as it was a combination of political strategy and "big thinking" stuff that was way above our paygrades. We just knew it was out there, and most of us thought it would never work.

Historically, the strategy of Vietnamization was announced to the American public in a speech on November 3, 1969. It was in contrast to the Americanization plan used by President Johnson, and it was initiated to provide for the gradual reduction of American forces in the country. By this time the war was extremely unpopular, and that grassroots sentiment only grew worse when Cambodia was invaded in 1970.

In a nutshell, to us, it meant turning our resources and control of the war over to the South Vietnamese Army, which would then take over the fighting and defend their country from being overrun by the Vietcong and North Vietnamese Army. That is a highly simplified explanation, of course, but that's what it meant to us.

Regardless, it represented very little to us in the way of real change. Our CA (combat assault) missions were all about inserting ARVN (South Vietnamese) Infantry troops into battle rather than Americans. So we were used to it from those very first days of 1970. But inserting ARVN troops into the field and picking them up again at the end of the day is a far cry from turning over the entire war to their leadership. That's where our skepticism crept in; we just didn't think it could be done.

Regarding the process of training South Vietnamese pilots to fly our helicopters, they actually enrolled ARVN flight students into US helicopter schools to learn the art and skills of flying. However, before a student could start the school, he first needed to take courses in English and achieve a set level of proficiency in the language. This was to be coupled with the flight school, then followed by several months of practice in the field. When everything was put into a single timeline, they concluded that the full training time, from acquisition until final qualification, was at least two years.

After hearing about this touted program for some time, we were finally brought face-to-face with it sometime around late July or early August. We were sitting in our revetment getting ready for our nightly mission, when suddenly, we noticed Olson approaching with another individual. We didn't recognize anything about this person other than that he was dressed in a flight suit and was apparently Vietnamese.

I remember thinking bad thoughts as soon as I saw this.

"This is not good!" was the thought running through my mind. Flying at night was dangerous enough already—and that was with an American pilot. Now we were being asked to train a new pilot who could barely speak our language and had almost zero stick time? I had a sinking feeling in my stomach as they approached the ship.

I angled my body so that I had a moment of private eye contact with Olson. I shot him a questioning look that conveyed my insecurity. It was a WTF expression that only he could see. He understood and gave me a reassuring nod and wink.

"I got this" was the message from Olson to me, and I understood. I didn't know what was coming, but I figured it would be good.

Olson climbed into the cockpit, followed by the Vietnamese pilot, and they both got strapped in for the flight. The Vietnamese pilot maintained absolute silence the entire time, not saying a word. Meanwhile, we prepared ourselves in the cargo area and got set for liftoff. We didn't know what Olson had up his sleeve, but we were ready for anything.

As soon as we lifted off, Olson came up to speed and gained a bit of altitude. Then for no apparent reason, he took the ship into a hard bank to port. Then he immediately reversed direction and went into a hard bank to starboard. This lasted for a matter of seconds before we reverted to the original bank to port. Then to starboard. Then to port. Then to starboard. And so on for the next two hours.

It took very little time, perhaps the first three minutes of the flight, before we realized Olson's intentions. Seeing up into the cockpit was difficult from the cargo bay, and getting a glimpse of the copilot's expression was even harder. But I have no doubt that our "Peter pilot" was a fine shade of green by the third or fourth banking maneuver.

Our shift lasted the traditional two hours, and the entire interval felt like a carnival Tilt-a-Whirl ride. Personally, I was grinning from ear to ear, and I think my door gunners were doing the same. Regardless, they couldn't have engaged any hostiles on the ground this shift anyway, as it would have been impossible to get a fix on a ground target while the ship was going through these crazy gyrations.

By the time we landed, the green copilot was looking pretty shaky. After clutching his midgut through his flight suit, he slowly rose and climbed out of the cockpit. He still hadn't said a word to any of us the entire time. I found myself wondering if he thought that all flights on Huey helicopters were like this. I could imagine him going back to his own platoon and filing an immediate request to transfer to infantry.

Once he was out of earshot range, Olson turned to me to provide his thoughts.

"He won't be back for our next two-hour patrol," he said. "Oh, and Feigel, you'll need to wash out the chin bubble. He puked in it."

After our two-hour break on the ground, Olson's assessment was confirmed. The South Vietnamese pilot never did return. We could only guess what he told his fellow ARVN pilots. It must have been something along the lines of "Those American pilots are crazy! They have no idea how to fly a ship!"

As we prepared to go up again for our next shift, Olson turned to me and said, "Come on up and hop in the left seat." I complied, and spent the next two hours flying copilot, which was a new experience for me. I never did master the art of hovering, but much of the rest was a lot like flying a fixed-wing aircraft. It was a great experience, although I still don't know what I would have done if anything had happened to Olson during our flight. Thankfully, we managed to stay out of harm's way.

Looking back on that night, I remember that it was the only time we ever had a Vietnamese pilot assigned to our ship. I don't know if that was a coincidence, but I rather doubt it. Super Slick was probably on the permanent blackball list from that night on.

Later on that year, on November 4, 1970, the Soc Trang Army Airfield was transferred to the Republic of Vietnam Air Force (VNAF). Our company, the 336th Assault Helicopter Company, transferred its aviation and support assets to the VNAF, which became the newly activated VNAF 227th Helicopter Squadron. In all, thirty-one UH-1 helicopters were transferred in the turnover, which was the fourth transfer of a complete helicopter company to the VNAF in the past two months. Following the official ceremony, only a few Americans remained behind to serve in advisory positions during the transition.

Years after all of us had departed Vietnam, the South Vietnamese government did fall to the armies of North Vietnam. Despite the peace talks and the treaties and the grand plans, all of us who were stationed over there knew it was coming. On countless occasions we'd fight to take over a tract of land and expel the VC intruders, only to lose that territory once it had been turned over to South Vietnamese forces. It wasn't that they were terrible fighters or lacked the will to contest the enemy in battle. Instead the common opinion is that it was a combination of unskilled leadership, poor command and control functions, and an inability to integrate their resources on a large-scale battle space. Once again, all that stuff was way above my paygrade.

Our American withdrawal was completed in 1973, and the country fell to the Communists in 1975. It was all what we expected, as well as the final result of Vietnamization.

Here is one last note: Our pilot is no longer green, but he left the airborne community forever.

## 21

# BREAKING UP THE CREW

So much had happened by the end of the summer of 1970 that it felt as though it would go on forever. Olson, Wilkes, Sandwith, and I (and now Dana Brown) had been through so much together that it seemed impossible to believe that we were all still alive and functioning on the same team. Both Sandwith and I had been shot by AK-47 rounds, Wilkes had been burned by a hand flare, and Olson had been completely drenched in Agent Orange. We had been shot at, ambushed, and watched as our friends and mates had been shot down and killed. This kind of living at death's door tends to mold shipmates into something more durable and cohesive than a team. Instead it produces a rock-solid bond that induces men to willingly sacrifice their lives for one another if the need arises.

This is the kind of crew and the kind of bonds we had formed by August of 1970. We had been through so much together that we really didn't need words at all to communicate. We each knew the needs of our shipmates and the needs of the mission. That's all there was. We barely needed to exchange glances to express our thoughts. It also kept us going because we knew that we were each indispensable parts of that unit, and we needed each one of us to function properly to achieve our mission.

That's why when Randy Olson left for home in August, it shattered something in my mind that I couldn't easily repair. But his one-year tour was over and his orders were in, so it was time to move on. I was actually glad to see him leave, in a way, because I wanted him to get home in one piece. Thinking back on Lucky Strike, I realized it seemed like fate was certainly on his side.

The interesting thing about Olson was that he left Vietnam and he left the Army, but he didn't leave the military. He ended up enlisting in the US Air Force and flying A10s, which were built for the combat assault roles he

201

knew so well. He ended up staying in the military and making a career of it. I think he was the only one of our Super Slick crew who stayed in the service after returning from Vietnam. Even after joining the US Air Force, he continued to use the call sign Slick for his A10 assignments.

Much of our leadership seemed to be rotating at the same time. Capt. Leandro had already left the month before, so we had a new Platoon Leader come in at the end of July. Leandro didn't stay away for long. He still had time remaining in the military, so he spent some time back in the States, but he then returned to Vietnam for a second tour, this time flying in a Cavalry unit.

Our new 2nd Platoon Leader was a fellow by the name of Capt. Don Franklin, whom I got to know briefly, although I was never as close with him as I had been with Leandro. It seemed like I wasn't getting too close with anyone new those days.

Meanwhile, Sandwith had become a genuine adrenaline junkie and had transferred to the scouts of Dark Horse Charlie Troop, 16th Air Cavalry. Scouts were the very smallest of all helicopters in Vietnam and were also probably the most dangerous missions to fly. These helicopters (which were mentioned in an earlier chapter) weighed less than a Volkswagen when empty and were notorious for getting shot down. But everyone in the aviation community always said that if you had to get shot down in a helicopter, make it a scout, as they had very high survivability rates in their crashes.

I did think it ironic, however, that by transferring to the Dark Horse Troop, Sandwith was heading to the same Cavalry unit from which we'd acquired Tom Wilkes. But he did great things there and eventually returned back to the States. He and I still communicate from time to time.

Tom Wilkes stayed for several more months, and we continued to fly together from time to time. I was still flying the nighttime base perimeter missions, but it was different now. We had Dana Brown as our Aircraft Commander sometimes, but not consistently. The door gunner position was also a revolving door of individuals. Our original crew, which had been in place since May, was now gone. Whoever showed up at our revetment at the start of the evening was part of our crew for the day. It just wasn't the same.

The times were changing, and I certainly felt it. In the back of my mind, I knew that I was getting short myself. I had but a couple of months left in-country, and I kept a mental calendar to remind me of the number of days remaining before my flight home. I contemplated transferring back into the safety of the hangar for my last couple of months, much the same as Ron Knight had done the month I arrived. After all, I had cheated death so many times already; who knew how long my luck would hold out?

In the end, though, my rebellious old nature won out, and the adrenaline rush I got from flying overrode my sense of logic. So I stayed in the air right up until the end. (Once again, sorry Mother.)

Lots of new faces appeared in our company and in my platoon. There were new Crew Chiefs and new door gunners all around me, but I rarely socialized with any of them. Every once in a while, I'd take the time to help out with some technical expertise or to pass along some words of wisdom to a new Crew Chief or door gunner. I felt that need, as many of the old veterans of my platoon had done that for me. But it got harder and harder, and it seemed as though my social skills were evaporating with the passage of time.

I also started noticing other changes within myself that were not pleasant. My startle response was off the charts, and a simple motion or sound could send me springing into the air or gasping for breath. The fight-or-flight syndrome seemed to arise in me from the most innocent stimuli, which was worrisome, if not embarrassing. I'd also catch myself staring at nothing, noticing nothing, and hearing nothing, with all noise canceled out. I was just there, somewhere, without feeling a thing. It was very strange, but I never thought much about it at the time other than to recognize that it existed in me.

It seemed as though I was running on autopilot about 80 to 90 percent of the time, doing the same things day after day, just picking one foot up and putting it down in front of the other. I was still very vigilant in my job; that never varied. But I was also becoming less and less social by the day, not talking to others while performing my Crew Chief tasks. Inside, I wondered to myself what had happened to the days when we used to joke around at the ship, playing tricks on each other while actually laughing. Those days were gone, never to return.

Later on in life, I'd find out that this phenomenon was common in troops who had fought together in combat. It is called PTSD.

# 22

# THE LAST FIREFIGHT

**September 11, 1970**
**This chapter describes a night that was fast-paced and violent throughout the entire episode. At times like these, I've found that my mind went into overdrive, causing me to lose perspective on events and, sometimes, to forget others. To assist with this section, I requested the perspective of our door gunner for the night, Spec 4 Dave Schap. Dave's actions that evening were not only heroic, but his recollections were critical to retelling this story as descriptively and accurately as it appears here.**

It only took a month or so in-country before you started developing a feel for things. Patterns seemed to present themselves more and more clearly, to the point where you could tell when something was wrong. It's as though your senses could anticipate an ambush or when the enemy was amassing a force with designs to attack your location. Some of those signs were easy to spot, such as excessive amounts of gunfire or observations of troops gathering at any given point, especially near your own base. But other signs were more difficult to spot, if not impossible. It all went back to the feel of the moment.

One of these precarious moments happened to our crew near the end of my tour, and it turned into a very wicked firefight that equaled anything I had seen in Super Slick. We were flying one of our nighttime base perimeter missions and were about to go airborne for our 0300–0400 stint. Before lifting off, we got word from Guardian Angel that enemy movement had been spotted south of Soc Trang Airfield. We were also told that another ship had already received fire from this area, so we knew what we'd be up against.

This wasn't a problem, as we were equipped with everything we needed to handle VC troops at night. That was our mission, so we knew what our targets would be on this particular night. So we lifted off and headed south to investigate.

It was already a different kind of night flight, just from the perspective of having a new crew member. Olson had returned to the States, and Sandwith had also moved. But we had the able-bodied assistance of another superb door gunner in the form of Spec 4 Dave Schap. It was the first time I'd ever flown with him, but he had a great reputation and was a willing volunteer for our mission, so we welcomed him aboard our ship.[14]

We flew directly south from our base and commenced looking for the enemy. We didn't have to go far. As a matter of fact, within a few minutes, we began taking fire—very, very accurate fire. This caught us a bit off guard, as we were still pretty close to the base. We would normally have had to fly a number of miles in any direction before encountering hostile fire in this concentration and accuracy, but not tonight.

The environmental factors were against us at first. It was a clear night with a very bright moon, which tended to give the enemy an unobstructed view of our ship. Our lack of cover was evidenced by the barrage of inbound fire during our first engagement of the fight. We witnessed many tracer rounds that were very close, even though none of them struck our ship. Tracers always seem to get much larger when they are close by, and these seemed abnormally large—at least, too large for comfort.

Upon receiving the inbound fire, we immediately opened up with our 50-cal, but the gun was not working properly. We pulled away from our original target area, and Schap tried making some adjustments to the head spacing and also increased the speed of the recoil setting, which enabled him to fire at a much faster rate. We then tested the gun in a river, and it appeared to be working much better.

We then began saturating the ground below from which the fire had originated. The response to our fire was quite unexpected. We started receiving additional fire—but from a completely different location. This was also unusual, and it was not a good sign. It meant that we were probably dealing with a large and spread-out force that was apparently well-equipped. And at least part of this force was located close to our own base. Not good.

---

14. Schap had become available for other assignments because his own helicopter had crashed during a POW rescue mission in the U Minh Forest.

We also spotted something that looked like a haystack on the ground that was about the size of a garage. We didn't pay much attention to it at first, but shortly after that, we saw a stream of white tracer rounds streaking by our five o'clock position, fairly close by. Schap engaged the machine gun position with about one hundred rounds until it stopped firing.

Deciding that we needed to quickly change our tactics, we immediately climbed to two thousand feet in elevation, where I deployed two large flares. These illumination devices were attached to small parachutes, which caused them to drift slowly to the ground below. We maneuvered to stay just above them, which allowed us to gain a better view of the tree-lined area below. It was a game changer in that it gave us the optical advantage. The flares turned the night into day, while blinding the enemy below. We had used this tactic before. It allowed us to see them clearly and direct very accurate fire into their locations, all while remaining cloaked in the glare of white light from the flares.

The scene below appeared to be a long line of trees bordering a river, which was the source of the enemy fire. We also saw some enemy bunkers and troop movement in the area that were caught in the white light of our flares. We took advantage of the light to open up with our 50-cal once again, focusing on the tree line and the bunkers. For the second time, we were immediately engaged with hostile fire, but this time, it was with heavier weapons. A combination of 51-cal shells and small arms munitions whizzed past our ship at close range, which again got our attention.

Seeing the 51-cal gun trained against us was a little unusual, although we had experienced this weapon while operating over the U Minh Forest. The 51-cal, which had the ominous nickname of Copter Killer, had been in existence since 1939, although its modification into its current configuration came about toward the end of World War II. It was usually mounted on a tripod, although Soviet forces mounted them on some of their tanks to counter enemy air superiority.

The next inbound rounds came from a series of three machine guns that were concealed in the tree line south of our position. We knew they were firing at us because we saw the muzzle flashes, although these guns had no tracers, so we couldn't determine how close they were to striking us. We engaged each location with quick bursts of ten to fifteen rounds, which appeared to silence all of them.

After this last round of returned fire, we broke off and climbed to two thousand feet for the second time in ten minutes. From our higher altitude, I once again deployed flares and lit up the skies above the Vietcong troops. We repeated the pattern and followed the flares down, all while tossing grenades out the door or firing the M79 grenade launcher. Schap was continuously picking out new targets and firing our own 50-cal gun, making for a ferocious engagement. This was about as hot an air-to-ground engagement as I'd ever seen.

Next, we flew directly over the haystack and headed down the north side of the tree line while firing rounds of armor-piercing ammo onto the sampans on the river. We could see flashes from the direct hits of our incendiary rounds exploding upon impact, which undoubtedly sunk those that we struck.

We also saw a small, twin-barreled antiaircraft gun that was firing up at us, although again, without using tracer rounds. We engaged that target using about one hundred rounds of our 50-cal gun, firing in a pattern all around the weapon on the ground. Even though it was probably protected by armor, Schap appeared to have put it out of commission, as it stopped firing.

Suddenly, we heard a voice over our radios that we recognized from other engagements. It was a US Air Force spotter plane that had been flying overhead, monitoring our firefight. I can't remember whether we even knew they were up there with us that night, but we were glad to hear them chime in over our radio.

The twin-engine aircraft was a Cessna O-2 Skymaster, which the US Air Force had begun operating in 1967. Used by the 20th Tactical Air Support Squadron, they were also employed for purposes of psychological warfare, dropping leaflets and broadcasting from large speakers inside the craft.

The normal form of attack involved the Cessnas flying in and firing Willie Peter rockets to mark the targets. Then the F4 Phantoms would follow, directing their ordnance at the marked area on the ground. The F4 was an exceedingly lethal platform that was capable of hypersonic speeds while carrying a payload of 18,000 lbs. of ordnance, including air-to-ground missiles and a variety of bombs. It became the primary air superiority fighter in Vietnam, along with a variety of other missions.

We had witnessed air strikes of this kind during the day but very seldom at night. Nighttime strike operations are much more challenging, as hitting the target with precision is a tougher task in the dark.

We heard the Cessna call us and ask whether the area was worthy of an air strike.

"That's a Roger," we responded, without delaying to consider.

We listened to the spotter plane calling his operations contact to request the air strike, and within minutes, we had a pair of Phantoms streaking inbound to our location. This was about to get good.

The F4s contacted their forward controller (we could tell they were F4 pilots from their muffled voices, which came through their face masks) and asked them if we could mark the ground targets for their strike run.

"Roger, we'll mark targets," said our AC.

We flew in low, marking the targets with our 50-cal tracer rounds, all the while receiving fire from the enemy's 51-cal gun. This time the inbound tracers were right on top of us, appearing as big as basketballs. We were taking hits throughout our ship as we returned fire with our own 50-cal. Then we broke off and peeled out of there. The Phantom pilots had seen our exchange and had attained a good fix on the enemy location.

"We've got it, Super Slick," said the pilot. "Break off and fly west. We'll be making our pass from north to south."

We couldn't see the Phantoms as they made their run over the target area, but we could see the large flashes from the explosions as the first jet dropped its load of bombs on top of the marked zone. We also observed the tracer fire directed upward at the craft as it pulled up from his run. The thought going through my mind was as follows: "These guys are hardcore. Maybe they weren't VC after all; maybe they were North Vietnamese regulars."

We also discovered that the haystack we had seen earlier was anything but an innocent pile of vegetation. As the jets were coming in to make their bombing runs, a number of VC troops emerged from the heap and opened up with automatic weapons, firing in patterns up and down their flight paths.

Next, the leader's wingman went in and delivered his payload right behind the first F4. Once again, we observed large explosions on the ground before he pulled out of his run. They were really lighting up the target area with some heavy explosives. Shortly thereafter, they came around again and made a second bombing run. Once again, the trail of hostile fire followed them as they gained altitude, which may have influenced their decision to make further attacks.

Their next request to us was one that we could not support. They asked that we go back in and deploy flares once again.

"Negative flares onboard," I replied.

Even as I said that, I knew what it meant. I knew we would have to go back and "mark" the targets again but in a different way. It would not be easy.

After this transmission, AC turned our ship around once again and started heading back into the area of the firefight. There was smoke still hanging in the air from the bomb blasts, as well as some haze from the fires now burning below from those same explosions.

We opened up with our 50-cal guns yet again, while also receiving the same heavy fire from below. We tried to continue with our own barrage, but we knew we'd already taken a lot of hits.

"Super Slick, we've got a good fix on the target," the spotter called. "Break off, fly west."

Following this call, we heard the spotter contact his Headquarters and again request another pair of F4s for a second air strike. However, sometime during this second strike, one of the jets took a hit from a 51-cal round. In a calm voice, we heard the pilot say that he'd taken a hit and would need to break off to return to base.

"Oh, great," I thought to myself. "We've been out here for almost two hours and had taken multiple hits *and from the same guns*. So why are we still up here, risking our necks, when we should be returning to our own base for repairs?"

As I mused over these thoughts, I turned a cautious eye toward the master caution panel to see if anything was flashing. Thankfully, there were no indicator lights that signaled any component damage. As "holey" as we were, it appeared as though nothing major had been hit that might take us down.

I looked at my watch and saw that we were closing in on 0400, which meant that we were nearing the end of our two-hour shift. Our sister ship, Tiger Surprise, would be relieving us soon and would take over until dawn.

I remember the relative calm of flying back to the base at Soc Trang and thinking, "Now that was a firefight." I had been in contact with the enemy on numerous skirmishes throughout the year, but this one stood out above the rest. Not only was it the most fierce and intense, but it was also my very last one. I felt lucky because it could also have been the one that took us down.

Fate must have been looking after us once again.

As we approached the base, the Aircraft Controller asked if we should land at the revetment. I told him no, we'd fly it up toward the hangar, as we had repairs we'd need to make. Based on the number of hits that I knew we had taken, we'd require the services of our sheet metal department (and the repairs/patch guy) for some time.

We made quite a scene as we touched down next to the hangar that morning. It was not quite light out yet, but those men who were out already approached our ship with wide eyes and looks of disbelief. We had more than our share of holes in the ship, including hits in the main rotor blade and the hydraulic reservoir. There was also a hit about a foot over the position where Schap's head would have been while firing his 50-cal, indicating that he, too, had a close brush with death. Several additional holes perforated the tail boom, thus rounding out the damage.

I still have photographs of the holes in our ship, which were not pretty. It was obvious that these were from the muzzles of 51-cal guns, not the much smaller caliber AK-47s. We were indeed lucky to survive intact, both our ship and crew, and to return safely to Soc Trang.

It was almost dawn by the time I was heading into the showers. In the distance, I could still hear the explosions of our bombs dropping on the enemy targets. It was time for me to sleep, even though the war never takes a time out.

**For their heroic actions on the night of September 11, 1970, Spec 5 Thomas Feigel and Spec 4 David Schap were among five members of the 336th Aviation Company to receive the Army Commendation Medal for Heroism, with the "V" Device for Valor.**

# 23

# TRANSFER TO THE CAVALRY

War has a funny way of changing people, each in their own way. I certainly never expected to find myself calling this place home. But somehow, over the course of the past year, Soc Trang had become a part of me. I had made and lost friends here, spilled my own blood on the soil, and done things that I never would have guessed possible as a twenty-year-old aviator. After going through so much at a place like this, I almost felt as though my own DNA had become part of the base and that I simply belonged here.

That's why it was so much of a shock to me when, on the morning after the September 11 firefight, I received the news. It was carried by our Company Clerk, who awakened me in my barracks.

"Hey, Feigel, you have orders in for a transfer."

I was barely awake and unable to comprehend the magnitude of the news.

"I have *what?*" I replied in surprise, wiping the sleep from my eyes. We had been flying our mission until dawn, and I wasn't used to being aroused at such an early hour.

"You have orders for a transfer. You're going to the 7th Squadron of the 1st Cavalry Regiment in Vinh Long."

He then casually dropped a copy of the transfer order on my bunk and disappeared out the door.

In my drowsy, half-asleep state of mind, I gazed at the orders through eyes that were still fogged over with sleepiness. I found myself thinking that there must have been some kind of administrative error in the order-writing system. After all, I only had a little more than a month left in-country. So why would they transfer me now? It just didn't make any sense.

I lowered myself out of my bunk and started getting dressed. As I did so, I overheard others discussing the same topic across the barracks rooms. Others were being transferred at the same time as me, so perhaps they were flying out everyone at the same time.

As I pondered these questions, I thought about the future of our base and our company. All of us realized that Soc Trang was to be transferred to the South Vietnamese Army in November, so perhaps they were relocating our entire battalion in advance of the handover. But that didn't make sense either, as not everyone had orders like me.

Once dressed, I walked down to the 336th Aviation Company Head-quarters building and confronted some of the admin clerks.

"Why the transfers?" I asked, my furrowed forehead and eyebrows emphasizing my confusion. "I only have a few weeks left. Let me finish my time here."

"Hey, orders are orders," they replied back. "We don't write the things. We just pass them out, OK?"

This obviously wasn't getting me anywhere.

"Well, when will this transfer take place?" I continued, looking for details on where I should be to catch the flight or ride.

"Tomorrow morning. Make sure you've got all your stuff together and assemble with the rest of the men being transferred. Be in the hangar at 1300."

"What about my ship?" I asked, still incredulous about the swiftness of the change.

"Someone else will crew your ship. Just be there on time with your stuff and your orders."

Vinh Long was a large base located not too far away. It was situated ninety-three miles to the north, although the road leading there was very primitive and seldom used. We instead covered that distance by air, which was much quicker and safer. The base had been home to the 7th Squadron since their arrival in 1968. They supported the same ARVN 21st Infantry as we had in Soc Trang, and they flew many of the same missions as our 2nd Platoon. I had known others who transferred to or from this location in the past year, but I was surprised to be now heading in the same direction.

I slowly walked out of the 336th Aviation Company Headquarters building and trailed back down the road in a dejected mood. I was in dis-belief that this had been done to me. I had worked, sweated, cheered, and cried at this base. Now all I wanted was to finish up my time here. I wanted to go back up and complete my final mission on Super Slick, to savor every minute and cherish the experience of each moment for one final time. I felt very cheated at the thought of being ripped away and sent elsewhere for my final month of duty.

Sorry, Mother. That's just the way I felt.

As I followed the road toward my barracks, every step felt bittersweet. I was having a very difficult time coming to grips with the fact that I'd be leaving the very next day and never coming back. All the friends I'd made, some of whom I'd since lost, would become nothing more than memories. But still, I was leaving for good. I should have been jumping for joy and shouting at the top of my lungs. I just couldn't bring myself to do that or to celebrate in any way.

Once inside my bunkroom, I opened my locker doors and prepared to start removing my clothes for packing. For some reason, I just had to stop and sit down to reflect. The barracks were very quiet, as it was a time of day when everyone was out working. In the solitude of the moment, I thought back over the past year and all that had happened. It was a bit like what I'd experienced back at Fort Eustis, except I was on the other side of my tour.

Visions flashed through my mind like photographs in the prism of a kaleidoscope: all those days, all those nights, the missions, my ship, and my crew. Passing through the viewer were the faces of my friends I'd lost on Lucky Strike, as well as all the others: my fellow hangar rats, the SEALs on Seafloat, and even Sergeant Barney Fife. I finally had to shake my head to rid my mind of these images and get remotivated for the task at hand.

Packing to leave Soc Trang, my home for the past twelve months.

I pulled out the contents of my locker and stacked up my pile of clean, folded combat fatigues. I noticed how faded they appeared, such a contrast to the bright green shade they'd been when I arrived. I was one of the newbies back then and had been every bit as green as my uniforms.

No longer.

My fatigues were now old and faded. I suppose parts of me were old and faded as well. Serving in a combat role in a combat zone will do that to you.

As I sat there, oblivious to my surroundings, my thoughts were interrupted by a familiar voice. It was my mamasan, who was standing by, watching me. It was the same woman who had greeted me a year ago by asking, "You want wash?" Since that time she had taken care of my personal requirements, including cleaning up my bunk area, doing my wash, and all the other little things that family members normally do for one another. She had become like family to me, and I knew I would miss her.

I'm not really sure how she knew that I was transferring away, but she definitely knew. I also knew it was going to be hard to say goodbye, but it had to be done.

"You leave tomorrow?" she asked in her stilted Vietnamese accent. As she spoke, her eyes welled up with tears.

"Yes," I replied. "You make sure that you take care of your children, and be good. Everything will work out for you."

She took my hand and placed it in her open palm, then put her other hand on top of it.

"You good man," she cried, her voice cracking with emotion.

I felt very badly about this exchange, as I knew that my own war was coming to an end, but her future would be cloudy for years to come. A widow, she was raising two children by herself since her husband was killed in action during the war. Life was going to be tough, although there was little or nothing that I could do to help. I always wondered about her fate. What would happen to her once the base was transferred from the US to the South Vietnamese? After that, things would become much more tenuous once the country fell to the Communist North Vietnamese.

I never heard from her after that day.

She went on her way while I continued packing. As I stuffed my personal belongings into my duffel bag, which had lain unused since my arrival at Soc Trang, other friends stopped by to say goodbye. Many people were not being transferred and would be remaining on base. Once again, the exchanges were bittersweet. There were lots of hugs and quite a few tears. We told each other, "Good luck, and take care," all the while knowing that we would never see each other again.

One of my friends who stopped by for a final visit was our company machinist, who had helped us on innumerous occasions on Super Slick with working fabrication on our Nighthawk system. He also flew with us from time to time as a door gunner, and we'd become close friends over the months. He presented me with a short-timer's stick, which is something given to an individual who is approaching the end of their tour.[15] This stick was very special. It was about sixteen inches long and was made out of turned aluminum, which he had polished to a mirror-like finish. Engraved on its side were the following words: "Sp/5 Thomas Feigel. Vietnam 69/70

---

15. A short-timer's stick, which can also take the form of a chain or other device, is a tradition that is seen across almost all of the US military forces. In the US Navy, the short-timer's chain is one composed of the small metal balls on which the member's dog tags are hung. The tradition is to cut one ball off the chain until it is completely gone, which takes place on the day the sailor departs at the end of his or her tour.

Night Hawk." I still have that stick today as a memory of our friendship and my year-long tour of duty at Soc Trang.

The following morning, I left my barracks for the last time. With my duffel bag over my shoulder and my square box fan in hand, I proceeded over to the hangar. I set my bag with all the others to be transferred, then sat down with all the other guys who were heading to the same place. It was a pretty good-sized group.

We stayed there for about an hour as we awaited further word. I think most of the guys were pretty happy about getting out of there, although no one was saying too much. I think most of them were experiencing the same reflective mood as me: coming to the end of a very tough year and finally heading home.

The next announcement informed us that our transport was on its way and asked us all to proceed to the pickup area. So we all hoisted our duffel bags once again and commenced our next shuffling movement in the direction of the flight line. There were about forty of us, so it was quite the procession. I had walked this path so many times over the past year, but this time, it felt different. We were leaving for someplace new, but this temporary stopover wouldn't last long. It would eventually lead us home. It seemed impossible.

The walk to the flight line would take me right past my ship, Super Slick, which sat resting in its revetment. It wasn't yet time for the ship to get ready for launch, so it sat quiet and empty, as though waiting for its master and crew to climb onboard and get things started. It felt like the ship was talking to me, saying goodbye, and asking if I wanted to go back up for a final ride. But that was impossible now, so I walked over and rested my hand for a few moments on the copilot's door.

"Goodbye, old friend." It felt very sad.

We then walked past the empty revetment that had been the home of Lucky Strike. It was still empty all these months after the blinding flash that had signaled the end of the ship and those six brave men. It was yet another bittersweet moment in my departure from this place.

Shortly thereafter, we heard the sounds of our transport approaching in the form of a CH-47 Chinook, which would carry us to Vinh Long. It landed, and we all queued up to climb onboard. Just before boarding, I turned around for one more glimpse of Super Slick. I silently said another goodbye before boarding the ship. It would be my last salutation, as I never looked back.

We lifted off from Soc Trang just before dusk. It was the first leg of my journey home.

# 24

# REUNION IN VINH LONG

The flight north to Vinh Long took less than an hour, although the sun had finished setting while we were in the air. All of us passengers climbed off the helo and assembled with our duffel bags on the flight line. The entire entourage had a kind of disheveled appearance, as though we'd been in transit for several days.

There were four of us who were identified as being on flight status, so they singled us out and loaded us into a designated Jeep that was headed in a different direction from the rest of the horde. Our destination was the Operations Office of the 7th Squadron, 1st Cavalry Regiment. Once we arrived there, we met a Sergeant who was holding on to a stack of orders, one of which belonged to me.

"Come on, boys, after I give you your orders, I'll get you to your platoon barracks," he said.

The Sergeant then assigned us to our various flight platoons, which was when I learned that I would be part of the Headhunters. This platoon was a lot like the Warriors back at the 336th, where I had spent the past year. The entire unit was made up of slicks, so I'd be spending my days carrying troops around, doing combat insertions, and other similar missions. In other words, there would be more flying around with a bull's-eye painted on my back. Wonderful. I'd already been shot there, so maybe it wouldn't feel as bad the second time around.

The Sergeant then loaded me, along with my duffel bag and box fan, into a tired-looking Jeep and drove me down the road to the Headhunters' barracks. I know he got a chuckle out of the way I guarded the fan while arranging it into the vehicle, but he understood its value. Box fans were like gold over in Vietnam—not easy to come by and a godsend in the heat and humidity. It was staying with me until I climbed aboard that last flight home.

We pulled up at the Headhunters' barracks, where I climbed out of the Jeep with my gear and entered the bunkhouse. It was early evening, so all the Crew Chiefs and door gunners were inside, and I immediately became the center of attention. It's always an interesting feeling when you walk into a new setting where everyone is busy and then suddenly *everyone* finds a reason to stop doing whatever it was that they were doing. It was awkward, to say the least. In a literary setting, I believe it is called the pregnant pause. Everyone has to stop to see the new guy. Except in this case, the "new guy" was not a newbie. I'm sure I'd had more time in-country than most of the guys there.

Finally, one fellow broke the ice by helpfully pointing out an empty spot in the barracks.

"No one's sleeping in that one," he said, nodding his head in the direction of an empty bunk. "Make yourself comfortable."

I dropped my duffel bag and fan next to the bed and mentally surveyed the place. Most of the guys were performing routine tasks, including cleaning their weapons and other typical flight platoon barracks activities.

I sat down on the bunk for a moment, but I then started thinking about empty bunks and how this particular one came to be empty. Some of these were the same thoughts I'd had looking at Dan Proctor's bunk back in Soc Trang, the night after Lucky Strike went down. Who had slept in this one until a month, a week, or even a day earlier? Worse yet, how many of the men around the room were watching me out of a corner of their eyes, thinking the same thing? "My best friend is dead, and you're sleeping in his bunk. And you don't even know it."

I suddenly had a very bad feeling about the place, and knew I wouldn't be able to stay there another minute. These people were totally new to me; I knew no one here. I didn't know the AO, any of the pilots, the door gunners, the ships, or anything else about the place. There were just too many unknowns for me here, especially since I only had a few weeks left in-country. I just wasn't willing to take any more chances. I had spit in fate's eye too many times already, and my next time might be my last.

Without saying another word, I grabbed my duffel and fan and walked out of the place. I'm sure there were those in the room who were stunned at my departure, but I really didn't care. They hadn't been through what I'd already experienced. I had nothing to prove here. It was really *they* who were the newbies.

Gear in hand, I walked back down to the Operations Office and opened the door. The same Sergeant was still inside, and he pivoted in his chair to see me. I'm sure he also noticed that I was carrying all my original possessions.

"Hey, is anything wrong?" he asked, staring over his desk.

He actually seemed like a nice guy, someone I could talk to without being derided or ridiculed. I just hoped he'd understand my request.

"Sarge, I've been flying for the 336th for a straight year now," I began. "I only have a week or two left in-country before I fly home to my family. My flying days are over."

The Sergeant just looked back at me, nodding his head in agreement. He had an understanding look in his eyes, and I suddenly knew he was going to help me stay out of harm's way.

"I understand. I'll put you in the hangar until you leave."

"Thanks, Sarge," I said, relieved that I wouldn't be going up in another ship. I suddenly had a much better understanding of how Ron Knight had felt when I first arrived for duty at Soc Trang. Luck only lasts as long as fate allows it to do so.

"Come with me," the Sergeant said as he directed me once again to the Jeep. "I'll drive you down to the Headquarter platoon barracks."

We hopped back in the vehicle for another ride, this time to the barracks of the office workers and clerks. The building was very similar to the Headhunters' bunkhouse, but the attitude and disposition of the men inside was very different. There were no guns in the room, and the guys were all involved in quiet activities like writing letters or reading books.

The Sergeant, who was still with me this time, pointed to an empty bunk.

"Here, this one looks empty. Go ahead and move yourself in."

I gratefully accepted the offer and thanked the Sergeant for his help. He then left to return to his office, leaving me to meet my new barracks mates.

Once again, as I unpacked my gear and arranged my personal items into my locker, I could feel the eyes of the other men on my back. But I also knew that these men could see my two-piece flight suit, which still carried the 336th patch for all to see. They could also see the faded colors of my fatigues, denoting the fact that I was *not* a newbie. I had been around and had the uniform to prove it. They could also tell that I had been on a flight crew, which meant that I had already seen significant combat. That meant a lot, especially to guys who spent their days working in an office on a typewriter. I had instant status with this gang.

A couple of guys came over to introduce themselves, which broke the ice with the rest of the men. They were all pretty friendly and wanted to know more about who I was and where I'd been. I could tell both by their questions as well as by the dark-green shade of their uniforms that they hadn't been in Vietnam for long.

"Where are you coming from?"

"How long have you been here?"

"Is this your first tour?"

The questions came fast and furious, but it was great to know that I was being recognized as someone who had been around rather than as the newbie.

When I told them that I was transferring in from the 336th Assault Helicopter Company down in Soc Trang, they looked totally confused. I might as well have been speaking in Latin, as they had no clue where Soc Trang was located. This platoon was comprised entirely of noncombatants, including clerks, supply specialists, and other administrative types. I doubt that any of them had actually fired a weapon since their boot camp training.

Our conversation continued on with questions about my duties as a Crew Chief and the close calls I'd had in the air. When asked about how long I'd been in-country, my reply of eleven months really got their attention. Most of these guys looked as though they had just stepped off the plane.

Instant respect. It felt good.

We soon ended our question-and-answer session by me telling them that I'd be flying home soon and would be working in the hangar for the next couple weeks until I got my flight. I then asked them where the showers were located (I badly needed one), took my shower, and was off to bed.

The following morning was the first day of my new assignment, and I wanted to get off on the right foot. I had to report to the armory to pick up my M16. That was no problem; my M16 and I had become very close friends over the past year, and I was comfortable with any version they wanted to hand me. The M16A1 had replaced the M14 in 1969, and I had used them in countless nighttime missions at Soc Trang. I could handle it with my eyes closed.

I walked into the armory building and addressed the clerk.

"I'm here to pick up my M16," I explained. "I had to turn in my last one when I left the 336th in Soc Trang yesterday."

The clerk retrieved one of the weapons and placed it on a counter along with a card.

"Here you go," he said, handing me a pen. "Fill out the card with all your personal information, but leave the bottom open. I'll fill out the serial number after you're finished."

I completed the card as he requested and handed it back to him. He then recorded the serial number of the weapon on the appropriate blank on the form, and then he started walking away with the card. And the weapon. He calmly placed the piece back in the rack as though he had just shown it to a customer in a gun store.

"*Wait!* What's the deal?" I asked. "Don't I get to keep the M16?"

"Nope. That's not how we do things here," he replied patiently. "Not unless you're a member of a flight platoon. Otherwise, all weapons remain here."

"But what happens if there's an emergency?" I asked. "Like if the base gets attacked and we have to defend ourselves?"

"If there's an emergency, you will come here, and we will issue you your M16, along with a clip to put in it."

"Great!" I thought (but didn't say). "So in the middle of an attack, they want me to run through the enemy fire to the armory, check out a weapon with a *single* clip, then counter the attack? What's up with that?"

"This base has had some racial issues in the past," he explained. "So our standard procedure is to keep all weapons locked up here and only issue them when needed."

This all seemed so unreal. Back at Soc Trang, which was a much smaller base, we'd had weapons of all kinds laying around all over the place. The M79 grenade launcher I'd carried wasn't even registered to me. I wished I'd brought it with me to Vinh Long.

I spent the first part of the day in administrative hell, filling out all kinds of forms and other paperwork, which I'm sure was needed by someone somewhere—but certainly not by me. Finally, around midmorning, I was driven out to the hangar to start my work. The ride was necessary, as it was a very big base. Back in Soc Trang, you could step outside your barracks and be at your destination in a few minutes. Here it would have been a very long walk, so I accepted the ride.

Upon arriving at the hangar, I stepped inside and was greeted by a Sergeant, who walked me over to one of the helo crews. They were organized the same as the crews back at Soc Trang: five men per team working under a team leader.

"You'll be working on Ron's team," said the Sergeant as he walked me over to the team leader, who was talking with another member of his group. "Ron is the team leader, and this is a great group of specialists who can do almost anything. You'll enjoy being here."

Ron, the team leader, quickly ended his previous conversation and turned toward us. The Sergeant quickly introduced us, then walked off to let us get acquainted. I noticed Ron's eyes as he glanced at my rank insignia sewn onto my fatigues. He was a spec 4, while I was a spec 5. I also saw his head drop in disappointment as he realized that he was now outranked on his own team.

"Well, I guess you're the team leader now," he said dejectedly, as he was already thinking of stepping aside for someone who outranked him. I didn't want to let that happen and quickly interrupted him to dispel that notion.

"No, Ron, absolutely not," I replied. "You're the team leader, and we're all part of the same team. You just let me know what you want done, and I'm all on it."

"Wow, really?" he asked, his eyes brightening noticeably.

"Sure, really," I replied. "I got my start in a hangar, so it's kind of fitting that I'm ending up in the same job. I'm ready to go to work, so you just tell me what you need me to do."

Ron's head instantly came up and his shoulders went back as he realized that he would still be in charge of his team. He was a good guy who appeared to have the respect of his team. I only wanted to help out as much as I could for my few remaining weeks in-country.

"Well, to start off, we're having a few issues with the hub assembly on this tail rotor," he said, looking up at the rear section of a Huey. "Maybe you could start out by jumping on that and helping the guys to get that wrapped up and inspected."

That's the way it went with us over the next few weeks. Ron never once pushed me. It was always "Hey, could you help us with this?" At this point, rank mattered very little to me. We worked together really well, and our time together was great. I also found interesting, both then as well as today, the kind of relationship I had with the rest of the guys on the team. Because of the fact that I was a spec 5 and that I had been in-country for almost a full year, I was considered the "old man"—this, in spite of the fact that I was still just a twenty-year-old kid. I often thought about how my father would have viewed this paradigm. Then again, in Vietnam, a great many things were upside down and backward.

Despite the fact that I was often blind to rank devices, there were times when I had to exercise care to avoid offending a senior officer. There was one occasion when I was walking down a road on base with another

Crew Chief, and we walked past a Major who was headed in the opposite direction. We didn't think anything of it until we heard him call us back.

"Hey, you two!" he barked.

We instantly came to a halt and turned around.

"Yes, Sir," we both replied in unison as we awaited his word, whatever it might be.

"Where are your hats?" he asked in a commanding voice.

"I'm sorry, Sir, we don't have them with us right now," I replied. "But we'll get them right away."

"And when you address an officer, you are supposed to salute."

"I'm sorry, Sir, but where we came from, we weren't supposed to salute," I explained. "We were always told that a salute let the enemy see who were the officers, so they'd know whom to shoot first if they were sniping on us."

The Major looked confused, but he probably thought we might be right on this matter, so he decided not to pursue it any further.

"OK, carry on. But make sure you get your hats on. It is part of the uniform!"

As we walked away, I found myself thinking, "This sure isn't Soc Trang." I never could have imagined Major Kilpatrick making such a fuss over something so trivial. Meanwhile, my Crew Chief accomplice mused out loud, "Where the hell are we going to find hats around here?"

On my second day in Vinh Long, as I was walking toward the hangar (probably without wearing a hat), a truck approached from the other direction. I idly glanced into the back of the vehicle, where I saw a familiar form seated. It was John! John Foley, my good friend whom I'd met back in basic training and with whom I'd traveled across to Vietnam. I could scarcely believe my eyes.

"John!" I called out at the top of my lungs while waving my arms in the air, hoping to attract his attention inside the truck. I succeeded in doing so, and he quickly asked the driver to pull over to the side of the road. He then jumped out and ran over to me, where we traded bear hugs.

It had been almost a full year since we'd parted ways back on that field in Long Bin. A lot had happened since that time, and even more *could* have happened. I had often wondered where he had been stationed and whether or not he had survived his tour. I was overjoyed to run into him like this.

"Hey, how the heck have you been?" we both asked each other. "We've got to find some time to get together and get caught up."

It turned out that John was not only located on the same base but worked in the same area as me. However, he was assigned to a team that worked the night shifts, so I hadn't run into him on my first day. Regardless, it felt great to discover that I had an old friend working in the same place as me and that our tours had been running parallel to each other even when I was down in Soc Trang.

John had also been functioning as a ship's Crew Chief, although their positions were much different than our own. John was assigned to a Cobra gunship, which had only two flight positions, both of which were manned with officers. The ship had no Crew Chief or door gunners who went up with them; the two officers did everything as a two-man show. So John did everything that was required on a Cobra—but only after the ship returned at night. His day began as most of us were hitting our bunks, and it ended when we were getting up in the morning. It was a "bass-ackwards" existence made necessary by the operational schedule of the ship.

Regardless of John's schedule, we made certain to arrange time to meet up, which we did the very next day.

"You're not going to believe this, but a couple more guys from our class are here too," John said, referring to our Helo Repair Course back at Fort Eustis. "Why don't we all get together at the service club tonight?"

Everything about that day was great: running into John after the year-long interlude, seeing some of the other guys I remembered from Eustis, and just getting out and enjoying myself for a change. It had been a very long time. (There really was no club like this back in Soc Trang either.) There were four of us: John and me, along with two others from our class back in the States. They all wanted to know where I'd been stationed, as well as all the details from the past year. There were drinks all around, and a general party atmosphere prevailed.

After that day, John and I managed to meet up at the club for dinner every night, which was a great change from the old mess hall. Even the food was better. But the base at Vinh Long was a lot different than Soc Trang, along with the attitudes of the men stationed there. They seemed to take some things a lot more seriously than we did at a smaller station.

I remember one night when we were in our bunks, a loud siren suddenly came blaring out of nowhere. Apparently, we had come under a mortar attack, and the guys in the barracks were going nuts.

"Incoming! Incoming!" they screamed. "Quick, everyone get to the bunker!"

Our men were running right, left, and every which way, but eventually, they made it out the door and to their assigned bunker. I was finally left alone in the darkness, thinking to myself, "I haven't heard any mortars." If only they knew how many real mortar attacks I'd been through, they might have understood my complacent reaction to the perceived bombardment.

Ho hum.

I did eventually make it out the door myself, thinking that I would follow them to the shelter. After all, I had no idea whether there really would be an attack or how bad it would be if one did start. But there wouldn't be any running. I just wasn't that worried. I calmly walked over to the bunker and let myself in before finding a comfortable place to take shelter through the attack.

The people here reacted so differently to attacks than my friends back at Soc Trang had. I never worried too much about these attacks, as most of them consisted of a few mortar rounds before they ceased firing and disappeared back into the woods. But I also remember one fellow back at the 336th who displayed even less fear than I had. He would often awaken in time to observe the men scurrying about and funneling out of the barracks, after which he yawned, rolled over, and went back to sleep. I wasn't going to be quite that smug. After all, I was due to go home soon, and I wanted to do so with all of my parts still connected.

My first week or so at Vinh Long went by without incident. I liked the guys on my hangar crew and had fun getting together with John and our buddies every night. Life was going along just great as I awaited my final orders, which should have been coming in about a month. Then, out of the blue, a surprise showed up in the form of a Sergeant from Headquarters, who drove up in a Jeep one morning while I was at the hangar. I had been at Vinh Long for about a week and a half, and I'd become accustomed to the new routine.

The Sergeant strode into the hangar without any fanfare, papers, or clipboard. He walked over to the area where I was working and found me returning some tools to the tool box.

"Hey, Feigel, I've got your orders for home," he said, probably waiting for me to celebrate.

Instead of breaking out in song, I had an alarm go off in my head, and I found myself saying, "What? How could this be possible?"

As good as it might sound, it was actually quite the opposite, as the timing would not work out for me. My total enlistment was for twenty-four months, with twelve of those months carried out in-country. That was the deal: You had twelve months to spend in Vietnam before you were sent home. The problem was that there was a "bonus" involved in the timing of your return to the US. If you arrived home with less than six months left on your enlistment, they discharged you immediately. With more than six months left, you had to serve out your full time. I had already extended in Vietnam for an extra month, so I'd have only five months left when I flew home. This early departure would spoil everything.

"No, Sergeant," I argued. "You've got something wrong here, or the orders were issued accidentally. I extended for an extra month so this wouldn't happen."

"No, and I'm sorry, but we've got your orders in the office," he replied.

"Someone definitely missed something here," I said, still full of disbelief.

The Sergeant clearly didn't feel like arguing with me. He shrugged his shoulders, gave a noncommittal nod of his head, and disappeared outside. I thought that was the end of it, so I went back to work, although certainly grumpier than before. I had planned this whole thing so that I'd be a civilian soon after returning home.

Or maybe not.

Within fifteen minutes of the Sergeant's retreat, the Jeep returned, but this time, it was driven by the Company Executive Officer (XO). The XO was a Captain and also a really good guy whom we all liked. He called me over to the vehicle to talk, so I was certain it was about the orders once again.

"Feigel, I'm not sure you understood what the Sergeant was telling you," he started, "but you're going home. We have your orders to put you on a plane and fly you back to the States."

"Oh no, here we go again," I thought. I didn't know how many times I'd have to explain this.

"Thank you, Sir. But as I tried explaining to Sarge, I extended for a month so that I could get discharged as soon as I flew back home. I've *got* to stay here another month."

"No, you don't," he countered. "Nixon approved a change that did away with the six-month requirement. It's all got to do with the troop strength reduction over here. We just don't need as many people. So if you're a draftee, and you served your full twelve-month tour over here, you're discharged as soon as you get home."

As he explained the new process, a smile appeared on my face that kept widening until it reached from ear to ear. I think someone could have slid a good-sized dinner plate into my mouth with room to spare.

Without waiting another second, I jumped into the Jeep in a single bound. I hadn't even stopped to talk to the guys on my crew, although they had overheard my conversation with the Sergeant, so I'm pretty sure they knew what was happening. I would be going home within a matter of days.

The ride to Headquarters was amazing, as I leaned back in the seat, the air flowing through my hair, reveling in a sense of freedom that I hadn't experienced in over a year. I wondered whether this is what prisoners felt when they were unexpectedly paroled from their cells. It was a feeling that was wonderful yet impossible to describe.

We arrived at the Headquarters building and walked inside. The Captain led me over to a clerk's desk and flipped through a stack of papers on a clipboard. Finding what he wanted, he removed a few pages and handed them to me.

Yup, there they were: orders for Spec 5 Thomas M. Feigel, United States Army, to commence the transit to a discharge center in Oakland, CA. I could hardly believe my eyes. I was most certainly going home.

As close as I was to returning home, one additional piece of tragic news arrived about two days before my leaving Vinh Long. We were out at the base club that night when I ran into another member of our 336th Assault Helicopter Company. He told me about an accident back at Soc Trang involving the crash of a night ship that, he thought, was my beloved Super Slick. It left me with a heavy heart, although I was later to learn, many years later, that it was a different ship that had gone down on that nighttime patrol. Errors such as these can be attributed to the confusion and mayhem of battle, commonly known as the fog of war.

The accident had taken place on the night of October 27, 1970. Many of the men with whom I'd served were involved in the heroic rescue attempts. The ship was Warrior 16, which was flown by 1st Platoon Leader, 1st Lt. Jack Bagley. They had been out on nighttime patrol and had seen something that had interested them in the trees about one mile from base. They had descended to a perilously low altitude in an attempt to identify and potentially engage the threat when the rotor struck a tree. The ship immediately plummeted thirty to forty feet through the branches and vegetation and crashed into the ground below.

The tower observed the crash and resulting fire and immediately scrambled at least one ship to attempt to rescue any survivors.[16] The first ship to get off the ground was Super Slick, Warrior 21. It lifted off shortly after 0200 and was able to immediately spot the fire. The downed ship, Warrior 16, had crashed about a mile outside the base. It appeared to be completely engulfed in flames.

Warrior 21 was able to set down about a quarter mile away from the burning ship. From there, Spec 4 Tom Wilkes led two others through the pitch-black forest to the site of the crash. They found that two of the four-man crew had somehow managed to escape the ship, including the copilot and the door gunner. However, the pilot (1st Platoon Leader, 1st Lt. Jack Bagley), and the Crew Chief, Spec 4 Alex Pysz, had been killed in the crash.

The rest of the night was an extremely intense rush of activity and flights, involving heroic actions all around. Piloting the various airships were 1st Lt. Franklin, Mr. Brown, and Mr. Barrett, plus additional pilots on the medevac ship that took the two survivors to the hospital in Binh Thuy. The personnel who had the gruesome task of removing the charred corpses from the burned-out ship have described the nightmares they'd suffered for many years after the incident. To make matters worse, they had to perform these grisly duties while protecting themselves from possible attack from nearby VC troops, who could see the burning hulk of Warrior 16 for miles around. Events such as these have been a major cause of the onset of post-traumatic stress syndrome (PTSD) in so many of our finest servicemen.

Learning about the circumstances behind the loss of another Warrior ship at Soc Trang certainly removed some of the happiness of my final week in-country. More friends lost, more weeping families back home, and more children who would grow up without getting to know their fathers. It was a never-ending tragedy that affected so many people, none of whom would ever know how or why.[17]

It also hammered home the point about fate; some people made it, while others didn't. It often didn't matter who was flying the aircraft or manning the guns. Sometimes, it just seemed like it was fate's call.

---

16. There are several accounts of the rescue flights and the individuals on those ships. However, these accounts differ from one another, which is to be expected since these memories are of one night a half a century ago. This section is a best attempt to correlate the various versions of this event with one another.

17. Flying at night was an inherently dangerous activity. Our sister company at Soc Trang, the 121st Attack Helo Company, lost one of their nighttime base perimeter ships as well. Around 0130 on the night of April 2, 1970, the lightship (call sign Tiger Surprise) was hit by a rocket about five miles from base. The two pilots, who were both badly burned, survived, but the entire crew (crew chief and two door gunners) died as a result of the blast.

Before departing on my transit home, I had to successfully "clear the base." While this sounded like something from a TV game show, it was actually just a series of stops at different locations around the base to collect signatures that showed you didn't owe anyone money or other base-owned items. These venues included the service club, the library (for checked-out books), the exchange, and other places where people spent money or borrowed things. I knew this would be quick for me, as I had only been in Vinh Long for two weeks.

I asked the Captain how long it took to clear base.

"Oh, probably a couple hours, depending on what you've done while you were here."

"To the best of my knowledge, I don't have anything to clear," I declared while shrugging my shoulders. "I haven't been here long enough to spend any money."

The Captain laughed at that and tossed me a set of keys.

"Here, take the Jeep," he said. "But put a hat on!" Sooner or later, I was going to remember to do that.

I took off in the Jeep, determined to clear the base in record time. That was before I realized that the first stop on my clear-the-base checklist was the recruiters' office. Oh, no, this was going to be good. I thought back to my first encounter with a recruiter back home, and it wasn't good. So what did they have here? A chair with iron manacles on it to shackle you down until you signed on the dotted line? Maybe a few wires inside the chair that were hooked up to a row of batteries that would deliver high voltage as encouragement? I could hardly wait to see.

Once inside the office, I was asked to sit in a chair across from the recruiter. But unlike my premonitions, I was not strapped in, and there were no batteries in sight.

The recruiter was a skilled negotiator, and he was armed with a boatload of incentives and bonuses. He presented the whole package as smoothly as a well-trained car salesman.

"Well, Feigel, you've done very well for yourself here, and you've done the Army proud. And now, we're ready to pay you back for all you've accomplished. We're willing to write you out a check for $10,000 if you extend for three more years."

*Ten thousand dollars!* That was a lot of money back in 1970, especially considering that a brand-new Pontiac GTO cost around $4,500–$5,000.

In today's dollars, that ten grand would be worth about $70,000. That's a *lot* of money.

As great as having all that cash in my pocket seemed, I had steeled myself for this bribery well before walking into the recruiters' office. I thought about all the risks here in Vietnam and also about my good job waiting for me back at Xerox. The decision quickly became a no-brainer.

"No thanks, Sarge, I'm just going to get out," I replied quickly, hoping to show my resolve in the matter.

"If you extend, there's also a really good chance that they'll give you a bump up to E-6, which means even better pay, better quarters, and all the benefits that come with it."

"No thanks," I repeated.

"And just for extending, we'll send you home for three extra weeks' leave, and we'll still keep paying your salary, and you'll still get all your regular leave for the entire year."

"No."

"And think of all the great educational benefits and the GI Bill and everything else that's part of your normal benefits package."

"*No!*" I found myself adding a little bit of emphasis and volume onto each successive "No" just to get my point across.

The recruiter finally realized that I was a lost cause. He scribbled his signature across his line on the checkout list and slid it across the table to me.

"Good luck, Feigel. I hope you find whatever it is you're looking for on the outside."

I would have said thank you, but his phone rang, and suddenly, I wasn't of interest to him in the least.

I took the Jeep and completed the list of designated stops, obtaining the required signatures at each. It didn't take me long, as I had never used most of the facilities on the list. Perhaps the most comical stop was at the armory, where I had to sign back in the weapon that I never had held in the first place. That was fun.

I was back to the Headquarters in near-record time to turn in my forms and finish the administrative sign-outs. I also took a minute to carefully read my orders, which provided the details of my upcoming journey across the ocean. It started with a flight to the processing center in Long Binh, which would be in just two days. That was fantastic; I could take anything for two days. It was time to start packing.

I walked back to my barracks, only to find them empty. It was midday, and everyone was either working or at the mess hall. I sat down on my bunk, just for a minute or two, and lost myself in thought. What a long, strange trip it had been.

Later on that night, I met up with John and a few of the others over at the club. We were going to have supper and enjoy the evening together, but deep inside, I was hiding a secret. As we all sat down and ordered our meals, I was practically bursting inside with excitement, which I couldn't keep concealed for long.

"Hey guys, guess what!" I started, once the waitress had left our table. "I have my orders, and I start for home in two days!"

The reaction I received was not what I'd expected. John, as well as our other two classmates, looked ready to burst into laughter.

"Me too," said John, pulling a folded paper out of his shirt pocket. "Same day and probably the same flight."

"Me too," echoed the other two men, both smiling and lifting identical papers from their pockets.

"You've got to be kidding me!" I exclaimed. "We all flew over here on the same flight, and now we're all going back on the same flight? That seems impossible!"

"Impossible but true," said John, his face alight. "What are the odds of that happening?"

It had to be fate.

## 25

# THE LONG TRIP HOME

The next two days seemed to go by in slow motion. Each moment, I expected someone to awaken me from a dream and tell me that I still had another year remaining in-country. Going home seemed like such a surreal idea, like a dream that would never come true. I found myself looking at my orders at least once an hour to convince myself that they were real and that I really was getting out of there within the next forty-eight hours.

The morning of the flight finally arrived, although I'm not certain whether I got much sleep that night. It was a very early departure, but I had packed the night before and had everything together long before my ride to the flight line. Upon my arrival out there, I found all the others who would be making the same trip. We all boarded a C130 transport, carting our duffel bags and other personal effects. One thing I didn't have with me was my box fan. It had been a prized possession while in Vietnam, but I no longer needed it when I stepped onto that aircraft. No place in the United States was as hot and humid as Southeast Asia, and it would be October when I got back to New York. I therefore decided to gift it to one of the newbies in the Headquarters barracks.

The first leg of the flight took us from Vinh Long to Long Binh, which was very short (about one hundred miles). Upon arrival, we filed off the plane with our duffels and were bused to the processing center, where we joined up with all the others going through the same process. From there it was on to the reception center, which was strikingly similar to the others I'd visited earlier that year. There were a lot of empty bunks, but many were without mattresses. Pillows, as usual, were almost nonexistent, so we improvised by using uniforms stuffed with other assorted pieces of clothing. At least it would only be for a couple more days.

As we were getting our things sorted out, a Sergeant walked in and addressed us in a loud voice.

"There will be formations every day at 0800 and 1800 hours," he announced. "At these formations, we will read off a list of names and flight numbers. If your name is called, you will write down your flight number and departure time. A bus will transport you to the airport. You *will* make sure to be on that bus."

His demand wasn't necessary and even sounded a bit comical to us at the time. Who among us wanted to spend a minute longer than required in this country? Each one of us would be on our respective plane with time to spare.

Before we did anything else, we were handed more forms and paperwork to fill out. Lots of paperwork. We were also going to be sized and fitted for new sets of khaki uniforms, which we were to wear for our final flight home. They must have wanted us to look good, as the new outfits were to have all our name tags, patches, medals, and so forth for our arrival back home.

Following the uniform fitting session, we were herded into a large, open-air building with tall tables arranged across the middle. We were arranged in groups around these tables so that each of us had our own little patch of tabletop, although none of us knew the reason behind this exercise. We waited expectantly for instructions.

Soon a Sergeant entered the space and keyed on a loud PA system to address the group.

"Soldiers, we are going to use this time to collect any forbidden contraband that you have in your possession," he intoned. "If you have any of these items in your possession, now is the time to place them on the table. We will collect them, and you will not be charged. These items include drugs of any kind, weapons or explosives of any kind, war prizes removed from the battlefield of any kind . . ." he continued.

The list was long and extensive. We all looked around the room at one another, waiting to see if anyone disclosed any illegal items.

"If any one of you has any of these items in your possession, you had better place them on the table immediately," he said. "If we search you and find any of these items after leaving this building, they will be confiscated, and you will be charged. They will then be held here until the time of your trial. Do you understand me?"

Yes, we did.

I doubt that anyone had drugs to dispose of, but there was a moderate amount of clattering as various knives of different lengths and descriptions were tossed on the tabletops. I don't know if those counted as weapons, but most people wouldn't have taken the chance and instead decided to play it safe by turning them in to the Sergeant. I thought back for a moment to the AK-47 that the ARVN Infantry soldier had handed to me during the troop extraction at VC Lake. But I had never kept the weapon beyond that night and couldn't even remember to whom I had given it. So personally, I had nothing to declare; I just wanted out.

Per the Sergeant's instructions, we all attended the 0800 formation the next morning. We all stood outside, smartly dressed in our new khaki uniforms, listening to the clerk as he read the list of names and flights.

"Come on, come on," I prayed, hoping that I'd be assigned to one of the first flights home. I didn't want to spend a single unnecessary day here, if possible.

Then I heard it. My name was announced with the flight number F2C3, which would leave the very next day. (Yes, that was the actual flight number. I remember F2C3 as though it were tattooed into my brain.) We were to be bused to the airport the following morning at 0800. To make matters even better, John would be on the same flight, along with two other classmates from our original Fort Eustis course.

To say that we were overjoyed would be a gross understatement. We headed directly to the base club to celebrate our last night in Vietnam and our pending flight home. We ordered drinks all around. Then we had another round of drinks, followed by lots of conversation, then more rounds of drinks. We were so hyped up on going home that no one wanted to sleep.

We ended up closing the club, but we still didn't want to turn in for the night. So we began walking the streets around the base, just talking and laughing and enjoying ourselves. We walked for hour after hour, trading stories about our year in-country and the things we'd seen. We also talked a lot about our future lives at home, including our families and jobs. There was so much to look forward to, and it was just nice to be able to discuss topics not related to our lives in the Army.

We spent the rest of the night lost in conversation and laughter, strolling up and down the same base roads hour after hour. It seemed like no time had gone by at all before morning arrived, with the dawn breaking over the installation and the sun peeking up over the trees. As we approached the mess hall, we saw a light come on through a side window, signaling that someone was starting to work on the morning breakfast. We walked through the door, only to find that the mess wasn't yet open for serving food. But we did meet a crusty old mess Sergeant who was sympathetic with our needs.

"Come on in and sit down, boys," he said with a crooked smile. "I've got some coffee brewing already, so you can help yourselves until breakfast is on."

We sat down and enjoyed the coffee, hoping that the caffeine would recharge our sleep-deprived bodies long enough to get us onto the plane. We stayed there until 0700, when we all headed back to get our duffel bags and other belongings. There was no way we were going to miss that 0800 bus.

The bus arrived right on schedule, and we all loaded onboard with all our gear. We must have looked sharp, all decked out in our new uniforms for the trip home. After a short ride to the airport, we were dropped off at a large hangar that was divided right down the middle with a chain link fence. All of us were directed to one side, where we collected as a group and commenced the wait for our plane.

Meanwhile, outside the hangar building, a plane pulled up that had just landed. We watched as they wheeled up two sets of portable stairs to the front and back of the plane. Within a minute, the front and rear doors opened and newbies began emerging from the aircraft. An endless stream of them started descending from the plane and filing through the wide doors and into the hangar. But there was one critical difference from our assemblage; they were funneled into the area on the other side of the fence.

Two groups: one going to war, the other going home. It felt incredibly good to be on the right side of the fence.

It didn't take long for a roar to go up from our group. It was partly a good-natured cheer and partly a taunt. But it was loud nonetheless.

"Newbies!" shouted a lot of the men on our side of the fence. "I'm going home!" screamed another.

The men on the other side of the fence didn't say much. They just queued up in yet another line, trying to figure out what it was all about. A few of them looked at us, probably wishing that they could trade places. Meanwhile, as I listened to all the yelling and commotion, I decided to remain silent. I could have joined in the ribbing, but I remembered how I'd felt when I arrived. It wasn't a good feeling, and I knew I wouldn't have enjoyed hearing someone jeering at me for being a newbie. I also remember thinking, "How many men in this newly arrived group won't be making the trip home? For how many of these soldiers will this turn out to be a one-way trip?"

It wasn't long before the plane was completely unloaded and the aircraft was serviced for the return flight. It took an amazingly short interval of time, after which they began boarding our group onto the plane. John and I boarded together and were quickly seated. It seemed as though the plane began taxiing out to the runway as soon as we'd gotten our seatbelts fastened.

Everything appeared to be happening in fast-forward, and the pilot was picking up speed even before turning onto the runway. He quickly revved the engines up to full thrust, and then he took us into the steepest climb I'd ever experienced in a commercial airliner. The entire cabin of passengers broke out in a rousing round of applause and cheers as soon as our wheels lifted off from the tarmac.

The pilot, who had remained silent until this point, decided to address us over the announcement system for a good-natured jest.

"Before we head home, I could fly along the coastline for a while so you men can look at the country for a little while longer."

A series of loud boos rang out inside the cabin to express our thoughts on the matter. The plane maintained its original easterly course, and we were soon out over the ocean. A number of the passengers craned their necks to look out the windows as we started our transit away from Vietnam and toward the United States. I made a conscious decision not to do that. I only wanted to look forward to my home. I didn't need to look back; I only wanted to forget about everything from the past year.

The plane soon reached its cruising altitude, and I found something to be quite surprising. Given that we were all now "free" and heading home, I would have expected a festive atmosphere in the plane, with lots of conversation, laughing, and perhaps even a spontaneous round of song. But there was none of that. I suspect that many of the passengers had spent the previous evening doing exactly as John and I had done: stayed awake talking and exorcising our mental demons from our time in-country. Instead of hearing celebratory voices throughout the cabin, I found the reality was the exact opposite: dead silence. All 225 men had crashed and were silently slumbering as we streaked eastward toward home.

After a lengthy flight, many of us were awakened as we heard the plane's engines start to throttle back, causing us to decelerate and lose altitude. The pilot then came on to address us once again.

"Men, we're going to touch down in Okinawa for a brief refueling stop," he informed us. "There will be no disembarking here, as we're going to get airborne again as soon as we're finished refueling."

In no time at all, we were back up, starting our next lengthy leg of the trip home. Our next stop would be in Hawaii so they could once again refuel the aircraft. This time we were permitted to get off the plane and stretch our legs in the terminal. That was great, and Hawaii looked like a splendid place through the terminal windows. But first and foremost, we wanted to get home to the red, white, and blue.

Our next stop would be Oakland, California!

One very long flight always feels like enough, but when two or three long flights are strung together, it can seem unbearable. But all of us were encouraged by the thought that this would be our last flight before setting down on American soil. A few hours later, our pilot once again spoke to us over the PA system.

"OK, boys, if you look out the windows as far forward as you can see, you'll catch your first glimpse of the California shoreline."

Everyone jumped up and put their heads as close to the windows as possible, trying to see the distant shoreline as it came into view. There was a big round of applause as some of the guys were able to see land in the distance.

"I want you to know that I am truly proud to have flown you guys home," he continued.

This brought on even more cheers and more applause. I can remember feeling the hairs on my neck standing up as I listened to the pilot speak. Even now, some fifty years later, I can vividly recall the sensation I felt as I listened to his words.

In another half hour, we landed and deboarded the plane at the Oakland Airport, back in our own homeland at last. As we walked down the stairs, we saw crowds of people standing behind a chain link fence, presumably waiting for members of our flight. They were all cheering and waving, doing their best to extend a welcome-home greeting to the returning soldiers on the flight. Some of the guys even took a moment to stop, get down on their knees, and kiss the ground. They may have promised themselves to do this in advance, or perhaps they were just so overcome by emotion that it was a spur-of-the-moment thing. Either way, it was a beautiful thing.

We were finally back on home soil.

⤜⤏

From the Oakland Airport, we were herded (one last time!) out the doors to a waiting bus. The final destination would be the Oakland Processing

Center, where we would complete our very last checkout en route to becoming civilians once again. We could hardly believe it.

Upon arriving at the center, we were greeted by a helpful Sergeant who pointed the way to a modern-looking barracks. Actually, everything looked clean and modern compared to the facilities we'd left behind. And there were none of the horrid, rotten smells to which we'd become accustomed. In fact, it smelled nice.

"You guys can use that one," called the Sergeant as he guided us to a series of empty bunks.

John and I followed the Sergeant's lead, along with our other two classmates, as we lugged our duffel bags into the facility. We were amazed to find nice, clean bunks with mattresses and sparkling-white sheets. Each bunk also had a pillow with a pillowcase, as well as blankets and all the other comforts of home. I was so taken aback by this that I wouldn't have been surprised to find a chocolate mint on the turned-down linens. Of course, the niceties didn't extend quite that far, but it sure was leap years ahead of anything we'd found in Vietnam. This was like heaven.

On top of everything, we also discovered that the barracks were equipped with nice, clean showers that were blessed with an unlimited supply of hot water. We all took advantage of that and jumped in, enjoying the sensation of fresh hot water cascading over our bodies. We all stayed in there for about an hour, which would have been longer had my appetite not started acting up. I think I opened my mouth and enjoyed a sip or two of the water just because I knew I could. It was clean. I loved being home.

After exiting the showers with completely waterlogged bodies, we dressed and were escorted to the dining hall—not a mess tent or chow hall but a genuine, bona fide dining hall. There were real wood tables covered with spotless white tablecloths that looked as though they'd never been used. Also, there was no chow line. Instead, we were seated at the tables, where we had the waiters bring our food.

There was steak! Really great, wonderful, magnificent steak, which was complemented by all the side dishes and fixings. They even served up some wonderful desserts to top off the feast. I hadn't eaten like that since I'd left home, well over a year ago. We all ate until we were ready to burst. It was a good thing they didn't measure us for uniforms as we walked out the door. Then it was back to the barracks to sleep on our immaculate new bedding.

The next day we started the paperwork carousel one more time. There were more papers and forms, more instructions, and more lines on which to sign. By the time it was over, I didn't have any idea what I was signing; I just did as I was told. We were then herded to yet another building, where we were fitted for our set of dress green uniforms. Then, there was even more paperwork. It was endless.

Another nice feature of this processing center was that it had pay phones, where we were welcome to call home to surprise our families with the fact that we were really back in the country. I had toyed with the idea of flying home without first calling, as is often seen in the World War II movies. (In these scenes, there is usually some big party with tons of family members going on at the house, and suddenly the victorious warrior son will arrive via taxi, in full uniform, and with a load of medals.) Instead, I opted for the more traditional arrival; I'd call home from here and let them know what time I'd arrive so they could pick me up at the airport.

I picked up the phone and dialed the number that I hadn't called in a full year. I knew it would be a shocking surprise, as I hadn't written a single letter since I was in Soc Trang. They would have thought that I was still at the base there, with a full month left of my remaining in-country.

The surprise was as complete and total as I had expected.

"Hi Mom, it's me!" were my first words when she answered the call. "I'm in California!"

"California!" she screeched in a high-pitched tone.

"Yes, California."

She turned and yelled into another room for my father.

"Joe, it's Tom! He's in California!"

I heard him reply in the background. He sounded just as surprised as my mother.

"What?" he shouted. I could picture him launching himself out of a chair as he bolted across the room to the phone.

We had a great conversation as I described the past couple months, of which they'd heard next to nothing. They were especially interested to learn about the series of events that had led me home and prompted me to receive the early discharge. The whole call was wonderful, although it was way too short. I promised to call them back with my flight information as soon as it became available.

As soon as I hung up the receiver, I knew that the phone lines would be lighting up around my hometown. News like that travels quickly.

It was hard to believe, but we still had another day of paperwork and processing ahead of us. We were then issued our spiffy new set of dress green uniforms, which went well with all the other fatigues and flight suits and khaki uniforms. I felt as though I were sufficiently outfitted to open up my own personal uniform shop.

Next, we were herded (again) into a room with lots of chairs, a movie projector, and a screen. The lights went out, and we were treated to a video of President Nixon thanking us for our service to our country. Then it was back to the processing area, where we received even more paperwork.

It was getting late in the day when we finished our last mountain of administrative sign-outs. Our last stop would be to the paymaster, which we knew would be followed by our long-awaited reentry into the civilian world. We were so close that the anticipation was overwhelming. We were almost there. I walked up to a small window with the clerk and handed him a sheaf of paperwork. It felt good to be handing my paperwork to someone else rather than being on the receiving end for a change.

The paymaster started by counting out my back pay for the past couple of weeks. Additionally, I had never used my two weeks of R&R (leave), so I ended up with a pile of money by the time he finished counting. I hadn't intended to walk away with so much money on hand, but I had decided long ago not to use my allotted R&R. I didn't need leave time; I only wanted to get home as soon as possible. And this time, I walked away with real American greenbacks, not the Monopoly money we were handed in Vietnam.

With my duffel bag thrown over my shoulder and my pockets flush with cash, I walked through the back door of the processing center, accompanied by John and our two classmates. This time, it was for real. Freedom. We were now "out."

A line of taxis was queued up on the street by the back door, waiting for those who needed a ride. We hailed one of the cabs and provided our destination: the San Francisco Airport, where we would catch our flights home. We were civilians once again.

## II

# MANY YEARS LATER

# 26

## NOT JUST ANOTHER NAME ON THE WALL

The Wall. Its official name is the Vietnam Veterans Memorial. Built to represent those who served there, both the living and the dead, it means so many things to so many people. For those of us who fought in Vietnam, it commemorates our own thoughts, our own memories, our grief, our sorrow, and our pain. The Wall symbolizes all of these emotions in each of us. It is indeed a single stark and somber representation of our collective soul.

By any measurement, the Wall is a powerful and massive undertaking. It touched a nerve in the psyche of this nation. Even the competition to design its construction drew over 2,500 entries. Over $9 million in contributions were received from over 275,000 donors across the United States, including American soldiers and civilians, public corporations and private citizens, who were all moved by the cause, all bound by the common message: "Remember."

The Wall. It's made with close to five hundred feet of granite forming two perpendicular walls: 140 panels of polished black rock, arranged in perfect symmetry, one after the other. Etched into these panels are the names of some 58,261 US service men and women. The list is all-inclusive, with not only US Army, Navy, Marines, Air Force, and Coast Guard but also mothers, fathers, brothers, and sisters. All were killed in action; all were casualties of the War. All are remembered on the Wall.

My own introduction to the Wall took place the week after its completion, in 1982. Indeed, the landscaping around the memorial was still ongoing. I was visiting the site with another veteran and long-term friend, Mick, who was equally as drawn to view the newly constructed monument. He had agreed to accompany me on my mission, which was to locate the names of the six men who'd perished when their helicopter, the

Lucky Strike, was shot down in February 1970. Six men, none of whom he knew. But it didn't matter. We were all brothers, all bonded by the common thread.

So much had been made of this site, including the radical design, which was very unlike any other memorial in this historic city. Even the ethnicity of the designer, an Asian American student at Yale University named Maya Ying Lin, drew mixed responses. Emotions run deep among the "band of brothers," and this memorial reached deeper into the soul than most. The Wall.

Mick and I approached the Wall from the back side, where we could not see the endless rows of names carved into the inscribed panels. We walked on through the November morning, feeling the cold and damp air pressing against our faces. With each step, our feet seemed to feel heavier, the sod soft and moist beneath our feet. An oppressive quietness hung in the air, suspended with the dew that had settled onto the grass. The only audible sounds were our own breaths, which quickened in concert with our heartbeats as we rounded the corner and gained our first glimpse of the Wall.

I was not fully prepared for the emotions I experienced as I stared down the polished, reflective surface, which seemed to stretch into infinity. An elderly couple stood nearby, rooted to a spot in front of a panel on the West wall. The woman held a scarf to her face, not as much to fend off the weather as to blot the cascade of tears, never abated. Their faces were fixated, grim and sorrowful, as they contemplated the loss of a loved one. A name on the Wall. One of over fifty-eight thousand, but one who was still missed, still loved.

It was Mick who finally broke the silence, suggesting that we search for the names of the six men killed in that one action. We leafed through a thick directory, not unlike a phone book, containing the names of all fifty-eight thousand mortalities that were engraved on the Wall. Then I saw it: "Daniel Proctor, Panel W11, date of casualty February 27, 1970." A name and a date, resurrected in my mind as I recalled his face from a dozen years earlier.

As we walked down the panels, counting them until we found the correct one, a flood of emotions came rushing into my head and heart. All these names—there were thousands and thousands of them. It was overwhelming, and it begged the question of why. Why were so many sent over? What a waste. And for what end? They were questions that I could not answer, and so I pushed them aside.

Mick soon spotted the name of "SP5 Daniel Vaughan Proctor, Killed in Action" in the middle of the polished granite surface. Then the others appeared: McCormack, Stafford, Swartz, Connelly, and Pace, their names emerging into view as though they were stepping through the mists of time. As I recognized them, one by one, I thought of what they would have accomplished had they lived, what they would have experienced, and the lives they would have touched. Once more I thought, "What a waste." My own tears soon transformed the carvings into blurred images, reminiscent of the fading memories from those war-torn years. My companion, meanwhile, stepped away, sensing my need to be alone with my thoughts. It was difficult, as well as perplexing. After all, why was I experiencing all this emotion? I barely knew these men, and it was so long ago. Were my tears really for these lost servicemen, or were they for myself and that part of my innocent soul I'd left behind in Vietnam as a nineteen-year-old soldier? I pondered the thought and wondered just how many times I had come close to becoming yet another name on the Wall.

The experiences of that day at the Wall were an awakening for both of us. We had put that phase of our lives behind us, buried behind careers, families, and a healthy dose of emotional cement. For many years, our only reminders of Vietnam were television documentaries and the occasional nightmare. This was one war that America seemed determined to forget. But now, embedded in this sacred soil for the nation to ponder, there was the overwhelming presence of the Wall. And whether it is because of the black granite surface itself, the endless rows of names, or my own vivid recollections that these have evoked, the result is the same. This memorial has finally succeeded in lifting my own self-inflicted veil of silence, enabling me to tell this story.

# 27

# FINDING SUPER SLICK

Like a lot of good stories, our tale of Super Slick had a wonderful surprise
ending. Long after all of us had left Vietnam and returned home to the
United States, we received a lightning bolt of news that shocked us to the
core. It came to us in a very unusual and roundabout way.

Our crew of Randy Olson, Rob Sandwith, Tom Wilkes, and I had
departed Soc Trang by the time we'd heard that Super Slick was shot
down on October 27, 1970. To the best of our knowledge, our ship was
gone—demolished and totally incinerated in a tragic accident within a
short distance of our base. Dana Brown would have known otherwise, as
he remained stationed there a few months longer than us. But none of us
were in close contact with him when we returned to the States, so we were
unaware of his knowledge about the real fate of our ship.[18]

Once I received the verbal news of Super Slick's demise from my
fellow company member at Vinh Long, I never corroborated the story. I
trusted that I'd heard the true accounting of the catastrophe and returned
home with that falsehood firmly taped in my mind as gospel. As sad as it
was, it really wasn't even a surprise to hear of the crash of our beloved ship.
After all, almost seven thousand Huey helos had been employed in the war
in Vietnam, and almost half of those had been lost in combat. We lost more
UH-1 helos in Vietnam than any other kind of aircraft. Super Slick was just
one more casualty of that war.

The fact that I had reestablished contact with Tom Wilkes was a bit of
a coincidence in its own right. I was a member of a VFW post in Fairport,
NY, which had a Huey helo on permanent display in front of its building.

---

18. Brown actually flew Super Slick out to the crash site of Warrior 16, the ship that actually
did go down on that tragic night mission.

I had decided to have Super Slick's nose art transferred (by decal) to the front of this ship. Tom Wilkes had been browsing the internet and came across a photo of the ship in Fairport, causing him to call our VFW post to ask for information. This was sometime around 2010. Once he was given my information, he decided to drive down from Connecticut and visit for a couple of days. It was the first time we had seen each other since Vietnam, which was forty years earlier. So we were already back in touch before we even learned of Super Slick's "reincarnation" stateside.

In 2012, Tom Wilkes received an email from an author named John Brennan. Brennan had been a Crew Chief with the 114th Assault Helicopter Company in Vinh Long from 1970 into 1971. Ironically, he was stationed there at the same time that I'd been temporarily working at that other base after leaving Soc Trang, although our paths never crossed at any time.

Brennan had a fascination with the helicopter nose art that proliferated in Vietnam between 1961 and 1973. His interest in the subject continued to grow, and he began carefully collecting and photographing as many of these paintings as he could find, with the idea of eventually writing a book on the topic. His first book on the subject was an authoritative accounting/collection of over three thousand examples of nose art. It included artwork from all helicopter companies, all helicopter models, and all years of service in the Vietnam War.[19]

Brennan had a photograph of the customized painting we had added to the nose of Super Slick in 1970, but he wanted to confirm the tail number on the ship. He somehow managed to obtain Tom Wilkes's email address, and Brennan sent him correspondence asking about this information. Tom Wilkes replied and told Brennan that he didn't have that number from the ship, but he was fairly certain that I did. He provided Brennan with my phone number and told him that he was sure I wouldn't mind the call.

John's phone call came from out of the blue. I wasn't expecting it, and I certainly couldn't have guessed at the outcome. It was that lightning bolt from out of nowhere.

"Hello, is this Thomas Feigel?" asked a voice I didn't recognize.

"Yes, who is this please?"

"My name is John Brennan, and I'm writing a book on helicopter nose art on Vietnam War era helicopters. A guy who said he was on your crew on a ship called Super Slick back in 1970 told me that you might know the tail number on that helicopter."

---

19. Brennan's book, titled *Vietnam War Helicopter Art*, was published by Stackpole Books in 2012. He has since gone on to publish follow-up editions and numerous other books on related subjects.

"Really?" I asked, caught a bit off guard. "What was his name?"

"Tom Wilkes. He's up in Connecticut."

"Yes, of course, I know Tom," I replied. "I saw him about two years ago, and he's correct; he was part of our crew on Super Slick, which was Warrior 21. We were part of the 2nd Platoon, 336th Assault Helicopter Company."

"Do you remember your tail number?" he asked, repeating his question.

"Of course. I was the Crew Chief. It was 16109," I replied without thinking. Those numbers were burned into my mind and will remain there until the day I die.

"OK, thanks. I just wanted to confirm that," he said nonchalantly.

We than chatted for a few minutes about the ship and the book he was writing. He seemed like a really interesting and well-informed person, and I enjoyed talking with him.

Evidently, Brennan knew more than he'd disclosed during our conversation, as he then sent another email back to Wilkes telling him about our ship.

"By the way, did you know that your ship is down at a war memorial in West Virginia?" he wrote in the email.

Wilkes had the same reaction as I would have felt had I received that same correspondence. It was a combination of excitement mixed in with a healthy dose of disbelief. When he told me about Brennan's research and the evidence he'd uncovered, I had to call John myself and hear it directly from the source.

Within the next day or two, I was able to reach Brennan at his office, and he repeated the same story to me about Super Slick's resting place. I paused for a moment, trying to make sense of his remarks. I was obviously talking to someone who didn't know the history of our ship or its fiery demise.

"Uh . . . no. Super Slick burned up in a crash in October of 1970," I said. "It went down after hitting a tree about a mile from our base in Soc Trang. From what I heard, there was very little of it left to even move from the site."

There was another pause on the end of the phone, followed by a calm voice that sounded like a school teacher trying to explain a difficult problem on the blackboard.

"Tom, if your helo really was a Huey with the tail number 16109, it is sitting on a cement pad display at a site in Fairmont, West Virginia," he said. "It's been sitting there since 1992, in case you'd like to see it for yourself."

I didn't know what to say. I was really lost beyond words, in total disbelief. What had happened? It was as though a living being that I thought had died years ago had been brought back to life. But how? How was this possible? The fog slowly started to clear enough for me to ask a question.

As skeptical as I was at first blush, I knew John Brennan, and I knew of his reputation. He was a solid researcher and a noted expert on Vietnam era helicopters. Because of this, I was inclined to take his word for it. But I also went online and read through the entire website of the Marion County Vietnam Veterans Memorial. It all appeared to add up and make sense. There was definitely a helo at that site that matched up with Super Slick's credentials.

When I spoke to Brennan on a subsequent phone call, I asked him the obvious question: "How did it come to be there? Do you know anything about it?"

## Helicopter UH-1D 66-16109

The following is Goldbook information on US Army helicopter UH-1D tail number 66-16109 This helicopter was purchased by the US Army in 0367.

| DATE | FLT | HRS | UIC | UNIT | | AREA | COUNTRY |
|------|-----|-----|-----|------|---|------|---------|
| 7001 | 97 | 1270 | WGPRAA | 336 ASLT HEL | CO | VIETNAM | RVN |
| 7002 | 100 | 1370 | WGPRAA | 336 ASLT HEL | CO | VIETNAM | RVN |
| 7003 | 96 | 1466 | WGPRAA | 336 ASLT HEL | CO | VIETNAM | RVN |
| 7004 | 45 | 1511 | WCLSAA | 388 TRANS | CO | VIETNAM | RVN |
| 7005 | 64 | 1575 | WGPRAA | 336 ASLT HEL | CO | VIETNAM | RVN |
| 7006 | 51 | 1626 | WGPRAA | 336 ASLT HEL | CO | VIETNAM | RVN |
| 7007 | 115 | 1741 | WGPRAA | 336 ASLT HEL | CO | VIETNAM | RVN |
| 7008 | 77 | 1818 | WGPRAA | 336 ASLT HEL | CO | VIETNAM | RVN |
| 7009 | 87 | 1905 | WGPRAA | 336 ASLT HEL | CO | VIETNAM | RVN |

*Record of 66-16109 at 336th Assault Helicopter Company in Vietnam.*

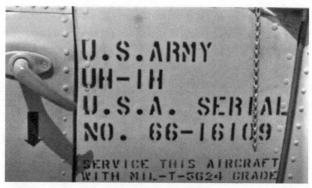

*Serial number (66-16109) on side of Super Slick. (Photo credit: Tom Fiegel)*

Brennan admitted that he didn't have the story regarding its voyage from the battlefield to the memorial setting, but I could investigate that myself. The important thing was that Super Slick had somehow survived and miraculously been transported halfway around the world to a location that was within a seven-hour drive from where I was living. It just didn't seem remotely possible.

I contacted Tom Wilkes again to review the conversation I'd had with the author, and he felt the same as me; we had to make our way to West Virginia to see our old ship as soon as possible.

Wilkes and I decided to make the trip to Fairmont in April 2012 to see it with our own eyes. After arriving, we walked around the ship, stepped onboard, and talked with Jeff Green, the site manager and coordinator of the memorial. At least a half a dozen officials representing the memorial, the town, and the state showed up. We met the mayor of Fairmont and some local elected representatives. Some of the memorial managers had the actual log books from the ship that documented its record. Once again, everything lined up.

Even as I looked over the records and thoroughly examined the ship, the thought kept hammering away inside my head, saying, "This couldn't be possible." But it was. I began searching for the little telltale signs that no one else would have thought to scrutinize: the patches on bullet holes we'd received in various skirmishes, the signs of heavy equipment and lighting systems when we'd flown the night missions. Everything. It was as though this ghost from the past were calling me, tapping me on the shoulder and saying, "Yes, it's really me."

The makeover performed by the Bombardier crew had been magnificent, although there was one discrepancy that they couldn't have avoided. There is a common misconception that the Huey helicopter in Vietnam was used for the single mission of being medical evacuations (medevacs). Super Slick was never used for that purpose, although we did sometimes remove injured ARVN soldiers from the battlefield during extractions. But the crew that restored Super Slick hadn't had access to the ship's historical records, so it painted the iconic red cross symbol and a white background on either side to symbolize its mistaken identity and mission. The symbol remained on the ship until its second repaint, circa 2017, when it was covered over with the regular Army-green paint.

The story of Warrior 21 (which became call sign Super Slick) and how it came to arrive at a small memorial in a picturesque West Virginia town is an interesting tale. It is also not without its twists and turns, along with a few gaps of blank time that cannot be filled. But we do know that the crew was disbanded in September 1970, when all of us scattered in different directions. After that, they removed a lot of the armament from the ship and converted it back into a regular slick. It was called only Warrior 21 from that time on. Even the nose cover with the painting came off and was replaced by a plain, unadorned cover. The artistic version with all the graphics ended up with the Soc Trang night Air Controller Baby Huey. He had been a good friend of our crew, and he'd conversed at length with us as we performed many of our nighttime base perimeter missions.[20]

From official records, we can tell that Warrior 21 was transferred from the 336th Assault Helo Company in Soc Trang to the 191st, after which it was transported back to Fort Hood, Texas, in 1971. Early in 1972 it moved on to the Army Aviation School at Fort Rucker, Alabama. Fort Rucker is a massive base that covers over sixty-three thousand acres of land and still serves as the US Army's Aviation Center of Excellence. It remained in use at the Army Aviation School until midway through 1973, although the ship itself stayed at Fort Rucker for many years after.

Almost twenty years later, in 1992, the citizens of Marion County wanted a Vietnam era helicopter to add to the memorial in the town of Fairmont. They were told that there was an inventory of decommissioned Hueys at Fort Rucker that were there for the taking. They just had to show up with the right paperwork, load it onto a truck, and take it away. It was everything they had hoped for, so they made arrangements for a trucking company in town to pick it up and bring it home to their town.

I was fortunate enough to speak with Ronnie Miller, the trucker who made that run to Alabama to retrieve the ship from the US Army facility. He took his son out of school for the day and made all the appropriate arrangements. However, when he'd arrived at Fort Rucker and walked into the office, he was told that the helicopter he wanted was no longer there.

"Sorry, but the helicopter you wanted was just given away to another city. But there are many more out there, so why don't you just take this one?" the clerk said, pointing out a very intact ship parked nearby.

The thing that interested the trucker was that the helicopter they'd offered was completely intact. Very often when a ship was decommissioned, they removed the engine. But they'd not done that on this one. Not on 16109. This thing not only had its engine, it looked completely flyable. The trucker, with help from the staff, took off the rotor blades and craned

---

20. The whereabouts of that nose cover with the original artwork is still unknown today. It had originally been designed by Tom Feigel using a graphic of a cartoon soldier that appeared in the *Stars and Stripes* newspaper in 1970. Randy Olson paid $10 to have an artist in downtown Soc Trang paint it onto the nose cover.

it onto the flatbed. The rotor blades then went onto the trailer with the fuselage.

From there, the truck brought the ship back to the war memorial site in West Virginia, where another crane was used to lift the helo off the truck and replace the rotor blades. It had arrived, and it attracted a lot of attention from the people of the town. But it was obvious that the fuselage needed a paint job. So, the locals in Fairmont decided to tackle the task head-on. They headed out to the site with paint, brushes, and sandpaper to repaint the ship in the same manner as they would repaint an old house. The problem, of course, is that an old helicopter is not an old house. As good as their intentions might have been, they were going about the repaint and restoration entirely the wrong way.

Coincidentally, as the well-intentioned work group was getting started, an official of Bombardier Inc. happened to be in the area and had witnessed the activity on the helicopter. Bombardier is a huge international corporation based out of Montreal, Quebec, that builds and maintains commercial aircraft, among other things. The company had a facility right down the road in Bridgeport, West Virginia. They offered to step in and contribute to the restoration efforts in the interests of public relations and for the integrity of the ship at the memorial site.

The helicopter was brought back to the Bombardier facility, where one of their work crews took over the entire reconditioning project. Everything was refurbished, including the sanding, painting, and even the decal work. When they were done, Super Slick looked like it had just come off the assembly line. They then wheeled the ship outside and actually started it up! Super Slick had a heartbeat once again!

The engine was then shut down, and the ship was trailered back to the memorial site in Fairmont, where it was once again placed in its permanent spot of honor. Since that time, the officials at Bombardier Inc. have graciously performed upkeep on the static display and its concrete base pad, which the town and the memorial site have greatly appreciated over the years.

Tom Wilkes and I returned home from our visit in 2012 thoroughly thrilled with our experience. Not only was the ship in magnificent shape, but we had irrefutable evidence that this was indeed our ship. We knew what our next move had to be: the next year (2013), we had to pull out all the stops and get the entire crew back together. The obvious choice was Memorial Day, when our celebration of finding our ship could be shared not only among ourselves but with all the members of the community.

As soon as we announced our plans for our small reunion, we had instantaneous buy-in from all hands. Rob Sandwith had the farthest to travel, but he didn't hesitate at the chance to come from his home in the state of Washington for the event. Randy Olson jumped at the chance to fly in from Texas, while Tom Wilkes and I had shorter drives from the East Coast. John Leandro and Dana Brown also said they wouldn't miss it and traveled to West Virginia to meet up with us.

Another interesting outgrowth of our 2012 visit came to life when I had dinner with my cousin, Donald Feigel, and his wife Karen in December of 2012. Donald was an instructor at the Rochester Institute of Technology, and he was a masterful producer of documentary programs. When I mentioned to Don and Karen our intentions of getting together with our original crew at the memorial site in West Virginia, their eyes almost popped out of their heads.

They looked at each other and exclaimed in unison, "We've got to make a documentary on the reunion of your crew!"

It seemed like a great public interest story, there for the taking. Immediately, their plans went into fast-forward as they planned the trip, the arrival, and the sequence of filming. They saw vast potential in the idea of a Vietnam War helicopter crew seeing each other for the first time in forty years against the backdrop of our long-lost ship. It represented the perfect setting.

Don decided to produce a DVD recording of the entire three-day weekend, from our arrival through the parade on the following Monday. It was a great conception that was bound to be packed with emotion and pride. Finally, in May of 2013, Don and Karen piled into my Ford Explorer and rode with me to West Virginia. They had been planning the setup and production of the documentary for months and were itching to get started. The ride itself was interesting, as the entire vehicle was crammed to the gills with equipment. Karen was in the back seat with lighting booms and microphones hanging over her head and across her lap. It was tight.

When we finally arrived at the hotel in Fairmont, Don helped us to compose our initial greetings. He wanted to ensure that he could capture the full emotional impact of the moment, so he asked us to keep apart until he gave the signal for us to walk into the foyer. But despite the choreography, our arrival and meeting in the front lobby of the hotel was about as sentimental as it gets. It was simply amazing to see everyone back together in one place again. We had all gained a few pounds and lost a few hairs, but none of that mattered. Handshakes gave way to big bear hugs, and the stories and ribbing started up almost immediately. No one in the vicinity would have guessed that we'd been apart for forty-three years.

Don also scripted the scene of us going down to see the ship at the memorial site, making sure to keep the area clear of other visitors. The documentary doesn't show all of our spouses who had made the trip, but they were standing in the background while the camera was rolling.

We all took turns climbing into the cargo area and finding our assigned stations in the craft. We got some great staged photos, but the real fun was swapping stories and trading memories of our days together during the war. We had become so bonded together as a group living on the edge every day that it seemed as though we'd never parted. All those statements you hear about the "band of brothers" and the bonds that hold them together really are true. And we felt the same way about our ship as well.

"This bird brought us through a lot of stuff," said Sandwith, looking wistfully at the ship. "Thank you for taking care of us."

Wilkes thought back on his days of flying with our crew with just as much emotion. "I just felt so much pride, knowing that I got to fly with the crew that I flew with."

Randy Olson described the commitment we'd all felt toward working together and getting the job done. "We never hesitated, ever, to complete the mission or do what we needed to do."

Meanwhile, I just thought back on the factor of fate: it had brought us all together forty years ago, and it had now brought us back together here again. I thought, "What a fitting place for our ship. It *earned* that spot."

Once we had completed our visit to Super Slick at the war memorial, we still had one more obligation to meet before parting ways and returning to our respective homes. Because our ship was now part of the community in Fairmont, we were invited to participate in the Memorial Day parade, which marched through the middle of nearby Grafton, WV. This was a complete honor, and we were all looking forward to fulfilling our roles as a part of living history in their towns.

West Virginia and Marion Country are very much "small town" America. There are American flags flying from every telephone pole and storefront. No one has to tell people to stand and remove their hat for the national anthem, because everyone already knows. This is gospel in locations such as these because they were raised in that tradition, and they still respect the flag for the principles it represents.

We rode on our own truck in that parade, carried through town on an old US Army utility truck with the 336th Assault Helo Company sign fastened to the front bumper. People applauded each group as they marched by, and we waved and said hello to our new friends. It was a very proud moment for all of us, as we felt like new members of their community.

Later on, we paid a formal visit to the Marion County Vietnam Veterans Memorial, where our crew laid a wreath at the base of the wall engraved with the names of the twenty-seven men from Fairmont who lost their lives in the war. It was a very solemn occasion. The officer presiding over the ceremony mentioned that the state of West Virginia had lost more young men in Vietnam than any other state in the union. That remark really struck home with the assemblage. Vietnam was a long time ago, but it was not so distant that many of the children and spouses of those killed in action aren't still with us today. Many of the tears shed during that ceremony were probably from those still grieving their losses.

Following the wreath laying, John Leandro continued with a speech to the Gold Star families about the ship and its history throughout the war. His words were concise, sensitive, and well-received by all.

In the years since 2012, we have continued to visit the ship, usually around Memorial Day, so we can continue to participate in the community's celebration. Meanwhile, the wonderful people at Bombardier have stayed the course and provided ongoing support and maintenance for our beloved ship. In 2016, they repainted the ship once again, so the four of us (Olson, Sandwith, Wilkes, and I) went over to their facility to thank them. They led us into the cafeteria where, much to our surprise, they had assembled everyone in the building to hear us speak. They literally shut the place down; there must have been over one hundred people in the room.

It's been that way every year since, as we continue to make our annual pilgrimage to the site. Prior to one of these trips, I discovered that one of the six men killed on Lucky Strike, door gunner Ron McCormick, had lived right down the road from the memorial in Fairmont. It seemed like yet another example of fate, just like my entire year in-country. When we contacted McCormick's sister and told her that we were going to visit his grave during our visit, she was blown away. We contacted a VFW hall in Clarksburg about the visit, and from there, things just took off. The media caught wind of the event, and the local police department provided an honor escort to the gravesite. Even the Patriot Guard motorcycle club showed up to ride with us along the route to the cemetery.

We were also glad to see that McCormick's entire surviving family was there to witness the ceremony and the 21-gun salute that fired in his honor. At the end of the service, John Leandro read the comments recorded by Lt. William Ahearn, the US Special Forces officer who'd witnessed the flash in the sky when Lucky Strike went down. Until that time, McCormick's family had never known how he died. It finally brought closure to a pain that had lingered for all those years.

As for us, we will continue to make this trip for as long as our tired bodies hold up and permit us to travel. We were part of something that was very special, and it's only been due to fate that we all survived and have made it this far to live the rest of our lives.

I've mentioned fate so many times throughout this book that it's become trite. Yet I firmly believe that certain things are preordained and are just bound to happen. I have no doubt that fate was responsible for the four of us becoming a team, staying together, and surviving to fight another day. I also have faith in the bonds we still share with those of us who didn't make it back: The crew of Lucky Strike. The men of Warrior 16. The US Navy Seals who perished en route to Saigon. And thousands more whose stories are told in other places. A part of each of them is still with us today, flying cover and protecting us from above.

# 28

## WHERE ARE THEY TODAY?

*Randy Olson in 1970.(Courtesy of Randy Olson)*

*Randy Olson in current era.(Courtesy of Randy Olson)*

### RANDY OLSON

Born Rock Island, IL, 1949, grew up in Tucson, AZ.

Warrant Officer, UH1 Huey pilot in Vietnam 1969–1970.

Logged 1,420 flight hours, mostly on Warrior 28 and Warrior 21, call sign Super Slick.

Went on to fly T-37 and A-10 in the US Air Force, served from 1974–2000.

Retired as Lt. Col., USAF, 2000, lives in Tucson, AZ.

### DECORATIONS

Distinguished Flying Cross
Air Medal

Army Commendation Medal
National Defense Medal
Vietnam Service Medal
RVN Campaign Medal

*Tom Feigel in 1970.(Courtesy of Tom Feigel)*

*Tom Feigel in current era.(Courtesy of Tom Feigel)*

## TOM FEIGEL

Born in Webster, NY, 1950.
Spec 5, UH1 Huey Crew Chief in Vietnam, 1969–1970, Warrior 28 and Warrior 21, call sign Super Slick.
Held numerous management positions as Xerox employee.
Retired in 2018.

## DECORATIONS

Purple Heart
Air Medal
Army Commendation Medal (with Valor "V")
National Defense Medal
Vietnam Service Medal
RVN Campaign Medal

*Robert Sandwith in 1970.(Courtesy of Robert Sandwith)*

*Robert Sandwith in current era.(Courtesy of Robert Sandwith)*

## ROBERT SANDWITH

Born, Bellingham, WA, 1950.

Spec 4, Door Gunner, served on UH1 Huey, 1969–1970, mostly on Warrior 28 and Warrior 21, call sign Super Slick.

Went on to serve in US Cavalry with C Troop, 16th Cavalry, 1st Aviation Brigade as door gunner.

After leaving the military, worked as tennis pro before entering the plumbing business. Owned and operated a plumbing business until retiring, 2017. Lives in Friday Harbor, WA.

## DECORATIONS

Purple Heart
Air Medal
Army Commendation Medal
National Defense Medal
Vietnam Service Medal
RVN Campaign Medal

*Tom Wilkes in 1970.(Courtesy of Tom Wilkes)*

*Tom Wilkes in current era.(Courtesy of Tom Wilkes)*

## TOM WILKES

Born, Danbury, CT, 1949.

Spec 4, Infantry and Door Gunner, Vietnam, 1969–1971. Served on crew of Warrior 21, call sign Super Slick.

Went on to serve in US Cavalry with C Troop, 16th Cavalry, 1st Aviation Brigade as an infantryman.

Worked as a carpenter, cabinet maker, and later as an employment specialist.

Retired in New Milford, CT, 2011.

## DECORATIONS

Air Medal
Army Commendation Medal
National Defense Medal
Vietnam Service Medal
RVN Gallantry Cross
RVN Campaign Medal

*John Leandro in 1970.(Courtesy of John Leandro)*

*John Leandro in current era.(Courtesy of John Leandro)*

## JOHN LEANDRO

Born in Fall River, MA, 1948.

The 336th Assault Helicopter Company, 1969–1970. 2nd Platoon Leader, January–July, 1970.

Returned to Vietnam for a second tour in July, 1971. Served with C Troop, 16th Cavalry, flying as an Air Mission Commander.

Returned to United States and worked in health care and assisted living industry until retirement.

Retired to Raeford, NC, 2018.

## DECORATIONS

Bronze Star
Distinguished Flying Cross
Air Medal
Army Commendation Medal
National Defense Medal
Vietnam Service Medal
RVN Gallantry Cross
RVN Campaign Medal

*Dana Brown in 1970.(Courtesy of Dana Brown)*

*Dana Brown in current era.(Courtesy of Dana Brown)*

## DANA BROWN

Born in Philadelphia, TN, 1948.

Warrant Officer, UH1 Huey pilot, served as pilot, Warrior 21, call sign Super Slick, 1970, and US Cavalry in Vin Long until 1972.

Went on to Flight Instructor School, served later in Korea, trained US Army, Air Force, and foreign pilots from Germany, Norway, and others. Became qualified in both helicopters and fixed-wing aircraft.

Served several more tours before retiring military in 1990 and later flew commercial aircraft for multiple companies before final retirement.

Retired to Loudon, TN.

## DECORATIONS

Bronze Star
Distinguished Flying Cross
Meritorious Service Medal
Air Medal
Army Commendation Medal
National Defense Medal
Vietnam Service Medal
RVN Gallantry Cross
RVN Campaign Medal

*Super Slick arriving at War Memorial Museum, Fairmont, West Virginia, 1992. Note: The red cross was added erroneously during the restoration of the ship. Super Slick never served as a medevac helicopter. Photo by Don Feigel.*

*Nose art plate from Super Slick. This piece of historic military art has been lost to posterity. Its whereabouts are unknown to this day. Photo by Tom Feigel.*

*Left to right: Rob Sandwith, Tom Wilkes, Tom Feigel, and Randy Olson around Warrior 21 at War Museum. Photo by Don Feigel.*

*Left to right: Dana Brown, Tom Wilkes, Randy Olson, John Leandro, Robert Sandwith, and Tom Feigel inside Warrior 21 at War Museum. Photo by Don Feigel.*

*Crew of Warrior 21 participating in the Memorial Day parade, Fairmont, West Virginia, 2013. Photo by Don Feigel.*

# ABOUT THE AUTHORS

## TOM FEIGEL

**Tom Feigel** was born in Rochester, NY, in 1950 and grew up in nearby Webster. His greatest interests included aviation, which led to him earning a pilot's license at an early age. He worked for Xerox Corporation in Webster both before and after his tour in Vietnam. In his forty years of employment inside Xerox, he held a number of middle management positions, including distribution program manager, advanced product strategies manager, and technical program manager. He also founded Conifer Logistics Inc.

Feigel's US Army career was centered around his year in Vietnam, where he served as a UH-1 Huey helicopter Crew Chief. While deployed to Vietnam, he logged over 750 flight hours, mostly on combat missions around the Mekong Delta. His combat awards include the Purple Heart, the Air Medal, and four Army Commendation Medals (including one for Valor).

Feigel retired in 2018 and currently resides in North Carolina.

## LARRY WEILL

**Larry Weill** has had a widely diverse life, including both in his professional careers as well as in his writing/authoring pursuits. Weill was a wilderness park ranger in the Adirondack Park of New York in the 1970s and early 1980s before he joined the US Navy in 1981. After being commissioned as an Ensign in 1982, he went on to a lengthy and successful career that included both active duty and reserve billets in the United States as well as throughout the Mediterranean Sea. He completed six command tours and retired as a Captain in 2008.

Weill joined the New York Naval Militia (NYNM), part of NY State Division of Military and Naval Affairs, after retiring from Federal Service. There he was promoted to Rear Admiral in 2022, and he went on to serve as Commander of the NYNM until his retirement in 2023.

Weill has also worked for Xerox Corporation as a senior analyst for almost thirty years, working as a logistics consultant in Webster, NY.

He has used his experiences in the Adirondack forests to author several series of books, beginning with his best seller, *Excuse Me, Sir . . . Your Socks Are on Fire*. He has since gone on to author six additional books while contributing to two others.

Weill currently lives in Rochester, NY, with his wife Patty. They have two children, Kelly and Erin, and two grandchildren.

# THOUGHTS OF A
# COLLABORATIVE AUTHOR

Greetings to the reader. My name is Larry Weill, although this story is not about me. I am simply a face behind the scenes, the person tapping keys as Tom Feigel tells his captivating tales of life as a helicopter ship Crew Chief in the thick of the Vietnam War. In other words, "pay no attention to the man behind the curtain." That's me. But I did want to introduce myself as the collaborative writer of this narrative, as well as explain how we came to work together to bring this book to fruition.

I met Tom in the early 1990s, when we were both employed by Xerox Corporation in Rochester, NY. At the time, he was a manager involved in Xerox logistics chains, while I was an analyst contracting inside the same Xerox organization. However, we'd never worked together closely until I was hired to work for a different contractor in 2007. I moved into an office with less than a dozen people, and Tom was one of the technical supervisors in the branch. We quickly discovered that we shared a military background, as different as those service careers had been.

My military career began when I was commissioned as an Ensign in the United States Navy in 1982. The closest I ever got to Vietnam was the draft card I received in 1973, which was the year that Nixon withdrew our troops. Even then, I was categorized as a 1-S, with any service deferred until after my graduation from college in 1977.

After completing a four-year degree and then going on to two years of graduate school and three years of employment for New York State as a wilderness park ranger, I took the test for the US Navy Officer Candidate School (OCS). I was accepted and reported for duty in February 1982. I was commissioned in June and went on to my first ship, *USS Concord* (AFS-5), based out of Norfolk, VA. Onboard *Concord*, I served in multiple Division Officer billets while I awaited my eventual discharge in 1986. I was there for four years, knowing that I never wanted to make the Navy a twenty-year career. I was strictly a "four and out" man, no more.

Little did I know that my retirement date would eventually come in November 2008, and that I would attain the rank of Captain in those twenty-six years. I was privileged to serve in six command tours over those years, although many of them came while serving in US Navy Reserve (USNR) status. Still, several of those USNR positions were very active in nature, requiring me to be on active duty orders for 100 to 150 days a year. I was very thankful to Xerox Corporation for tolerating all those weeks and months when I was deployed overseas, leaving a hole to fill at my Xerox job.

Sometime around 1994, after starting my work at Xerox, I began to write. My first several books were about my life and times in the woods as a wilderness park ranger in the late 1970s. I had lived in a tent for three years in a wilderness region located *way* back in the Adirondack Mountains of upstate New York, and I'd encountered a plethora of interesting characters who were continuously getting themselves into unusual predicaments. Those books, starting with *Excuse Me, Sir . . . Your Socks Are on Fire*, resonated well with outdoor enthusiasts, and thus was my publishing career launched.

In the interim since 2005, I have had eight books published, with several more in the pipeline. These books are all about the Adirondack Park, including its majestic mountains, pristine waterways, and storybook residents. It is indeed a magical place, and I do consider myself to be primarily an "Adirondack author."

However, one day late in 2007, Tom and I were swapping stories in his office in Rochester when he learned that I was a published author. Additionally, he was interested in the fact that I was still writing books, enthralled with the pursuit of telling tales and spinning the yarn. He relayed to me that he, too, was interested in writing a book, but one about his experiences as a helo Crew Chief in Vietnam.

It sounded fascinating. We spent an hour or two of lunch time that week discussing his subject material, including ideas for chapters, themes, and titles. I recognized immediately that he had some great content that could be written into a real page-turner of a book. But Tom was more of an action guy and storyteller than a sit-down writer, so I decided to offer my assistance. I rewrote a single, three-page section about his visit to the Vietnam War Memorial ("the Wall") in Washington, DC. I enjoyed writing it, and he was pleased with the end result.

That was the extent of it. The year was 2007, and Tom left us a couple years later. He retired to Florida before later relocating to North Carolina, where he still resides today.

At this point, we have to fast-forward to 2020, when I was entering my final year with Xerox. I was "cleaning out" my work laptop and deleting as many files as possible when I came across the chapter I wrote for Tom back in 2007. As I glanced at the file name, remembering the content, my finger paused over the "Delete" key on my keyboard. Then, instead of deleting the file, I opened it and reread the three pages of text. I was enthralled, just as I had been twelve years earlier. It told a great story.

My next move was to press down on a button. But it wasn't the "Delete" key I depressed. Instead, it was the "Dial" button on my cell phone, connecting me to Tom's cell phone in North Carolina. He answered immediately, and we spoke for quite a while. No, he had never written the book, although he had helped produce a documentary on the subject, including his discovery of his actual Vietnam Huey, Super Slick, which he had located back here in the States.

Tom's first question to me was, "Are you sure you want to do this?" He wanted to confirm that my interest was serious and that we could combine our time and talent to write and produce this memoir of his time spent on Super Slick in the Vietnam War. I assured him that I was indeed serious, and we cemented our agreement to bring this project to completion.

Writing *Super Slick* was, for me, more than a book-writing task. It was an eye-opening journey that allowed me to view the world of the helo Crew Chief first hand, as though I'd been in on the action and perched inside the UH-1 Huey flying into battle. Although I spent almost twenty-seven years in uniform, I never experienced a single day that could compare with the daily heart-stopping, adrenaline-filled action incurred by the men who flew these aircraft.

It was also interesting to me to be able to capture the action from an alternate viewpoint to the vast majority of Vietnam helicopter books. Whereas those tell the story of the ship's pilot (or Aircraft Commander), this story is told from the vantage point of the Crew Chief. This is the individual who runs the crew, directs the gunfire, and is responsible for the rest of the ship outside the pilot's chair. Because of this nuance, *Super Slick* is written from a new and unique perspective that will be of interest to all readers of military memoirs and students of Vietnam history.

Over the course of this book's development, Tom and I spoke almost every day as he relayed pertinent details about the many exciting operations and missions. Several of those memories of combat missions, including the tragic loss of Lucky Strike with its entire crew, are just as painful today as they were fifty years ago. Tom's searing memories, along with those of his crewmates, are notable for their clarity, conciseness, and emotion. I can honestly say that it was a complete privilege to work with Tom on the composition of this volume. Hopefully, it will add a new chapter to the overall history of the Vietnam War while also serving as a literary pressure relief valve to those who served in those troubling and violent times.